BUILDING A
Full-Service School

A Step-by-Step Guide

by
Carol Calfee, Frank Wittwer, *and*
Mimi Meredith

JOSSEY-BASS PUBLISHERS • SAN FRANCISCO

A previous iteration of this book, entitled *Building a Full Service School: Florida's Model of Collaboration for School-Based and School-Linked Services,* was developed under the auspices of the Florida Department of Education.

We gratefully acknowledge permission from the Florida Department of Education and the Santa Rosa County (Florida) School District to describe experiences, reproduce documents, and quote from materials developed as part of their full-service schools initiatives.

Chapter opening icons and Figures 1.1 through 1.4 courtesy of ClickArt® Art Parts™ ©1996 Brøderbund Software, Inc. All rights reserved. Used by Permission. Art Parts is a trademark of Art Parts. ClickArt and Brøderbund are registered trademarks of Brøderbund Software, Inc.

Jossey-Bass books and products are available through most bookstores. To contact Jossey-Bass directly, call (888) 378-2537, fax to (800) 605-2665, or visit our website at www.josseybass.com.

Substantial discounts on bulk quantities of Jossey-Bass books are available to corporations, professional associations, and other organizations. For details and discount information, contact the special sales department at Jossey-Bass.

For sales outside the United States, please contact your local Simon & Schuster International Office.

Manufactured in the United States of America.

LIBRARY OF CONGRESS CATALOGING-IN-PUBLICATION DATA

Calfee, Carol, date.
    Building a full-service school : a step-by-step guide / Carol Calfee, Frank Wittwer, Mimi Meredith. — 1st ed.
        p. cm.
    Includes bibliographical references and index.
    ISBN 0-7879-4058-5 (acid-free paper)
    1. Community and school—Florida—Case studies. 2. Social service—Florida—Case studies. 3. School children—Services for—Florida—Case studies. 4. Family services—Florida—Case studies. 5. School facilities—Extended use—Florida—Case studies. I. Wittwer, Frank, date. II. Meredith, Mimi, date. III. Title.
    LC221.2.F6 C35 1998
    371.19'09759—ddc21   98–25318

FIRST EDITION

PB Printing   10 9 8 7 6 5 4 3 2 1

Contents

Preface

School reform continues to be a lively topic in the media, educational journals, state legislatures, and the Congress. There is no shortage of opinions, expert or otherwise, on solving the schools' problems. However, the problems facing schools are also the problems facing communities. Perhaps the topic of school reform should be reexamined as community reform. The concept of full-service schools is one of the models being explored by school systems nationwide to provide a collaborative school and community approach to solving the problems of our changing society.

In earlier times—"the good old days," when populations were less mobile and the economy and families appeared to be more stable—schools could concentrate on the three Rs. Local businesses, churches, families, and friends (along with a few social service organizations) seemed able to fulfill most of the employment, civic, social, health, and welfare needs of children and their families.

Time has a way of changing our minds, our needs, and even our memories. The good old days really were not that good. Children and families had many unmet needs. If a health and human services agency was not there to meet a need, the child or family did without. Today, the concentration of populations in our cities and schools continues to create more stress and greater demand for support services. Ignoring or delaying service provision has costly consequences for the future. Both the nuclear and extended families are endangered species. The days of Ozzie and Harriet are over. The definitions and roles of home, employment, school, and community have drastically changed.

The concept of full-service schools, where schools and communities work together in coordinated delivery of services to families and children, is ready for realization. The academic and social service needs of children cannot be separated from the needs of the family unit. Nor can delivery of these services be neatly separated according to agency. Whether we like it or not, we as a society are very interdependent.

This book is designed to guide readers in their consideration of establishing a full-service school in their community. Actually, this is a book about

> *To make a difference, you must have two things in the same place at the same time. One is a caring attitude, and the other is a service to provide what really works. (Both are hard to find!) Either one alone will have limited effectiveness.*
>
> **—Susan Danahy, psychologist**

building a sense of community in which the school has a central role. This book presents various ways in which schools and social service agencies can work together without competition, without the need to protect their own narrow interests, and without duplicating their efforts—while efficiently delivering comprehensive services to families. Unlike much of the reform rhetoric of speculation, the information in this book is based on a working model with an eight-year history of development and implementation. It all began with an idea that was shared in conversation among three people. The idea survived the conversation, was piloted in a rural elementary school, and has since expanded into six elementary schools, two middle schools, two high schools, an adult school, and a vocational center in one school district in the Panhandle of Florida.

There are over 350 models of full-service schools in the state of Florida. Each is unique because it is shaped by the needs, resources, and political reality of its particular community. In other words, no single model is best.

This idea of schools and community social, welfare, and health agencies working together to deliver services to children and their families is not a new concept. Review of the literature indicates that this idea is also known by a host of other names: school-linked services, school-based services, assessment centers, one-stop shopping, community education, family service centers. Multiple-agency service delivery to children and families need not be sponsored by or even include the schools, however. Many community-based interagency delivery systems exist without any link to a school. Even under current definitions of full-service school, a number of models exist. These include programs in which community agencies co-locate on the school campus, in some instances using existing space in the school building. In others, a school-based coordinator may direct school children and their families to service agencies located off site but nearby.

There is no single way in which services can be delivered; the best model is the one that works in a particular community. The authors of this text advocate that if a current program is working, don't fix it. But *do* look at the possibilities suggested in the following chapters to determine whether your existing program might be enhanced or extended.

There is no cure-all for the problems of providing quality education. However, our experiences and the data we have collected indicate that implementing a full-service school model does build a sense of community and collective ownership of "the problems." We invite you to read on.

Acknowledgments

Building a Full-Service School was made possible through grant funding from the Florida Department of Education and support from the Santa Rosa County School Board.

Special thanks go to Lynn H. Groves, Mary Jo Butler, and Bob Smith for their leadership at the state level; and to Bill, Jimmy, and Shane for all their patience, encouragement, and lost time on weekends!

So many people have helped along the way that we are afraid we'll miss a few. We have listed below the folks who are the original "Project Vision Gang," the ones who sought the vision, brought it to reality, and still lead it to fruition.

- Bennett C. Russell, superintendent of schools, Santa Rosa County: charismatic leader and risk taker

- Morris Marx, president, University of West Florida: facilitator and divergent thinker

- Chelly Schembera and Chuck Bates, district administrators, Florida Department of Health and Rehabilitative Services (HRS), District One: provider pioneers

- Sandee Williams, Joyce Berry, and George Dahlgren, principals: kid advocates and visionary leaders

- Frank Green, assistant superintendent of schools (retired): organizer, politician, communicator, and mentor

- Sam Mathews, research scholar, University of West Florida: evaluation designer, rabble rouser, and friend

- Billy J. Williams, emeritus professor, University of West Florida: molder of the vision

- Ken Hardy, IBM marketing representative: technical assistant and program advocate

- Burt Sutton, director, Santa Rosa County Public Health Unit: health care advocate

- Butch Miller, program administrator, HRS District One: family advocate

- Freda Carroll, of the Florida Private Industry Council: community and family consultant

- Walt Wooten, director, information systems, HRS District One: technical assistant, program advocate, and empathizer

- Cynthia Descher, caseworker, HRS District One: the first of the troops in the trenches

- Patty Kowalski and Eleanor Williams, educational researchers, University of West Florida: translators of impersonal statistics into human needs

In addition, we would like to thank our partners from the following agencies and funding sources:

Adult Learning Center of Santa Rosa County; ARC/Santa Rosa; Avalon Center of Baptist Health Care, Inc.; Big Brothers/Big Sisters of Northwest Florida; Community Drug and Alcohol Commission (CDAC); Child Protection Team, Prevention Project; Children's Services Center; Children's Home Society; City of Milton; Educational Opportunity Center, Pensacola Junior College; Even Start; Family Preservation and Support Services Program; First Start; Florida Healthy Kids Corp.; Florida Teaching Professionals (NEA); Gulf Power Co.; Head Start and Early Intervention Program; Healthy Start of Santa Rosa County; HRS District One; Human Health Care Plans; IBM; Job Service of Florida; Juvenile Alternative Services Program, SEDNET; Lutheran Ministries of Florida, Gulf Coast Youth and Family Services; Monsanto; National Foundation for the Improvement of Education; Naval Air Station, Whiting Field; Navarre Beach Chamber of Commerce; Florida Private Industry Council; Retired Senior Volunteers of Santa Rosa County; Santa Rosa County Extension Service; Santa Rosa County Sheriff's Department; Santa Rosa Educational Foundation; Santa Rosa County Public Health Department; Santa Rosa County Commissioners; Santa Rosa County Press Gazette; Santa Rosa Medical Center; Santa Rosa County Chamber of Commerce; Think First of Northwest Florida; USA+ Health Foundation; University of West Florida; Florida Division of Vocational Rehabilitation; WEAR Channel 3 ABC Television; and Women, Infants, and Children's Program (WIC).

About the Authors

Carol Calfee was balancing her time as a mom and wife in 1990, while simultaneously working as an elementary and middle school teacher of gifted and technology-education classes. One day, she heard about a new idea for including health and human services as part of a "holistic" way to facilitate children's learning through family advocacy. She became a teacher on special assignment to coordinate Project Vision, the Santa Rosa County (Florida) Full-Service Schools Program, and is currently an administrator in the district's Student Services and Exceptional Student Education Department. This book is a documentation of her work—from blue sky to concrete—intended to assist others with an idea that really works.

Her educational training includes certification in administration, endorsement in gifted education, and a master's degree in elementary education from the University of West Florida (UWF). She is known throughout Florida as the project manager for Project Vision, but she is also recognized as a teacher, software consultant, grant writer, and presenter. In addition, she is proud to work with a cadre of veteran project directors who in turn work with the National Foundation for the Improvement of Education. She has authored numerous articles for state and national publications on collaboration and the full-service school concept, on using technology to motivate the underachiever, on health issues, and on software evaluation.

Frank Wittwer is the founder and director of the University of West Florida's Educational Research and Development Center (ERDC) in Pensacola and professor emeritus in the College of Education. His career in education began with a five-year stint as a high school teacher and with work in the Illinois Department of Education. After receiving his Ph.D. from the University of Wisconsin, Madison, in 1967, he joined UWF and initiated the ERDC's development and its focus: at-risk children, youth, and families. The center provides planning, training, and technical and evaluation assistance to schools and community agencies for programs in alternative education, delinquency diversion, in-school suspensions, interagency consortia, and full-service schools. He is renowned for his personal, caring approach to adults and children alike, whether he's playing Santa for the children in the ERDC's prekindergarten enrichment program or counseling a school principal on how to overcome truancy.

Mimi Meredith operates Wordsmiths Unlimited, writing, editing, and designing newsletters, training manuals, and books such as *Building a Full-Service School*. She has a master's degree in computer science, has been a social worker and a trainer, and spent five years as a research associate in UWF's Educational Research and Development Center. In the late 1980s, she directed development of Florida teacher certification tests in drama, speech, humanities, journalism, and for teachers of the visually and physically impaired. She has taught business and professional communication as an adjunct instructor in communication arts at UWF. Her community involvement has included board membership in a domestic violence prevention and intervention program called FavorHouse, and chairmanship of the annual fundraising effort Pensacola's Art Against AIDS.

BUILDING A
Full-Service
School

Introduction

Understanding Paradigm Shifts, Applying Them to Full-Service Schools, and Using This Guidebook

Think of us as the general contractor you have hired to design, construct, and close on the full-service school "house" of your community's dreams. We have experience, we have enthusiasm, and we have professional know-how—all of which we want to share with you in an understandable and usable guidebook format. By way of introduction, we first fill you in on pertinent shifts in the market for education and social services in the United States, shifts in paradigm and service models. Next, we draw the blueprint for this guidebook: "rooms" for each function of a full-service school's development. Finally, we lay out the contents of our toolbox: icons, design elements, and text markers to help you move comfortably among the rooms. This introduction is therefore your "key" to the guidebook's contents.

Shifts in the Education and Social Services Paradigm

Over the past one hundred years, U.S. society has settled on a particular mind-set regarding how its system of support for children and families should work. Operating in this model, or *paradigm,* our society labels individuals and their "problems" and hires public and private agencies to solve the problems. In order to make a family's complex problem understandable, the paradigm segregates the problem into small pieces; in order to evaluate a program's effectiveness, it counts "cases" instead of individual successes; in order to "treat" the problem, the paradigm assumes that only a professional knows best. But labeling, segregating, counting, and treating the family's complex problems have served only to create a system that funds countless agencies; duplicates services; functions inefficiently; and fails to improve the educational, social, medical, and financial lives of the people it is meant to serve.

The paradigm, however, is shifting. By analyzing our society's current situation in terms of twelve major shifts in focus—or *paradigm shifts*—we can

The amount of time and effort put into establishing a full-service school program will come back in rewards threefold.

—Kathleen Long, facilitator, Adult Learning Center

Figure I.1. Major Paradigm Shifts

Major Paradigm Shifts

• Grouping	Segregation	→	Inclusion
• Structure	Categorical programs	→	Shared service networks
• Services	Bundled slots	→	Unbundled wraparounds
• Design logic	Isolated problems	→	Whole systems (holistic)
	Mechanical parts	→	Organic relationships
• Focus	Process	→	Result
• Strategy	Clinical treatment	→	Social support
• Control	Professional control	→	Consumer choice
• Authority	Central hierarchy	→	Local network control
• Evaluation	Process compliance	→	Outcome/satisfaction
• Funding	Program budgets	→	Block grants/managed care
• Resources	Increasing public funds	→	Declining public funds
• Public trust	Public monopoly	→	Open competition/choice

SOURCE: reprinted by permission from Ray E. Foster, Improvement Concepts Incorporated (1995).

begin to transform frustration and anxiety into productive, proactive approaches to problem solving (Figure I.1).

The full-service school initiative is a product of these shifts in thinking. The initiative focuses not on segregated programs, each with its separate label and working in isolation from others, but on *inclusion* for children and families in the mainstream of life and a *holistic* approach to their educational, social, emotional, and physical needs. Education, social, and human service agencies collaborate in *shared service networks* to ensure *unbundled wraparound funding*—continuous funding over time and across programs—for programs that address families' needs. Program evaluation, then, shifts from counting the numbers of people receiving services to measuring outcomes and *results.* Instead of succumbing to professional control, families are encouraged to make *consumer choices* about the services they need, and they are asked to assess services with *satisfaction* surveys. Because public funding for family support programs is declining, formerly isolated programs have combined forces to apply for *block grants,* distributed under *local network control* and encouraging *open competition* and *choice.*

By design, then, full-service schools fulfill the intent of these shifts in paradigm or mind-set.

A "Room" for Each Function in the Development of a Full-Service School

When you build a house, you may begin with a paradigm that suggests an orderly and linear approach to its construction, but you soon discover that no single activity occurs in isolation. The architects do not wait for the lot to be cleared before asking the owners how many square feet of living area to sketch. The framers do not wait for the concrete foundation to dry before planning how much lumber to order. The roofers do not wait for the drywall to go up before nailing on the decking.

When you "build" a full-service school, the same principles apply. Although a 1-2-3 stepwise approach would be simple to design and follow, you are likely to find that the steps to your full-service school are sometimes uneven, occasionally run parallel to each other, and often overlap. Other authors have developed stages or phases that describe a full-service school's development, such as those of Melaville and Blank with Asayesh:[1]

Stage One: Getting together

Stage Two: Building trust and ownership

Stage Three: Developing a strategic plan

Stage Four: Taking action

Stage Five: Going to scale

We have drawn the blueprint for this guidebook by designating a room or chapter for each developmental function. But this does not mean you must start in Chapter One and end in Chapter Six. Each chapter has a "window" onto every other chapter, so you may move freely within this house plan for a full-service school.

- *Chapter One: Why build a full-service school?* Learn what defines full-service schools, why they are needed, how they differ from traditional schools, what myths you may have to overcome, and how a real one functions.

- *Chapter Two: Draw a blueprint for collaboration.* Identify your community's stakeholder "crew"; define the program manager's role; decide on a governance structure, whether site-focused or community-focused.

- *Chapter Three: Pour a foundation of knowledge.* Design your full-service school based on assessment of your community's needs, problems, services, target populations, agencies, resources, and barriers.

- *Chapter Four: Finance the construction.* Discover how to maximize existing resources and tap new funding sources.

- *Chapter Five: Frame the funding request.* Ask for and justify the funds you need with this guide to writing proposals and evaluations.

- *Chapter Six: Furnish the house.* Implement your program effectively by developing confidentiality guidelines, designing interagency cross-training programs and working agreements, and publicizing your efforts.

- *Resources (appendixes):* Move into your full-service school program with sample interagency agreements, family support plans, floor plans, and needs assessment surveys; information on sources of funding; and more.

- Finally, an *annotated bibliography,* a *glossary,* and an *index* offer expanded and supplemental information to support your full-service school's foundation.

A Toolbox for a Guidebook

What's a construction project without tools? We pull our tools out of the box one by one.

Text markers

- Words in bold *and* italic (for example, ***community agency***) indicate a term used for the first time. It is then defined in the narrow margin on the page. The definitions given are not necessarily universal but are specific to the purposes of this book. These words and their definitions also appear in the Glossary.

- Superscript numbers like this one[1] indicate reference to a source to be found in the corresponding endnote of the chapter. The annotated bibliography at the end of the book lists these and many other references alphabetically by title.

Design elements

- Wide columns of text contain the guidebook's main content.

- Narrower columns of text contain these elements:

    Quotations from other authors and from stakeholders in our full-service school program

    Key terms used in a process, approach, or system

    Lists of pointers for developing, conducting, or implementing some aspect of the full-service school program

- Text boxes hold checklists or (like the "Focus on Stakeholders" texts) relate real-life accounts of people undergoing the full-service school experience.

- Figures offer tables of information, pictures, forms, or diagrams that visually reinforce the main content.

- Diskette icons indicate sections of this book available on diskette (see p. 228).

If the full-service school concept is familiar ground for you, jump into this guidebook at whatever point interests you or answers a particular question. If the concept is totally new, you will probably want to start at the beginning and work your way to the end. If you decide to use this book to guide the construction of your own full-service school, you may find yourself referring to Chapter Three for ways to assess what services your community needs, at the same time you are evaluating Chapter Two's governance structures for your *stakeholder* crew or identifying funding sources suggested in Chapter Four. The important thing is not the order in which you read what we've written, but that you use the information contained here to effect change that benefits your community and its families. So get out your bookmarks, highlighters, and pencils. Make notes in the margins, mark off completed jobs on the checklists, jot down things to do. Make this book—and a full-service school program—your own.

Endnote

1.   Melaville, A. I., and Blank, M. J., with Asayesh, G. *Together We Can: A Guide for Crafting a Profamily System of Education and Human Services.* (U.S. Department of Education Office of Educational Research and Improvement; U.S. Department of Health and Human Services, Office of the Assistant Secretary for Planning and Evaluation.) Washington, D.C.: U.S. Government Printing Office, 1993.

Stakeholder
any potential participant in the full-service school: children, parents, extended family, neighbors, school personnel at all levels, community agencies (mental health, child welfare, juvenile justice, health, vocational, recreational, economic), businesspeople, and college faculty and staff

Chapter 1

Why Build a Full-Service School?

Understanding How Full-Service Schools Work

A full-service school . . . integrates educational, medical, and/or social and human services that are beneficial to meeting the needs of children and youth and their families on school grounds or in locations that are easily accessible.

—Concept Paper, Florida Department of Education

Because every community is unique, there is no single blueprint for building a full-service school. Each community has some characteristics in common with every other community, though, so there are tools common to the design of all full-service schools. We want to share with you a definition of full-service schools, and we want to lend you our design tools. In doing so, we hope to help you decide whether building a full-service school will meet the needs of your community.

We are acting as your general contractor, so to speak, in guiding you through the building process: developing blueprints for collaboration, laying a foundation of community knowledge, seeking financing, framing proposals, passing evaluation inspections, raising the roof, and publicizing your "open house." Along the way, you will meet the multitude of subcontractors—or stakeholders—whose skills are critical to constructing a full-service school: families, educators, health care providers, politicians, government regulators, social service caseworkers, and members of other community organizations. But before you design a full-service school, you must become familiar with the "building code":

- What characteristics define a full-service school
- Why full-service schools are needed: the basis for a philosophy of school reform
- Where a full-service school differs from others: three models
- What myths your community may harbor about full-service schools, and how to overcome them
- How a "real" full-service school functions: one family's story

What Is a Full-Service School?

For each school in our nation, the setting is uniquely shaped by the interaction of geography, history, economics, government, and population. In each community, then, the school's response to its setting must be unique. In the state of Florida, the full-service school concept is the foundation for such response, as the 1992 Interagency Workgroup on Full-Service Schools describes: "a full-service school means a school which serves as a central point of delivery, a single 'community hub,' for whatever education, health, social/human, and/or employment services have been determined locally to be needed to support a child's success in school and in the community. Such a school is locally planned and designed to meet the holistic needs of students within the context of their families. The full-service school becomes a family resource center, a 'one stop service,' for children and families and, where appropriate, for people in the surrounding community."[1]

But not all services must be located on site; the full-service school concept provides for coordination of services as well as for co-location of services. A full-service school expands its conceptual boundaries beyond the traditional educational model to a school-community model, where the lines of distinction between school and community are barely visible and where gaps in family support services disappear.

Why Do We Need Full-Service Schools?

Social and cultural changes demand reform. Responsibilities once assumed by families are now assumed by the community, and our existing educational and social systems are perceived to have failed. Listen to the observations of several concerned thinkers.

"The time has come for a new conception of the responsibilities of the school," a reformer writes. The lives of youth are desperate, parents "bring up their children in surroundings which make them in large numbers vicious and criminally dangerous," and some agencies must take charge of "the entire problem of child life and master it. If the school does not assume this responsibility, how shall the work be done?"[2] An urban superintendent agrees that the school should "serve as a clearinghouse for children's activities so that all child welfare agencies may be working simultaneously and efficiently, thus creating a child's world within the city wherein all children may have a wholesome environment all of the day and every day."[3] A sociologist echoes the idea: all agencies dealing with "neglected or behavior-problem children [should] be closely coordinated" under the aegis of the school, including "medical inspection, school nursing, attendance control, vocational guidance and placement, psychological testing, visiting teachers, and special schools and classes."[4]

The reformer was Robert Hunter—writing in 1904. The superintendent was William Wirt of Gary, Indiana, speaking in 1923. The sociologist was Thomas D. Eliot, who in 1928 urged a blending of education and other forms of child welfare. Although their comments were made years ago, their message sounds contemporary. Traditional schools can no longer meet the expanding needs and expectations of children, families, or communities. Times and needs have changed.

Raising Children Has Become a Community Responsibility

The traditional school was limited to teaching children basic literacy and social responsibility. Traditional schools were expected to prepare students for their transition to the world of work, or to a technical school or institution of higher learning. Other *community agencies* had responsibility for health, social services, and juvenile law.

These traditional patterns no longer fit. Societal problems have grown increasingly complex: more single-parent families and more households where both parents work outside the home, hunger and poverty, drug and alcohol abuse, high unemployment, child abuse and neglect, violent crimes, homelessness, long-term emotional problems, and vandalism. Because children bring these problems into the school setting, growing numbers of children are less ready to learn, and academic success is severely affected.

Responding to the profoundly complex problems presented by today's families is not the sole responsibility of one agency, organization, or institution—or of the school. Teachers, administrators, and counselors seeking to improve children's academic performance are beginning to accept that delivery of human services and restructuring of education are inextricably linked. As an African proverb proposes, "It takes the whole village to raise a child."

The Existing System Has Failed

Why is it that existing delivery systems for educating children and caring for families do not work? There are five basic reasons.

1. **Most existing services are crisis-oriented.** Instead of taking a preventive orientation, we wait until a critical incident forces us to commit resources to the problem. This orientation is not only more costly but also less effective in resolving chronic problems. As a result, Susan is not eligible for counseling to overcome her attention deficit disorder unless her behavior causes harm to another child in the classroom. Sean does not receive academic tutoring until he actually fails a subject.

2. **The existing social welfare system divides the problems of children and families into rigid and distinct categories that fail to reflect interrelated causes and solutions.** In our rush to sim-

Community agency

an organization, local in scope, public or private, for profit or not for profit, including those that offer assessment, prevention, and intervention services such as mental health, child welfare, juvenile justice, educational, medical, vocational, recreational, or operational services plify complex issues, we succeed only in assigning labels, prescribing solutions, and treating symptoms of isolated problems. Services designed to address each problem are offered by dozens of different agencies, each with its own eligibility criteria, funding sources, and program goals. As a learning-disabled teen who is a parent, Carmella may not be adequately prepared to understand what is taught in a standard teen parenting program. T. J.'s emotional handicap is addressed in a special program at school, but he goes home to parents who are unable to deal with his problems because of their own (financial stress from unemployment).

3. **The current service delivery system is inadequate to meet families' needs because no functional communication exists among the myriad public and private community service agencies.** Families with multiple needs are served by more than one agency; they must travel to each agency; they reproduce the same paperwork for each agency; they repeat the same story to each agency. The agency and the school seldom share information, even though both are involved with the same family. Family, agency, and school are therefore all needlessly handicapped by duplicate paperwork and effort. Tran, who speaks English but cannot write it, asks a neighbor for help in completing his application for employment services; but he is embarrassed to ask again when his wife Anna comes home from their children's school with an application for free lunch.

4. **Specialized community agencies are incapable of crafting comprehensive solutions to complex problems; thus they cannot offer solutions to families with multiple problems.** Specialized agencies operating independently do not interact with others in an environment rich in the professional talent and expertise that is needed to plan, finance, and implement programs that respond to complex needs. This is why Joanne is forced to drop out of a local job training program, because she cannot afford child care for her three children. Jacob is eligible for two different counseling programs, but no such programs are available for his mother, the perpetrator of his physical abuse.

5. **Existing community agencies are insufficiently funded. The "response-ability" of both schools and community agencies has greatly diminished, while their responsibilities have greatly increased.** Every day, newspapers print stories of agencies forced to reduce the size of their staff, despite being burdened with larger caseloads. Schools must lobby state legislatures for the most basic operational funding and harbor little hope of funding

any prevention or intervention services. So Lianna languishes on Head Start's waiting list because there are not enough funds to hire a sufficient number of teachers. Her brother, Jabal, finds himself at loose ends after school—and in danger of joining his delinquent buddies—because funding for his after-school athletic program was not renewed.

Communities feel the impact of the intense competition for resources brought about by changing times. The time has come when schools and related community agencies must work together to offer a broader continuum of coordinated services. Schools are a logical hub in the wheel of delivery, *coordination*, and integration of these services.

Where Do Full-Service and Traditional Schools Differ?

School-community relationships can be characterized as existing on a continuum of involvement having infinite variations. On one end, there is little or no interaction, coordination, or communication between school and community. On the other end, the school and the community are almost indistinguishable. Since each community is unique, full-service school stakeholders must determine the existing level of interaction between individual schools and their communities. Doing so establishes a starting point for change, which helps you determine whether your school and community want to move toward a shared system for delivery of educational, medical, social, and human services.

Model One: Traditional School-Community Relationship

In some communities there may be few or no interactions between the school and the community. In the traditional model, the family teaches values; the school delivers academics; and community agencies provide medical, social, and human services. If a child in school presents a health problem, the school sends the child home to the parents, who presumably take the child to a separate facility for treatment. There is no tracking system for problems or solutions, no way of knowing if, when, or how a particular problem is resolved. Separation of school and community is complete (Figure 1.1).

As communities struggle with the increasing variety and number of societal problems, many feel that the distance between the school and the community must be reduced, and that *collaboration* and *cooperation* more efficiently and effectively address these problems.

Model Two: School-Community Partnership

In another community, the relationships and interactions between school and community are closer than in the traditional model. The school and the com-

Coordination
process of linking the functions of autonomous entities in an effort to achieve the most effective results and to avoid duplication

Collaboration
process of working jointly with others, including those with whom one is not normally or immediately connected, to develop and achieve common goals

Cooperation
process of associating and acting together for mutual benefit

Figure 1.1. Model One: Traditional School-Community Relationship

munity are starting to raise their children together, as in the African proverb. The emerging partnership is strengthened by invitations from the school to the community, or from the community to the school, to participate in activities that create bonds between them. The school opens its doors to business partnerships, parent organizations, volunteer programs, evening adult literacy activities, and on-campus after-school youth groups. Community sporting events, choral and dance recitals, band, and theater productions all take place in the school's facilities (Figure 1.2).

However, there is clearly a line separating school and community as to function. The school still teaches academics, but it neither delivers nor coordinates human services to children and their families on or near the school site. If there are family problems, they still are referred to the family and the community. The common ground is the physical school site and the opportunity for the community to see the school as a user-friendly place.

Model Three: School-Community Collaboration

The full-service school concept is recognized when the lines of distinction between the school and the community start to become invisible. The gap

Figure 1.2. Model Two: School-Community Partnership

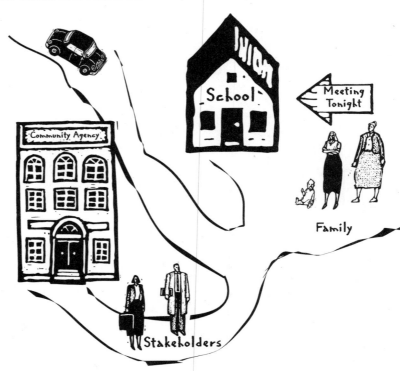

Co-locate

the act of relocating community agencies or their representatives to the campus of a full-service school

between them completely disappears. The school is the community and the community is the school.

In this collaborative model (Figure 1.3), the school and community are highly interactive and mutually involved. Community agencies are either *co-located* on the school property or housed within the school building. Partnerships between local businesses and the full-service school provide the school with technical equipment, and business owners even teach some classes. The school is open at night and on Saturdays. Social service agencies serve children and families as a unit. Health screenings and inoculations are routinely provided by county medical staff. Services not available on site are arranged by an interagency referral system. Parents are no longer forced to drive long distances to obtain basic health, economic, or social services for themselves or their children. Agency caseworkers do not have to drive long distances to deliver services.

The community agencies' staff routinely consult with teachers and school administrators. Agency staff members are invited into the classroom to assist teachers, and their skills and knowledge have a direct impact on the curriculum. Interagency agreements establish partnerships between the school and community agencies. Cost sharing, problem solving, and information exchanges reduce duplication and bureaucratic red tape.

These three models of school and community interactions are not moving pictures. They are snapshots, at just three intervals along the continuum

Figure 1.3. Model Three: School-Community Collaboration

of possibilities. Selecting snapshots does not capture all the possibilities that exist between the interval points. The purpose of the models is to provide points of reference as you consider the relationship between your own school and community, before you pursue the idea of developing your own full-service school model. The more distance there is between your school and community, the more difficult it may be to build a full-service school. This does not mean that the school cannot be built. It just implies that the community and the school have not yet had the experience of sharing information, resources, and trust. To create your own model, first define where your school and community are located on the continuum of possibilities in Figure 1.4. Then, decide where you want to go.

Where on the continuum do your school and community lie? Which model most closely approximates the existing relationship between your school and your community? Which model best describes the school-community relationship you would like to see develop?

You may doubt whether your school, agency, or community can assemble the leadership, motivation, and other logistics to initiate a full-service school venture. As an individual, you may feel overwhelmed that the task of initiating this concept is your responsibility. If you feel that your voice is too small, the challenge is too big, and someone so insignificant couldn't

From my point of view, the most important aspect of full-service schools is that we are more intimately bound to the ongoing life of our community. We are not just touching a part of it. The hardest part is rethinking the idea of what a school is.

**—Tom Kennell,
elementary school
assistant principal**

Figure 1.4. School-Community Relationship Continuum

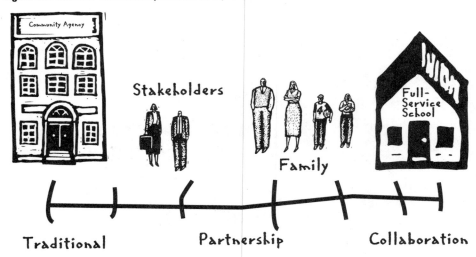

possibly have an impact, then recall the effect of one tiny mosquito being in your bedroom at night. Recognize that you probably already have significant experience in utilizing the skills needed to assemble a full-service school.

Does your school have a PTA or PTO program? Or a Business and Education project? Do you have students from a university or college doing practicums or internships? If the answer is yes, you have the initial skills, experience, and credentials. A full-service school is simply an expanded version of what you are already doing. The biggest challenge you face is remembering to start small, insist on quality, focus on the needs of children and their families, keep the lines of communication open, invite feedback, don't give up when a glitch appears, and put personal egos in the refrigerator.

Now, let's do the rest of our homework by reading on.

What Myths Exist About Full-Service Schools?

Be prepared to face some of the prevailing notions that we list here in the form of quotations from community members. Countering these myths with valid information about full-service schools produces an accurate picture in the public's mind and helps turn community opposition into the community support so critical to your program's success. Responding to these and other myths also validates the *why* of your full-service school.

Myth 1   *Overload* Our school district already has enough to do, working to meet our goals. There's no time to initiate another program. It takes just one example of a typical goal to dispel this myth: "The schools, district, and state ensure the professionalism of teachers and staff." Here are just a few of the full-service school programs that respond to such a goal: professionalization institutes, staff wellness, in-service training on available community resources, and technology initiatives. Instead of increasing the burden, full-service schools actually resolve issues required by existing programs or mandates (see Resource A, "Matching Full-Service Goals and Services").

Myth 2   *No Problem*   **We don't have those problems in this school, and we don't need help from the community. This school has always resolved its own problems.** Believers in this myth live in a state of denial. There is not a school in the country free of problems that are beyond its present capabilities. If this myth prevails in your community, orchestrate the development of a communication plan to disseminate facts about the needs confronting families in your community. The plan might include newspaper articles, presentations by experts at special school or community functions, or a local television special on complex family problems.

Myth 3   *Turf*   **Those agencies should just stay in their own space instead of using our school to house their personnel and offer their services.** This attitude stems from the philosophy of separate functions, that schools take care of academics, health service agencies take care of health problems, and social service agencies take care of social problems. You can counter this myth by agreeing that, ideally, schools are supposed to take care of academics; in reality, schools are struggling to deal with health problems, mental illness, abuse and neglect, teen pregnancy, and violence. Because most schools do not have the support staff necessary to resolve nonacademic problems, they need support from community agencies. In this way, educators can better concentrate on education. Although schools alone may not be able to provide a complete array of services, a full-service school approach means that schools and school boards play key roles in ensuring that students receive the services they need.

Myth 4   *Liability*   **Schools should not get involved in providing all of these services for families and students, because doing so increases the school's liability.** Often proposed by school administrators and principals, this myth ignores the truth that properly written interagency agreements minimize the school's liability. Actually, experienced full-service school principals are often less liable because they share responsibilities with other agencies. One full-service school principal reports sleeping better after making a child-abuse-and-neglect referral because she knew the onsite social worker, and she knew the social worker would report the results the next day. The same school principal expresses relief at having interagency teams, not just the school, share responsibility for service delivery decisions.

Myth 5   *Parental Resistance*   **Parents aren't going to support this idea of providing full service at school sites. It will never work here.** This myth reflects a lack of understanding about the benefits of full-service schools for families. The truth is that parental involvement and volunteer hours usually skyrocket at full-service school sites. Families involved in the planning and implementation stages of the program are its strongest advocates!

Myth 6   *Unsuitability*   **A program like this won't work in our school. We are urban . . . rural . . . suburban. We are a middle school . . . a high school . . . an intermediate school . . . an elementary school.** When a full-service school responds to the community's needs and when decisions about services are based on needs of families in that community, no two full-service schools are the same. Your program uniquely reflects your community's needs, whether the neighborhood is rural or urban, whether the school is elementary or middle.

Myth 7   *Those People*   **We don't want "those people" on our school's campus. They will fraternize with our students, and it's not safe.** "Those people" may have a mental health or substance abuse problem, or a need for economic or health services, or whatever. In short, they may be like any one of us at some period in our lives. This is a sensitive issue in every community, best overcome by a reminder that "those people" benefit the community by taking advantage of services located in the full-service school. Do be careful to steer high-risk adults away from the general traffic flow of students. If your community is extraordinarily sensitive about this issue, implement less-controversial services first, and then expand your program as the community's trust grows.

Myth 8   *Increased Taxes*   **We will end up paying for all those extra services at the full-service school, and our taxes will go up.** Collaborative services often result from complicated funding mechanisms, and members of your community may assume that additional services on or near a school campus require additional tax dollars from their pockets. Counteract this myth by educating the community about program funding. (See Figure 1.5 for a sample matrix of services and funding sources. Resource A offers you a template for this community-education purpose.)

Myth 9   *Diversion*   **Providing all these additional services at school sites will take children away from valuable educational activities.** Counteracting this myth is a communication challenge. Stress that additional services are often integrated into the existing curriculum, offered before and after normal school hours, and provided during evening hours that are convenient for parents. A service matrix (Figure 1.5 and Resource A) is a good tool for counteracting misinformation.

Myth 10   *Space*   **Adding community services will take up school space that could be used for our children's education.** Avoid converting regular classrooms to community agency space if at all possible—unless you can honestly say that the lost space has no detrimental effect on students.

Myth 11   *Responsibility*   **Why are schools becoming full service anyway? It's the parents' responsibility to make sure their children get the help they need.** A properly planned full-service school reinforces the idea that it is the parents' responsibility to obtain needed services for their children. Full-service schools fully support the concept of family empowerment and remove barriers so that families can help themselves.

Myth 12   *Administration*   **Having "other agency" support staff on our school campus will cause a whole new set of problems: supervision, performance evaluations, resistance from the school faculty, confusion of roles, and more.** This is an administrator's argument. If the principal at the proposed site of your full-service school makes this argument, that site may not be your best choice. Most such issues, however, can be worked out by employing cross-training techniques (Chapter Six).

Myth 13   *Impossibility*   **This full-service school stuff is just too complicated. I don't believe it can be done! You are wasting our time trying to do this.** The good news is that communities all over the nation operate successful (though diverse) full-service schools. It can be done! Yes, it does take time and patience. Yes, it is worth the trouble. Just ask a participating family.

All the coordination, cooperation, and collaboration that your school and community agencies muster cannot keep some stakeholders from clinging to these myths unless you plan ahead to dispel them. Present the facts, and listen for protesters' underlying concerns and fears. It is possible that such opposition may eventually fuel development of an even more responsive program than you envision.

Figure 1.5. Service Matrix for a Real Full-Service School

Service	Description/Clientele	Location/Hours	Funding Sources
Adult Education	Basic education and remediation for adults 16+ Undergraduate and graduate coursework	Middle School, Monday and Thursday 5–8 P.M. College and enrichment classes by semester	• Adult Learning Center • Community schools • Community college • State university
Casework	Protective services, Project Vision Referrals for delinquency, foster care, developmental and economic services, alcohol/drug abuse, mental health counseling, home visits	Middle School, weekdays	• State Dept. of Children and Families (DCF)
Child Care	Free or reduced, subsidized child care for children 3 months to 12 years Some restrictions apply	Appointments taken for location convenient to parent	• Children's Services
Community Use of School Facilities	Civic and parent groups apply for permission Available to all, free	Primary, Intermediate, and Middle Schools	• County School Board
Economic Services	AFDC, Medicaid, food stamps: intake, screening, application, review Referrals to other community resources	Middle School, M–F, 8 A.M.–5 P.M. Appointments preferred; walk-ins accepted	• DCF
Educational Opportunity Center	Career options counseling and financial aid for students 19+	Community Center, Tuesdays 1–4 P.M.	• Community college
First Call for Help	Toll-free community resource information hotline	Available districtwide	• Center for Community Mental Health • United Way • Retired senior volunteers
Graduation Enhancement Program	Technology-based early intervention to promote student learning	Intermediate and Middle Schools	• County School Board
Health Services	RN and psychologist: prevention, early detection, early intervention, and community referrals Mobile health unit Emergency food and clothing Affordable health insurance for school-age children	Intermediate and Middle Schools, M–F, school hours	• Supplemental School Health Grant: DCF and State Dept. of Education • Sacred Heart Hospital • Community resources • Healthy Kids Corp.

Figure 1.5. Service Matrix for a Real Full-Service School *(continued)*

Service	Description/Clientele	Location/Hours	Funding Sources
Healthy Kids	Affordable health insurance for children ages 3–19	Available districtwide Enrollment by toll-free number	• State legislature • Healthy Kids Corp. • County School Board • County commissioners • Blue Cross/Blue Shield Health Options
Home Visitor High-Risk Infant Program	Home visits by social worker for at-risk infants Training in parenting skills, immunizations, etc.	South end of county	• DCF
Job Services	Employment services for job training and placement with computer access to regional job listings	Middle School, M–F, 8 A.M.–5 P.M.	• DCF • Private Industry Council (PIC) • Job Training Partnership Act
Juvenile Alternative Services Program (JASP)	Meaningful sanctions and services for certain juvenile offenders and their families, designed to divert from judicial processing and to reduce incidence of law violations	Intermediate and Middle Schools	• DCF
Latchkey	State-licensed after-school programs until 6 P.M. schooldays and some holidays Summer camp program, 7:30 A.M.–6:30 P.M.	Primary, Intermediate, and Middle Schools Campers picked up and returned to Intermediate School	• Community schools • Parent tuition • Title XX funding for qualified families
Mental Health Counseling	Counseling for students and families Exceptional student education specialist Full-time therapist for emotionally or severely emotionally handicapped	Primary, Intermediate, and Middle Schools	• Center for Community Mental Health • Medicaid • Private insurance
Parent Involvement Center	Educational and counseling materials available for checkout by parents for use with students at home	Primary, Intermediate, and Middle Schools	• Project Vision • National Foundation for the Improvement of Education (NFIE) • Junior League • Community resources • Parent-teacher association (PTA) • Parent advisory boards

(continued on next page)

Figure 1.5. Service Matrix for a Real Full-Service School *(continued)*

Service	Description/Clientele	Location/Hours	Funding Sources
Parent Workshops	Hosted periodically during the school year for all interested persons	Primary, Intermediate, and Middle Schools	• Project Vision • Community resources • PTA • Parent advisory boards
Prekindergarten	Head Start or early intervention programs for 4-year-olds Placement on space-available basis Some restrictions	Intermediate School	• Federal and state funding in collaboration with County School Board
Private Industry Council (PIC)	Employability skills for middle school, 16+ students, and adults	Middle School	• PIC
Protective Services	Onsite investigator for abuse or neglect complaints through State Protective Services System's Abuse Registry	Middle School	• DCF
Research	Ongoing research activity supervised by state university	Primary, Intermediate, and Middle Schools	• Full-service schools • State university
Sheriff's Department	Onsite deputy available for assistance with law enforcement issues, education, and prevention activities	Primary, Intermediate, and Middle Schools	• County Sheriff's Department • Full-service schools
Volunteers	Volunteers act as tutors, teacher helpers, mentors, etc.	Primary, Intermediate, and Middle Schools	• Retired senior volunteers • County School Board • Community organizations
Women, Infants, and Children Program	Offers nutrition counseling and supplemental food for prenatal and postnatal care and for children from birth to 5 years	Community Center, 1st Wednesday and 2nd Friday each month, 9 A.M.–3 P.M.	• PIC • Federal funding through County Public Health Unit

See Resource A for template listing suggested services.

How Does a "Real" Full-Service School Work?

Illustrating an eight-year history of survival and expansion, our subject full-service school is a composite of four school sites physically located within one Florida community. Students attend classes in prekindergarten through grade twelve, so their ages range from three to about seventeen. Many services offered at the schools are available to the entire community, whether or not families have children enrolled in one of the four schools.

This site was chosen for a full-service school because the community wanted it, needed it, and was ready for it. Keep in mind that the model presented here may have changed further by the time you read this documentary. The program was never meant to be static; rather, it is dynamic, meeting emerging and changing needs of the community's students and families.

The concept of a full-service school is based on the bold philosophy that schools can produce academic literacy only when students are ready and able to learn. Success in school is directly related to family environment and to students' physical and mental health. If we are to reach the goal of school reform—to maximize every student's learning potential—then we must identify the problems our students face, and we must become proactive participants in the solutions, not promoters of quick fixes. We must explore less costly and more efficient ways of "doing business." We may not be able to work any harder, but we can work smarter.

The array of services offered at these schools runs almost from A to Z: from adult education, through economic services and a latchkey program, to the Women, Infants, and Children program (Figure 1.5). Although most of the services are located on one of the four school campuses, some of them are offered from a community center, a student's home, a child care center, or a family service center linked to the schools. Funding sources, too, constitute quite an array: local retired senior volunteers, the county school board, the state Department of Children and Families, and the National Foundation for the Improvement of Education (NFIE), to name just a few.

At the middle school level, the school building is open six days per week from 7:00 A.M. to 9:30 P.M. and on Sunday from 8:00 A.M. to 1:00 P.M. This is how services and clientele come together at this location:

- Adult basic education and college-level coursework (evening hours)
- Protective services casework (weekdays)
- Civic and parent groups (after hours)
- Economic services (weekdays, walk-in, or by appointment)
- Graduation enhancement program
- Health services: registered nurse, psychologist, mobile health unit (school hours)
- Juvenile Alternative Services Program (school hours)
- Parent involvement center and workshops
- Sheriff's department prevention activities
- Volunteer tutors

Far from being static, however, the sites, services, sources, and clientele are likely to change since the community's needs are in flux. Over an eight-year period, the sustainability rate of cooperative services is an impressive

FOCUS ON STAKEHOLDERS:

Children—and a Family—in Need

Meet the Young family. They live two miles from the site of our full-service school, and they have been involved with the program for about four years. Alice and Sam Young have two children. Amy, twelve, is a seventh grader with multiple physical and educational challenges; she has been in the exceptional-student education class since second grade. John, ten, is a handful: he performs poorly, disrupts the class, and may fail the fifth grade. His teacher has tried numerous interventions, unsuccessfully. It is because of John's classroom behavior—and the rumor that he recently broke into a neighbor's home—that John's teacher refers the Youngs to an interagency problem-solving "care team" by way of the school counselor. The care team consists of members of the child's family, the classroom teacher, the school counselor and social worker, a project psychologist, an administrator, a registered nurse, a resource officer, a caseworker specializing in child abuse and neglect, and other members of the community support system as needed. The care team meets to help the family decide on a course of action to promote student success.

The school counselor tells the other team members about John's classroom problems. The sheriff's department resource officer explains John's recent brush with the law. The health nurse voices her concerns about Amy. Having considered the facts, the team decides that the school's onsite social worker should join the health nurse for a home visit and conference with Mr. and Mrs. Young.

The visit provides evidence that the Youngs are struggling, both economically and emotionally, and John's acting-out behaviors are symptomatic of high levels of stress at home. Sam, a truck driver, is in and out of work and rarely at home. There is very little food in the Youngs' dilapidated two-bedroom trailer. Alice, overwhelmed and confused by the family's circumstances, shows signs of stress and depression. She has no job, no car, and few friends; her health is poor. Daughter Amy is obviously unhappy, and John's behavior at school is getting worse.

When the team meets with Alice, they discover some important strengths. Alice is very eager to participate in any available services, she has significant support from her extended family, her family unit is intact, and her husband is currently employed. There are critical deficits as well: Alice did not finish high school, she worries because Amy has not had a physical exam in over four years, she confides that John tried to run away from home last month, and she admits she frequently argues with her husband over family finances.

Together, the team and the Youngs work to develop the *family care coordination plan*. The plan

Family care coordination plan
a written document resulting from a family-centered process that identifies the family's strengths, concerns, and goals, and that coordinates community resources and services in support of those goals

92 percent. New programs, of course, join existing ones to create an ever-changing, but increasingly responsive, array.

Now you understand the building code for a full-service school: the characteristics that define such a school, why such a school is needed, how the full-service school model differs from more traditional ones, and what myths you are likely to have to overcome if you decide to build your own full-service school. You have also seen firsthand (in Figure 1.5 and Resource A) the extensive matrix of services created by a real full-service school, and you have witnessed real results in a stakeholder family.

Many more such experiences await you. Chapter Two offers a blueprint for planning and decision making with community stakeholders. Chapter

includes health services for Amy, counseling for John, career counseling for Alice, and economic and educational services for the family.

With the plan in place, the Youngs' situation starts to improve. After talking with the full-service school's adult career options counselor, Alice enrolls in nighttime adult basic education classes. She also volunteers in the school's computer lab and signs up for dance lessons on Wednesday nights, all on site at the full-service school. The school's onsite registered nurse assesses Amy's condition and refers her to Children's Medical Services for a complete physical exam. Amy is also found eligible for a Private Industry Council program that pays students while they learn practical job skills. Through the school's onsite child care referral office, John is certified for an after-school latchkey program—instead of after-school mischief. He is placed in an onsite early intervention program that incorporates technology into the curriculum, and the health service psychologist provides insight into effective behavioral interventions for his teacher.

Alice and Sam begin family counseling sessions with a mental health professional who offers evening appointments at the full-service school, and at the suggestion of John's teacher they check out educational materials from the parent involvement center. At the school's economic services office, the Youngs apply for and are approved for food stamps. Alice attends a parenting workshop on adolescents, sponsored by the school counselors.

Where are the Youngs today? Fours years after becoming involved with the full-service school, Alice has received her GED and is employed as a data entry clerk. Amy, diagnosed with a rare disorder, is undergoing a regimen of medication designed to help her body develop normally. She recently won a gold medal at the Special Olympics. John has had no further brushes with the law, and his grades, attendance, and attitude improved so much he was mainstreamed to regular education classes. Sam, still a truck driver, recently began more stable employment, thanks to information he received from the full-service school's new job-services terminal. The family no longer receives, or needs, food stamps. When the family became ineligible for Medicaid because of their increased income, Amy and John were able to enroll in a new school-based, affordable, comprehensive health insurance plan called Healthy Kids, for a fee of $5 each per month.

The Youngs' story is true; only their names and identifying details have been changed to ensure confidentiality. Alice is involved with school and school-related issues every day. She works with the classroom teacher to keep both children on track. She attends parenting sessions and checks out educational materials for use at home. Her new interest in education for herself has made her a powerful role model for her children. The Youngs grow and learn—as a family—every day because of their involvement with a full-service school.

Three contains strategies for needs assessments. Look to Chapter Four for funding approaches and sources, and to Chapter Five for pointers on writing proposals and evaluations. In Chapter Six, you will find ways to develop interagency agreements and training programs and to handle public relations and confidentiality. So, it's time to break ground on your full-service school!

Endnotes

1. Florida Department of Education, Interagency Workgroup on Full-Service Schools. *Concept Paper.* Tallahassee: Florida Department of Education, 1992.

2. Tyack, D. "Health and Social Services in Public Schools: Historical Perspectives." *Future of Children,* 1992, *20*(1), 19–31.

3. Melaville, A. I., and Blank, M. J., with Asayesh, G. *Together We Can: A Guide for Crafting a Profamily System of Education and Human Services.* (U.S. Department of Education Office of Educational Research and Improvement; U.S. Department of Health and Human Services, Office of the Assistant Secretary for Planning and Evaluation.) Washington, D.C.: U.S. Government Printing Office, 1993.

4. Tyack (1992).

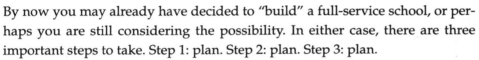

Chapter 2

Draw a Blueprint for Collaboration

Planning and Decision Making with Stakeholders

By now you may already have decided to "build" a full-service school, or perhaps you are still considering the possibility. In either case, there are three important steps to take. Step 1: plan. Step 2: plan. Step 3: plan.

Resist the urge to start a program without *lots* of planning. A quickly poured but poorly planned foundation may doom your program before it rises from the ground. Our intent in this chapter is to help you develop a blueprint (plan), one that calls for collaboration among the key subcontractors (stakeholders) in your full-service school program.

Planning in the context of the full-service school is the careful and deliberate process of using decision making to build collaboration. Planning is the basis for sound implementation. Since it is also a constant event in the life cycle of a full-service school, this chapter's blueprint is drawn in a way that gives you practice in planning. It does so by answering these questions:

- Who are the key stakeholders in your community's full-service school?

- What family support services should your full-service school offer, based on the community's needs?

- Where will these services be offered?

- When will services be delivered to the community?

- How will services be delivered effectively?

In this chapter, we assume that you already possess current, valid data about your community's composition in terms of children and families, about your community's agencies and activists, and about what services are available or lacking. If you do not yet have these data, see Chapter Three for tools with which you can conduct a comprehensive community needs assessment.

The most important results of our full-service school program are the collaboration and cooperation that take place. They enable us to better serve the citizens of our county. If you build a full-service school, be willing to give as much as you take!

—Betty Arnold, operations director, Children's Services Center

Who Are the Stakeholders, and What Are Their Roles?

Planning
the careful and deliberate process of using decision making to build collaboration; the basis for sound implementation of a full-service school program

The strength and longevity of your full-service school program depends upon the direct, real, and early involvement and collaboration of key stakeholders. Stakeholders can be students; families; teachers; local civic organization or church members; or representatives from education, health, and human service agencies. *Planning* is simply where their collaborative relationship begins. Although one person may initiate your full-service school program, significant others must quickly be allowed to share the vision and the ownership, as well as their skills and knowledge. Mutual trust and respect evolve naturally among stakeholders who work together and who share responsibility for the program's success.

To select the *who* in your collaborative planning effort, you need to complete these steps:

1. Identify the stakeholders.
2. Decide who is to take the lead.
3. Choose a program manager.
4. Establish the governance structure.

Step One: Identify the Stakeholders

The stakeholders play the primary role in planning, policy development, and implementation of services specified in the blueprint for your full-service school. The process of identifying stakeholders is guided by the philosophy that you are planning with—not for—the community. From the very start, stakeholder decisions have dramatic impact on the success of your program. Through the decision-making process, the stakeholders begin immediately to develop a common understanding of the community's problems, become supportive of collaboration among community agencies, lay a foundation of mutual trust, and share a vision for the future of your full-service school program.

Selecting stakeholders to participate in development of your full-service school may come down to choosing those individuals who want to participate. There are probably some stakeholders in your community who should be involved but are reluctant; in that case, it is better to leave them out. They might be motivated to join your construction crew later, perhaps once there is evidence that your full-service school is really going to be built. You might recruit more people if you provide potential stakeholders with a written proposal or action plan for design of the full-service school.

Carefully evaluate the number of stakeholders you select for your crew. Weigh members' potential contributions against the danger of making the

Pointers

Ask these questions to help identify key stakeholders:

- Who are the major stakeholders (families, schools, community agencies, corporations, parent organizations, churches, media representatives, university personnel)?

- Who collects data that document the needs of children and their families?

- Which stakeholders have a history of quality and timely service delivery?

- How can the stakeholder group be balanced to match the community's ethnic and racial composition?

- How can you balance representation from school personnel, community agencies, businesses, and families so that one group does not "own" or dominate the program?

crew's membership too large. If rapid movement toward achieving your program goals is important, limit the group to ten or fewer individuals; any more, and your program's implementation is likely to slow considerably.

One cluster of potential crew members needs special attention during the planning process: the superintendent of schools, the school board, and the principal at the proposed site of your full-service school. A program planted at a school site without the involvement of these stakeholders is doomed, sure to fall victim to passive resistance and sabotage. Because the full-service school concept is based on the idea that family support services are to be located at or near school sites, most traditional schools must broaden their vision considerably in order to successfully develop into full-service schools. Ensuring that the school system's leading officials are included in the decision-making process, then, is critical.

One more tip about selecting stakeholders: be sure to include any significantly influential community group, and do so before making any public announcements about the program. If a key group is left out, you then spend valuable time and energy trying to repair a public relations problem. Selecting stakeholders is truly the key to gaining communitywide support for your full-service school program.

Step Two: Decide Who Is to Take the Lead

As your collaborative effort begins, decide whether one person or a combination of people, groups, or organizations is going to take the lead. The person or agency that started the ball rolling should lead the stakeholder crew at the outset. An election process can then ensure continuity of leadership after the program gets under way. In many full-service school programs, a school is designated the program's lead partner; note that some funding sources specify a lead agency (whether a school or otherwise; see Chapter Four). There are logical reasons for this decision to have a school be the lead partner:

- Schools have access to more children than any other branch of the community service system.

- Schools often initiate collaboration because they recognize the dramatic need for family support services.

- Schools are already required to collect extensive data about children.

There are potential problems, however, if a school dominates an interagency effort:

- Difficulty in attracting additional dollars from agencies that have not traditionally collaborated with schools

- Demands for space that a full-service school requires in an already overcrowded system

- Perceived burden of adding health and social services to the school's responsibility for academic services
- Difficulty in restructuring the school hierarchy—one that is independent and historically resistant to change—to include other community agencies

Although it is vital to your program's success to have a designated leader, it is equally important for that leader to draw other stakeholders into leadership roles. All major decisions should be made within the collaborative structure of the stakeholder crew.

Step Three: Choose a Program Manager

The choice of a program manager to manage and coordinate your full-service school program is quite likely to determine its success. Ideally, this person does not have ten other major responsibilities: this is a full-time job! Because the right person can jump-start your program by facilitating communication and implementation, he or she should be hired very early in the planning process.

In all likelihood, there is no shortage of candidates for program manager. The head of each collaborating agency is, by definition, in a leadership position. But behind every leader you find the rubber-meets-the-road staff, people who take the blue-sky planning documents and convert them to action. Such is the role of the full-service school program manager. The ideal manager anticipates needs and gets the job done smoothly and efficiently, brings stakeholders to the table and keeps them involved, and maintains clarity about the program's vision. The manager recognizes when the program stalls and is able to spark movement on new ideas and initiatives. A traditional job description is shown in full in Resource B, but you may want to add these special qualifications to it: the patience of Job, the work ethic of a pioneer, and the heart of a saint!

Because a full-service school program assumes that schools are participating, the stakeholders may want to seek out a program manager experienced with both the school system and family support services and programs. Special education teachers who understand at-risk students, who have at least some experience with collaborative efforts, and who show strong leadership skills are good candidates for the job. Personnel from community agencies who have a working knowledge of how school systems operate are also promising candidates. Take time to find the best candidates, hire a manager early, and treat him or her well. The manager must provide the program with continuity and momentum long after the bloom fades from the rose of first publicity, so investing in a quality program manager is both necessary and wise.

Step Four: Establish the Governance Structure

After the key stakeholders are identified, a lead person or agency chosen, and a program manager selected, the next item on your agenda is to establish a *governance structure*. When your stakeholder crew reaches this point, it is completing the last of the initial planning steps but simultaneously beginning implementation. Keep in mind that planning and implementation are an ongoing effort in the life of your full-service school. You are constantly in a state of "construction," with new crews coming in for remodeling while old crews are adding on to the original structure.

Governance structure
an organizational arrangement designed to guide or influence a program's initiation, development, evaluation, and sustainability

Explore two alternative governance structures with your stakeholders: site-based (designed to get a program started fairly quickly at a particular site) and community-based (designed to lay the foundation for continuing collaborative relationships on a broader scale within a larger community and over a longer period of time).

Site-Based Governance

A simple but effective *site-based governance* structure is a three-tiered pyramid, having as stakeholders a planning committee, a policy committee, and a steering committee. All of them interact through the program manager (Figure 2.1). The pyramid is built on the ideas of site-based decision making, communication between natural levels of administrative power, and total involvement of the community.

Site-based governance
organizational plan based on the premise that those individuals working directly with students and families at the site of a full-service school should have the most influence on initiating, developing, evaluating, and sustaining the program

Each tier of the pyramid houses specific stakeholders who are assigned specific tasks. The advantage of this governance structure is that decisions are made by stakeholders who deal daily with the problems that families face. Bottom-up management is implicit in site-based governance, keeping the

Figure 2.1. Site-Based Governance

program design closest to the families it is designed to serve. Using this governance structure, you have a built-in communication mechanism to deal with the constant and dynamic change inherent in your program's design: new personnel, changes in funding, and identification of additional needs, to name a few. Keep in mind, too, that this governance structure can be adapted to accommodate fewer than three levels if your program is very small or if you have a limited number of stakeholders.

Members of the planning committee are on the front line of your program's planning and implementation. The members of this group are likely to fall into two categories: those who are risk takers and leaders in their field, and those who have the potential to create major barriers to implementation. The first group is important for the communication and problem-solving skills they contribute; the second is important because involving them early in the planning process may diffuse opposition and turn them into committed proponents. Planning committee members, all of whom should have a working knowledge of your community's needs, are representative of groups such as these:

- Families
- Caseworkers
- Teachers
- Counselors
- Parents
- Community health and human service workers
- School staff (counselors, social workers, psychologists) and mental health and health professionals who are stationed or work with families associated with the school
- At least one teacher

Full-service schools serve our students with an education that addresses personal needs as well as learning environment. Solicit ideas from your community's service agencies. Make every agency a part of your school.

—James Albritton, employment representative

The school site administrator may serve on both this committee and the policy committee. As your full-service school adds to or alters its services, the composition of the planning committee changes as well.

The planning committee is to be responsible for your program's day-to-day operation. Of the three layers in the pyramid, the committee meets most often (we recommend weekly) to maintain communication among stakeholders and minimize barriers to implementation. With the program manager, the planning committee identifies and clarifies changing student and family needs, identifies resources to address those needs, and makes recommendations to the policy committee on such major issues as the need for additional resources or for streamlining access to existing resources (Chapter Four).

Members of the policy committee are managers, the supervisors of the planning committee members. This group consists of such people as the school principal, a community agency administrator, or a health department director. As your program expands to include additional services, invite the supervisors of new planning committee members to join the policy committee. If, for example, a mental health professional is a member of the planning committee, that person's supervisor becomes a member of the policy committee. The role of the policy committee is to establish policy and procedures for site-specific program implementation and operation. Primarily responsible for funding and streamlining access to services, policy committee members receive information from the planning committee and in turn request action: changes in policy, changes in resource allocations, and requests for additional funding. Their requests are directed to the steering committee. The policy committee should meet at least monthly.

Solicit members for the steering committee from among community power-hitters:

- Chief administrative positions of community agencies
- Superintendent of schools
- Sheriff
- Local judges
- Administrators of social service organizations
- Community and business leaders
- School board members
- County commissioners
- Local community college or university presidents, provosts, and deans
- Other local government officials
- Representatives of state departments of education and social services

The role of the steering committee is to address any issues left unresolved by the planning or policy committees, advocate for program funding, and maintain a political basis of community support. Although this group is located at the top of the site-based governance pyramid, the bottom-up management philosophy reinforces the steering committee's role of working for and in support of the planning and policy committees. Ideally, the steering committee takes the lead in program design and implementation, assisted by the program manager; this is accomplished through joint meetings with the policy committee on a monthly or bimonthly basis.

In summary, the roles of committee members at each level in the site-based governance structure are based on the same individuals' roles in the community support system for families. Those working directly with families are closer to the bottom of the pyramid, where program recommendations originate. Figure 2.2 provides a summary of the committees in the model, the membership selection process, and a comparison of responsibilities.

Figure 2.2. Site-Based Governance Components, Membership, and Roles

Site-Based Governance		
Components	**Membership**	**Roles**
Planning committee	Workers with direct contact with families, e.g., social workers, teacher, family members, school counselors, health professionals	Day-to-day operation of program; make recommendations to policy committee
Policy committee	Supervisors of members of site-based planning committee, e.g., school principal, supervisors, managers	Receive recommendations from the planning committee; take action for or make requests to steering committee
Steering committee	Highest-level administrators, e.g., superintendent, administrators, presidents, elected officials	Receive recommendations from site-based planning and policy committees; seek additional funding and political support

Community-based governance
organizational structure involving broad representation from community agencies; designed to guide or influence initiation, development, evaluation, and sustainability of a full-service school; based on the premise that long-term viability requires community involvement and participation at all levels of the program

Care coordination
activities that link families to needed service providers through screening, referral, delivery, and follow-up

Community-Based Governance

A *community-based governance* structure may be the alternative of choice for either of two reasons. First, instead of relying solely on interactions at the local school site, the community-based model utilizes existing interagency councils that specialize in collaborative efforts for particular populations, for example prekindergarten councils, networks for severely emotionally disturbed children, jobs committees, child protection teams, and juvenile justice councils. Many such councils already have interagency family *care coordination* teams, and they are an invaluable source of information and services. By communicating with these councils, you can effectively minimize misunderstandings about how your program's goals relate to the entire community.

The second reason you might choose this structure is if you plan to implement more than one full-service school program at more than one site. This model (Figure 2.3) promotes the program manager's ability to network throughout the community and to keep communication flowing among all the program's stakeholders. It is absolutely imperative, then, that your stakeholders become knowledgeable about the functions of any and all existing interagency councils.

The membership of the steering committee in community-based governance is similar in composition to that of the steering committee in site-based governance: judges, superintendents, district administrators, chiefs of police, and so forth. The role of the steering committee is to act as advisors and decision makers for the full-service school program. In concert with the program manager, the members of the group respond to requests from other levels in the governance structure.

Members of the local oversight council represent these groups:

- Community agencies
- Families
- School personnel
- Caseworkers
- Health and human service providers
- Local oversight officers
- Ad hoc workgroups
- Representatives from family care coordination teams
- Members of existing interagency councils
- Representatives of full-service school sites

Make sure that the faculty and staff of each school are involved in the planning. This will ensure that everyone has an understanding of the full-service school concept— an understanding that will enhance the program's effectiveness. Such involvement also helps fulfill the program's potential for meeting our students' needs— physical, emotional, and educational.

**—Elton Nowling,
elementary school
principal**

Figure 2.3. Community-Based Governance

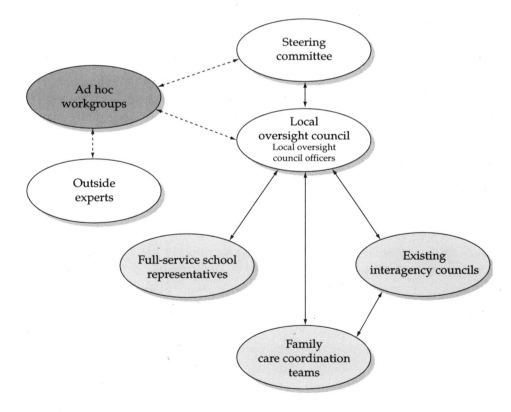

NOTES:

▨ Local oversight council members come from these sources.

☐ Ad hoc workgroup members can come from the steering committee, the local oversight council, or from outside experts, depending on the job at hand.

◄--► Temporary, task-specific relationships

◄—► Ongoing network of relationships

The local oversight council promotes expanded collaboration within the community to support development of one or more full-service school programs.

Officers of the local oversight council form a core group of leaders identified or elected from the larger council. Their role is to accomplish very specific tasks:

1. Provide staff services, that is, meeting agendas and minutes, data collection for special programs, grant referrals, and special assignments to ad hoc workgroups.

2. Encourage program development and documentation of the full-service school program's outcomes.

3. Develop plans for program implementation and grant proposals.

4. Mediate conflict within the group or between other groups when needed.

Ad hoc workgroups derive their membership from any combination of the community-based governance structure. Representatives from the local oversight council, for example, are periodically assigned to special ad hoc workgroups. Community experts who are not regular members of the oversight council may also be recruited for special programs. These groups are assigned to research specific problems and brainstorm solutions. An ad hoc workgroup might develop an interagency confidentiality form, research barriers to transportation or child care needs in the community, or work to pursue a specific grant proposal or alternative funding source. The groups are short-lived, very task-specific, and highly focused.

Interagency council members are representatives and advisors from community agencies who operate as a network. Having these councils represented in community-based governance avoids duplication of services and efforts within the community. Bringing these groups together ensures a comprehensive and seamless network of services within the larger community setting. The role of interagency council representatives is to offer valuable expertise and training for the new full-service school program.

Family care coordination team members are representatives and advisors from existing interagency teams that are currently working with families with such special needs as teenage parenting, mental health, or transition planning. These members provide valuable cross-training about existing resources within the community. They offer technical expertise on how to initiate and institutionalize interagency efforts.

Full-service school site representatives are personnel from all levels of the proposed full-service school. As members of the community-based governance structure, they interact with a wider spectrum of stakeholders. Keep in mind that, traditionally, school representatives have not been involved in health and human service planning and decision making. Cross-training between community agencies and the school under the community-based governance structure builds the trust and personal relationships needed to establish, expand, and institutionalize a full-service school program.

Figure 2.4 summarizes the membership components and roles in a community-based governance structure. The business relationships among community agencies can be formalized in *interagency agreements* (described in Chapter Six).

Where Will the Services Be Based?

Simply stated, there are three potential sites for a full-service school program:

1. *School-based*: services are actually co-located, relocated, or coordinated in or near a school that serves a large number of *at-risk* families.

2. Community-based: services are *school-linked,* meaning an effort is made to coordinate activities in a separate center at or near the school. A family resource center located in an at-risk neighborhood is an example of a community-based site.

3. Combination: if it is not possible to deliver all of the needed services from an accessible school site, the combination approach is used so that more services can be included in your action plan. Selected programs are actually located on the school campus, while coordinated efforts are made to refer students and families to other services off campus.

Your choice of site is influenced by availability of resources both in the community and at the school. See Chapter Three for needs assessment strategies that identify community resources and Chapter Four for ways to streamline access to services.

Now that your full-service school stakeholder crew is organized into a working body of individuals and a site has been selected, you may begin to feel that the blueprint is complete. But there are some lines left to be drawn: the *what, how,* and *when* of your program.

What Services Are Needed?

The six steps required in planning for your full-service school can be taken in any order you choose. Just remember to involve the members of your stakeholder crew from the beginning. For example, if you choose the

Interagency agreement
a mutually agreed-upon, signed contract among collaborating community agencies in a full-service school program; specifies contributions each partner is to make to the program

School-based services
basic economic, social, and health services that are integrated, available, and delivered from or near a school site

At risk
the concept that any person at any time may be exposed to the chance of injury or loss, or that a person may not be able to achieve full potential because of inhibiting factors

School-linked services
services offered by schools, linked to at least two or more other children and family service agencies in an ongoing, collaborative relationship

Figure 2.4. Community-Based Governance Components, Membership, and Roles

Community-Based Governance		
Components	**Membership**	**Roles**
Steering committee	Community power-hitters, e.g., judges, chiefs of police, superintendents, district administrators, elected officials	Acts as advisors and decision makers for full-service school planning and implementation
Local oversight council	Community representatives at large, such as families, teachers, caseworkers, health care providers	Promotes community collaboration to support full-service school development
Local oversight council officers	Core group of leaders from local oversight council	Provide staff services, encourage program development and documentation, plan for implementation and funding, mediate among other members
Ad hoc workgroups	Temporarily assigned local oversight council members, joined by community experts	Research problems and brainstorm solutions to particular community issues
Existing interagency councils	Network of representatives from established community agency advisory councils	Provide service-specific expertise and prevent duplication of services offered in the community
Family care coordination teams	Representatives and advisors from existing interagency teams working with special-needs families	Offer cross-training and technical expertise in implementing and institutionalizing community-based programs
Full-service school representative	Personnel at all levels of the school's operations: clerical, educational, administrative	Interacts with community to develop relationships necessary to establish, expand, and institutionalize the full-service school program

community-based governance structure, ad hoc workgroups may be assigned to research each of the first five steps and write an action plan; the ad hoc groups may choose to use the needs assessment strategies in Chapter Three to complete their assignments. The local oversight council writes the action plan and submits it to the steering committee for approval. If you choose the site-based governance model, the policy and planning committees complete steps one through five, develop an action plan, and present it to the steering committee.

The six steps in planning are as follows:

1. Identify significant health, social, and economic problems facing families.

2. Identify services that families need and want.

3. Identify duplication of effort and gaps in services offered by community agencies.

4. Identify a target group of children, youth, and families to be served based on need.

5. Identify barriers to service delivery, from within families and from within agencies providing services.

6. Develop an action plan (including a funding strategy; see Chapter Four) for program implementation that defines how and when each component of your full-service school program is implemented.

The comprehensive needs assessment strategies listed in Chapter Three are designed to help you gather the information required in these six steps.

In reviewing your community's needs, you may find many more needs than resources. As an alternative to wringing your hands in despair, find a need that is manageable in size, that does not exceed your current resources, and that can clearly benefit from your interagency effort. Remember, there is no such thing as a small success. You can always grow and expand, but an early success does wonders for the sustainability of your program.

One way to give the community a preview of the kind and quality of service you plan to deliver is to designate a small ad hoc workgroup with the purpose of publishing a community resource directory. List all existing public and private family service agencies (see the community service inventory of Figure 3.2 and Resource C). Include telephone number, eligibility guidelines, costs, and location for each agency. Then sit back and bask in the interagency communication that results. (Naturally, before you propose such ideas, you gather most of the information so that when you present the ideas to your community-based or site-based governance structure, the members are sure to agree to pay the publishing and distribution costs—and you are ready with a final document in a short time span!) Add some well-timed publicity that focuses attention on the community effort (Chapter Six), and you are on your way to beginning a full-service school initiative.

How Will Services Be Delivered?

At this point, you may be overwhelmed by the number of decisions and choices necessary to establish a full-service school. However, it is time to focus on one specific decision: how to deliver the services you choose to offer.

You could begin your full-service school program by involving only one agency at a time, adding others after the dust clears and the program stabilizes. Starting small and limiting your targeted population also makes your program more manageable. Consider the *triage* model, used in medical emergencies. The triage system ensures the greatest benefit from limited facilities or resources by giving priority treatment to those who must have services now, and little or no treatment to those who can survive without it (as well as those who have no chance of survival). Although this model seems a bit harsh in humanistic terms, it does offer sound advice to a new program with limited resources. The triage model can be used to establish your initial service offerings, but remember that a full-service school program ultimately intends to provide a full range of services to prevent unmet needs in the future.

As you plan for delivery of the full range of service, include these aspects of care coordination—a method of service delivery that effectively links families to needed services—in your full-service school's blueprint:

- Screening
- Referral
- Type of delivery
- Follow-up and monitoring

Screening

Screening, or determining the family's or individual's risk and eligibility for services, includes such activities as completing a social history profile, collecting economic information, administering educational or vocational tests, and conducting a medical examination designed to identify developmental delays. Any one or all of three types of screening may be necessary in your full-service school's design:

1. Universal screening targets all individuals within a particular demographic group, such as infants screened at birth for developmental delays, or third graders screened for scoliosis.

2. Informal screening targets a population at large, as when a service provider routinely screens all families the agency works with for speech and hearing problems.

3. Selective screening also targets a population at large but does so at special events such as semiannual immunization days or an annual voter registration drive.

Triage
system that ensures the greatest benefit from limited facilities or resources by giving priority treatment to those who must have it and little or no treatment to those who can survive without it

Screening
determining the nature of the family's or individual's risk and their eligibility for needed services

FOCUS ON STAKEHOLDERS:

Multidisciplinary Team and Social Services Approaches

The Young family (whom we met in Chapter One) ultimately became part of the family care coordination approach to case management. Here are descriptions from one county's version of alternative case management approaches: the multidisciplinary team approach and the social services approach.

Six months ago, two middle-school-age brothers were referred to the school counselor for what was described as a problem of significant academic underachievement. Even though both brothers are extremely bright, their grades were falling dramatically and their "inappropriate social skills" were causing behavior problems. The counselor, who was active in a multidisciplinary, interagency team, contacted Retired Senior Volunteers, two of whom now act as mentors for the brothers and meet with them weekly. Other team members joined in. The school's onsite caseworker discovered that the boys' mother was blind and their father unemployed; this resulted in referrals to other team members for economic assistance, training services for visual impairment, and JTPA (Job Training Partnership Act) training. The brothers are joining a small intervention group led by their school's onsite resource officer, a deputy sheriff. In the meantime, the boys have made dramatic improvements in both behavior and academics. One made the honor roll last term.

Although the school's resource officer is a member of the multidisciplinary team, there are occasions when this deputy acts as the case manager. This demonstrates a social service approach:

> Upon arrival at one of the school sites where I am stationed, I was contacted by a patrol deputy who notified me of a suicide attempt by a student at the middle school. I realized that we would need to help not only the student who attempted suicide but also the students who were her classmates or friends. I immediately contacted the school's principal, nurse, and counselor and proposed a response plan. Fortunately, the response plan did not have to be implemented. However, if the need had arisen, we were prepared to handle student behavior, address their emotions, or answer their questions arising from the situation. This forewarning of a potential crisis could not have occurred if a school resource officer had not been on site to receive this law enforcement information.

In another instance, the resource officer acted in a supportive role to the case manager, a child welfare caseworker:

> Another middle school student had to be removed from his parents' home in order to protect him from the drug and sexual abuse going on there. He didn't trust many people, and the case manager worried that he might run away from a foster home. I had talked with the boy at school on several occasions, and although I did not know him well, our conversations had formed the foundation for a relationship. When the case manager asked me to help transport the boy to his foster home, I agreed. During the trip, he and I talked about his fears and succeeded in reducing some of his anxiety. I like to think that our relationship, begun at the school site, was at least partly responsible for his settling into foster care placement more easily.

Referrals

If the screening agency or program is unable to deliver the needed services itself, it must make referrals to other agencies, or to other programs within its own organization. Your full-service school program accomplishes referral in a combination of approaches.

External referral is necessary in a full-service school program that has limited service offerings or personnel. In this case, an intake and referral specialist is assigned the job of handling referrals and utilizing existing telephone hotlines, central referral agencies, and one-on-one contact with community agencies. If the specialist position cannot be funded, consider redefining an existing school or community agency position; a school counselor can be trained to match service needs with existing community resources, or a social worker's job description can be modified to include a greater time commitment to interagency referrals.

Mobile rapid response is a referral system that is temporary, short-term, and quickly implemented to respond to specific crises such as gang fights, suicide, or other trauma. As an example, a task force of doctors, ministers, parents, students, and school personnel can refer adolescents who are in crisis over a recent suicide of a classmate to appropriate social or psychological service agencies.

Type of Delivery

The type of service delivery your full-service school offers can be as distinctive as your community. Here are some options:

- Circulating or itinerant service occurs when your full-service school offers a significant number and variety of services on site or near the site, but not every day of the week. Mental health counseling is available on site every Wednesday, for example, and health services every other Thursday. A service provider makes a site visit whenever ten referrals from the school accumulate through the provider's toll-free telephone system. This approach fosters service delivery that fully utilizes existing physical facilities; one room in your school can offer four or five different services.

- Multiservice units provide a combination of specific services for a specific population, on site. If, for example, your full-service school wants to deliver services to families with children under the age of five, enlist collaborating agencies that offer adult education, day care, economic services, home visiting programs, and parenting classes. The advantage of this type of service delivery is its comprehensiveness.

- Combination approaches to service delivery offer perhaps the greatest opportunity for creativity and innovation. By combining expanded office hours with child care during parent-teacher conferences and transportation assistance, your service delivery system becomes more user-friendly. Consider reorganizing your staff, utilizing paraprofessionals and volunteers, and developing specialized problem-solving teams to fulfill your community's needs.

Follow-up and Monitoring

Follow-up and monitoring ensure that screening, referral, and type of service delivery are valid for a family or individual on a continuing, evolving basis. Together with the other aspects of care coordination, follow-up and monitoring constitute what is sometimes also referred to as *case management*. No matter which term you use, remember that family involvement and empowerment are the goals, from beginning to end, of care coordination. Inherent in follow-up and monitoring is the idea that as a family utilizes one service they overcome their need for it, require another service instead, or need a service that supplements the first one.

Case management
process that identifies, assesses, plans, implements, and evaluates client needs and service delivery; sometimes used interchangeably with *care coordination*

Follow-up and monitoring constantly seek to assess these changing needs through one of three care coordination approaches.

1. The social service approach assigns one case manager to follow the family through all care coordination steps and to play a key, ongoing role in developing the family's plans and decision making. The case manager could be a social worker, school resource officer, or mental health professional.

2. The multidisciplinary approach requires representatives from all agencies serving the family to divide care coordination responsibilities, adding their own perspectives and knowledge to the family's immediate and long-term plans. The school nurse contributes health assessments, the school resource officer adds data on the family's involvement with law enforcement, and the teacher provides current education-related information, evaluating progress with the family and coordinating access to new services as needed.

3. The family care coordination approach actually makes the family its own case manager. A social service or multidisciplinary team case manager acts as an information resource, helps with interagency coordination, and offers periodic feedback to family members as follow-up to service delivery, but the family develops, monitors, and revises its own family care coordination plan (Chapter Six).

The *how* part of planning for your program's service delivery requires your stakeholders to make collaborative decisions about screening, referral, delivery types, and follow-up, all of which are integral parts of a care coordination system.

When Will Services Be Delivered?

You have clarified your choices as to the *who, where, what,* and *how* elements of your action plan. You know that planning requires six steps: identify families' problems, identify needed services, identify duplication of effort and service gaps among community agencies, identify a target population, identify barriers to service delivery, and develop an action plan. Now, what makes an action plan active? The answer is: establishing when to take action.

Figure 2.5 is a sample structure for tying all the elements of your plan to target completion dates. Adapt it to your own needs, or design a timetable that uniquely matches your full-service school program's blueprint.

Figure 2.5. Sample Action Plan

Action Plan					
Identified Need	**Services**	**Service Providers**	**Type of Delivery**	**Funding Sources**	**Target Completion Date**
In our town, 1,153 adults work at minimum wage. Of those adults, 57% express a desire to obtain a GED, with the expectation that education will help them find higher-paying jobs or encourage them to pursue additional skill training or education	Adult basic education courses Adult remedial courses in reading and mathematics	County school board Local community college	School-based Extended hours two nights per week (M and Th 5–8 P.M.) Screening, referrals, and follow-up handled via collaborative interagency team consisting of full-service school site-based ABE instructor, public school adult education counselor, and community college remediation specialist	Adult Learning Center Community schools	Review existing and develop new screening and enrollment eligibility guidelines: December 30, 19xx Review and revise existing ABE curriculum to match community needs: March 1, 19xx Develop promotional materials: March 30, 19xx Announce and promote awareness of program's availability: April 30, 19xx Open early enrollment: May 1, 19xx Assess results of promotion (enrollment data) and revise approach if necessary: June 15, 19xx Classes start: September 12, 19xx

The point is this: start small and offer quality service in a reasonably short span of time. It is better to plow a small field deep than a large field shallow. Choose stakeholders and a program manager wisely, evaluate what services your community needs most and soonest, decide where and how to offer those services, and complete your plan of action (your blueprint) with a time frame. Invest your community's limited resources where they achieve maximum results; this is the full-service school concept in action.

Speaking of action, Chapter Three will have you "acting," all right—as you begin to pour your full-service school's foundation with solid knowledge about your community's needs.

Endnote

1.   Hawkins, J. D. "Controlling Crime Before It Happens: Risk-Focused Prevention." *National Institute of Justice Journal*, Aug. 1995, 10–17.

Chapter 3

Pour a Foundation of Knowledge

Strategies for Assessing Community Needs

A founder of the humanistic psychology movement, Abraham Maslow grouped human needs into categories and arranged them in order of importance: physiological, safety and security, love and belongingness, self-esteem, and self-actualization. According to Maslow's motivational theory, needs that appear lower in the hierarchy must be satisfied before higher needs are felt. We do not realize that we need love, belongingness, and self-esteem if our physiological and security needs are not first satisfied. If we live in fear for our safety or in anxiety about where our next meal will come from, Maslow believes that there is little hope of ever reaching the level of self-actualization, "to become whatever one is capable of becoming."[1]

When you decide to initiate a full-service school program, your stake-holder crew is likely to face the issues addressed by the lower needs of Maslow's hierarchy. The community must first reach consensus on a standard for quality of family life. By promoting this standard, stakeholders can decide what resources are available to meet those standards. Once you know what resources are available, then you can begin to strategize how to reduce or eliminate the service delivery gaps, barriers, or duplications that prevent families from meeting their potential, or self-actualization.

In order for your full-service school program to self-actualize, you must pour a foundation of solid knowledge about your community's needs and resources. There are many effective and appropriate ways to gain this knowledge. The method or methods you choose depend on how much you already know. In this chapter, we propose ten strategies (tools) for assessing needs and resources; we provide detailed worksheets embracing the strategies. If you have the luxury of time, you may choose to use all ten. Keep in mind, though, that needs assessment is an ongoing process. Thus you may use one or two strategies to begin a small full-service school program, and then use additional strategies as your program expands.

Full-service schools offer one-stop shopping by focusing on families and making services convenient and accessible for special populations. Single parents, for example, often don't have reliable transportation and may not fully understand how the system works. Assess the needs of your community and strive to provide what is not always readily available.

—Suanne Locklin-Johnson,
coordinator,
Single Parent Program

Ten Strategies for Assessing Needs and Resources

Decisions about which services to offer and how to deliver them should be based on the perspectives of both the family receiving the service and the provider of the service. Although the needs of families in your community may be complex, the services your program delivers must be practical, acceptable, and beneficial to the providers. So be sure that your needs and resource assessments are as simple but as comprehensive as possible. Your assessment data are your most important tool in deciding—and justifying—whether to utilize existing resources, pursue additional resources, or solicit funding. The more information you have about the families you wish to serve, the more persuasive you are in recruiting organization and agency involvement.

We offer you these tools to gather information that strengthens your full-service school's foundation, whether you are trying to identify stakeholders or inventorying available physical facilities, whether you want to design an effective funding proposal or prepare an authoritative press release.

1. *Conduct a demographic survey*: how can you obtain knowledge of the community's present strengths and weaknesses?

2. *Inventory existing community services*: what services are needed, duplicated, deficient, or nonexistent?

3. *Inventory physical facilities*: what actual physical space and facilities can be used for service provision?

4. *Assess community interaction*: how does your community currently rate in interacting with at-risk families?

5. *Design a unique community survey*: if you need particular information, how can you create a survey that effectively elicits what you need to know?

6. *Use computer-based mapping*: how can the visual effectiveness of maps help in designing better service delivery?

7. *Conduct a stakeholder analysis*: how can input from your key players shape the design-in-progress (while heightening their commitment)?

8. *Lead a focus group*: how can a quick query supplement the deeper analysis of the community survey (and train people in greater awareness of resources)?

9. *Take an action research approach*: is it too soon to place professionals at the proposed full-service school site? What can be gained by doing it now?

10. *Conduct a transition study*: how can a continuum of services be designed to help people moving in and out of crisis or time of need?

Strategy One: Conduct a Demographic Survey

Demographic surveys provide snapshots of a moment in time within a targeted geographic region. Start your demographic survey by seeking existing information that describes the students and the school, community, district, region, or state in which you want to implement a full-service school. Increase the number of snapshots to get a more complete collage, hence a better image of the community and a more reliable database. Keep in mind that you can also use this information to document funding requests.

Remember, too, that you must determine strengths as well as weaknesses within your community. There are many excellent sources of ready information. School boards keep very detailed data about the communities they serve in order to predict enrollment patterns and special program needs. Chambers of commerce often access data on income levels. Builders associations use statistics to forecast population growth in a particular area. Utility companies use demographic data to predict community growth patterns. Law enforcement offices have data on migrant populations or highly transient areas within the community. Local interagency councils may have already generated a demographic profile of your area. Census data are another valuable source of information. Use the worksheet outlined in Figure 3.1 (and given in full detail in Resource D) to compile demographic information and document its source.

Completing a demographic survey and analyzing the data ensures that you identify significant problems and the target group most in need of services. Use the data to answer these questions:

- What general conclusions can you draw? For instance, do most problems seem to be health-related? Or are health problems being adequately addressed but crime is a major concern? Does the unemployment rate indicate that vocational services should be a focal point?

- Can you identify a population that needs services? Use the demographic survey to describe that population and rank its service needs in order of their significance.

- What are the current strengths of this population?

- What are the critical or unsolved problems of this population? What portions of the population are underserved or unserved?

Strategy Two: Inventory Existing Community Services

Use this strategy to identify existing community services and match them to the services families need and want; to identify duplication of effort; and to target gaps in service among agencies. One of the fundamental principles guiding the full-service school concept is to supplement—not supplant—existing services. In collecting the information targeted by this strategy, you discover opportunities to streamline, relocate, or reallocate existing resources to meet at least some community needs without additional funding.

Demographics
information such as age, sex, marital status, occupation, income, education, or zip code; often used as "predictor variables" in data analysis to establish whether subjects with similar demographics will respond to survey questions similarly

Pointers

Share the survey's results by helping your audience picture "one month in the life of a child":
    During the month of May in Ourtown USA,
- Thirty-one babies were born
- Six babies were born to teen mothers
- One baby had low birth-weight
- Twenty-two children were reportedly mistreated
- Eighteen students were suspended from local schools
- Twelve delinquencies were reported

Figure 3.1. Demographic Survey

💾 Demographic Survey

Data	Source and Date

A. Community Status: rural, urban, suburban, mixture

_____   _____

B. Geographic Barriers: describe physical barriers to service delivery (such as isolated farmlands, two large bodies of water that create transportation barriers, thirty miles to existing social services, dense population, and so on.)

_____   _____
_____   _____
_____   _____
_____   _____

C. Key Facts About Children

1. Number of children younger than eighteen   _____   _____

2. Percentage of total population younger than eighteen   _____   _____

3. Percentage of children living in
   - two-parent households   _____   _____
   - single-parent households   _____   _____
   - households headed by someone other than a parent   _____   _____

4. Ethnicity:
   - percentage of children who are white   _____   _____
   - percentage of children who are black   _____   _____
   - percentage of children who are of mixed race   _____   _____
   - percentage of children who are of Asian heritage   _____   _____
   - other significant groups   _____   _____

5. Ages
   - number of children under one year of age   _____   _____
   - number of children between one and five   _____   _____
   - number of children between five and ten   _____   _____
   - number of children in other significant age groups   _____   _____

D. Community Descriptors

1. Population (number)   _____   _____
   Political description (e.g., 80,000, in urban county)

_____   _____

This resource assessment strategy can be difficult and confusing to use, given agency jargon, myriad program names and acronyms, and complex eligibility requirements. The community service inventory (outlined in Figure 3.2; the complete inventory is in Resource C) is best completed by a group of stakeholders who have a wide knowledge of the human services available in your community. The planning and policy committees of a site-based governance structure (Chapter Two) are excellent resources to complete this task because these groups are usually made up of experienced health and human services workers as well as family and school representatives.

If you elect not to complete the entire inventory, an alternative is to select sections that apply to the more critical needs of your community.

Before completing this inventory, of course, look for existing community service inventories. Many communities have agency service directories and family hotlines for information and referrals. State departments of health, human services, and education frequently have extensive inventories.

The ten major categories of service assessed by the community service inventory (adapted from the *Survey of Full-Service School Sites in Florida*)[2] are not meant to be exhaustive. Your stakeholders will want to add categories that are unique to your community. If an inventory of your community's services has never been completed, then using the results of this inventory to publish a directory of community services (as suggested in Chapter Two) can be an outstanding first achievement for your stakeholder crew.

To complete the community service inventory, first read the descriptive paragraph accompanying each service category (see Resource C). Ask the group that is completing the inventory to discuss the descriptions. Then choose a target population (a school population, a cluster of schools, a community), one that has been identified by the demographic survey or one you are considering for a full-service school program. As your stakeholder crew works down the list, determine whether each service is available to the target population and what the source of the service is. Contact each source agency to verify that the service is still available.

Using the community service inventory helps you accomplish steps two and three of the planning process: identify services that families need and want, and identify areas of duplication of effort and gaps between services offered by community agencies. If you have also conducted a demographic survey, you can combine the results of strategies one and two to ask these revealing questions:

• Is there a need to increase specific services?

• Are there services that should be decreased?

• Which services should remain at their current levels?

• Is there duplication of effort among several agencies serving the same population? Where?

Know your service providers and what they have to offer. It is important to know them as people, too—you can go a lot further together when you understand each other and know when you can depend on each other.

—Jane Prewitt, mental health center therapist

Figure 3.2. Community Service Inventory

Community Needs Assessment

💾 Part One: Community Service Inventory

1. **Assessment services** may be defined as diagnostic and evaluative. Assessments usually involve professional determination of the nature of a child's or family's problems and consideration of the strengths and weaknesses of the child and his or her family environment. Assessments may be conducted to determine eligibility for a particular program and/or to develop a plan of services to be provided. These may be conducted for a single program or in a multiprogram environment.

Service Available?		Category	Source (e.g., agency, school, program, or support group)
Yes	No		
		Behavioral	
		Psychiatric	
		Psychological educational	
		Psychological	
		Social	
		Social and family	
		Other	

2. **Child welfare services** are provided to students and their families to assist and support the family unit. Supportive services, such as financial assistance and protective supervision, assist the child to remain within the home. If the family is so stressed that it cannot remain intact, substitute services may be provided. Respite care may be considered a child welfare service or a mental health service, depending on the level of focus of the service provided.

Service Available?		Category	Source
Yes	No		
		Supportive services	
		Child advocacy	
		Crisis intervention	
		Flexible funding, e.g., housing deposits	
		Food and clothing banks	
		Home services, e.g., homemaker, housekeeper	
		Housing	
		Interagency case management	
		Nonresidential runaway services	
		Parent effectiveness training and support groups	

Figure 3.2. Community Service Inventory *(continued)*

Service Available?		Category	Source
Yes	No		
		Supportive services *(continued)*	
		Parent training	
		Protective supervision for child abuse and neglect cases	
		Voluntary family services	
		Substitute care services	
		Adoption services	
		Economic services (e.g., food stamps AFDC)	
		Emergency shelter services	
		Family group homes	
		Foster care	
		Independent living services	
		Pregnancy and parenting for teenage students	
		Runaway shelter	
		Other	

3. **Educational services** are intended to provide knowledge and socialization skills, development for students. By law, all students are entitled to free and appropriate public education. Students with emotional and behavioral problems may require special services to help them obtain an education.

Service Available?		Category	Source
Yes	No		
		Adult basic education	
		Adult GED classes (general equivalency diploma)	
		Alternative schools and programs	
		Child care, extended day (before, after school)	
		Child care, prekindergarten disadvantaged	
		Child care prekindergarten handicapped	
		Child care, weekends, intersessions, summer	
		Child care for adultssessions	
		Community education	
		Community service programs	
		Computerized literacy center	
		Curriculum development and improvement	
		Dropout prevention programs	
		Educational guidance counseling	
		Educational homework help	
		Exceptional education	

• Discuss the services that are not available. Is there a call for initiating these services based on the needs of the clientele that you are serving? What is the best way for the service to be accessed (refer, relocate, expand, or change service delivery pattern)?

• Prioritize the results of the inventory. Rank the services that are not available in order of importance as determined by the needs identified in the demographic survey.

• Discuss how to improve access to and information about the resources that are available (see also Chapter Six).

The community service inventory does not begin to address all there is to know about service availability. You may want to use additional strategies to identify service providers, facilitate timely service delivery, and coordinate and monitor service provision. You could, for instance, use strategy four, a survey of community interaction, to assess your community's knowledge of these issues:

Public awareness	Outreach activities
Contact points for service	Identification system for referrals
Location of services	Referral systems
Screening	Assessment and evaluation
Tracking	Monitoring
Follow-up	Fee structures
Annual reviews	Eligibility guidelines
Parental consent	Caseloads

Strategy Three: Inventory Physical Facilities

Knowing what physical facilities are potentially available to your full-service school program is critical in determining where you locate service providers so they are easily accessible to families. In the ideal world, one of three situations exists. First, as new school buildings are constructed, adequate space for community agency representatives is included in the plans—constructing a new high school that serves as a college, vocational training center, and full-service school site, for example. The second possibility is that the full-service school obtains *capital outlay* funds to renovate or add facilities later. Third, participating agencies can pool their resources to lease or construct facilities, perhaps renovating an old school site with community funding that promotes co-locating services. All of these ideal-world options require thorough and visionary planning, however, so this strategy entails surveying available facilities and defining those that are needed but do not yet exist.

Consider these practical, more real-world options for utilizing existing physical facilities imaginatively:

• Use community buildings during unscheduled hours.

• Convert existing space (such as garages, closets, unused office space, vacant apartments, or vacated stores) into usable space.

Capital outlay
funds used for fixed assets such as land or buildings, improvements to grounds, construction of or additions to buildings, remodeling, or equipment

- Use portable buildings and house trailers.

- Share existing space with other agencies. Reorganize schedules, offer alternative schedules for services, and encourage flexible hours. School sites that are typically not operational after school hours are particularly suited for this option. Working families are more apt to utilize services in the evening.

- Organize mobile units to travel to specified community sites at scheduled intervals. Communities across the country have equipped mobile health vans, mobile parent literacy centers, and traveling teams of professionals who go where the families are.

- Deliver services in the home environment. Early childhood programs, specialized services for at-risk families, and literacy programs are particularly adaptable to delivery in the family's own environment. This has the added advantage of eliminating two of the major barriers to service delivery: transportation and child care. An example of delivering services in the home environment is a unit in a subsidized housing complex being dedicated as a family support center.

- Organize teams of professionals to float among service delivery sites. On the day that the team is scheduled on the site, a counseling room or office space is made available.

- Look for rooms that are not used 100 percent of the time. There are few buildings where every room is used all day, all evening, and on weekends.

- Find ways to consolidate resources to provide additional space. This may have the added benefit of co-locating resources at more than one site.

- Approach churches in the community; they have a history of collaboration, outreach, and family support. Most churches have the advantage of being located within concentrated population areas, and they often have excellent facilities that are used only on Sundays and a few evenings each week. Churches may also have buses or vans that can provide transportation.

- Seek out space in schools with declining enrollment or agencies that are cutting back on personnel.

- Assess the political climate for additional funding and grant resources. What is the hot topic in your state's legislature? Is it possible to align your need for space with another initiative that is likely to receive funding and resources?

For additional information on sizes of facilities and suggested design criteria, refer to Resource E, which defines three areas commonly found in full-service school settings: the school health room, reading resource room, and waiting room.

Strategy Four: Assess Community Interaction

More than fifty national organizations concerned with the well-being of children, youth, and families met in January 1994 to develop consensus on a set of principles for effective family service delivery systems. The consensus was published in a report, "Principles to Link by," subtitled "Integrating Education, Health, and Human Services for Children, Youth, and Families: Systems That Are Community-Based and School-Linked."[3] The community

Figure 3.3. Community Interaction Survey

💾 Community Interaction Survey[1]

Rank the following in order of their effectiveness within your community setting.

1	2	3	4	5
no evidence	in existence but not effective	moderately successful	successful but needs improvement	strength of the community

1. Services should be community-based and community-delivered.

Services and support programs are locally planned, operated, and evaluated with broad public and private community involvement.	1	2	3	4	5
Families and youth are essential partners with professionals in planning and implementing services and programs.	1	2	3	4	5

2. Services should be family-centered; driven by the needs of children, youth, and families; and built on strengths.

Families and providers (and whenever possible, young people themselves) are involved in planning and implementing services that support family independence and strengthen community ties.	1	2	3	4	5
There are current family assessment initiatives in place.	1	2	3	4	5
There are current family-focused initiatives, including programs offering home development specialists or in-the-home services.	1	2	3	4	5
Parent and family involvement is encouraged in all settings.	1	2	3	4	5
Professionals believe in family support planning and the concept of interagency collaboration to meet the needs of students and families.	1	2	3	4	5
Parents take an active role in educational and support activities.	1	2	3	4	5
There is a single point of intake for families to receive information, complete paperwork, and participate in a family-focused plan of delivery for services.	1	2	3	4	5

---

[1] A portion of *Survey of Full-Service School Sites in Florida*. Tallahassee: Florida Department of Education, University of South Florida Institute for At-Risk Children and Their Families, 1993.

interaction survey (shown in outline form in Figure 3.3 and in detail in Resource F) uses the group's ten principles as the basis for assessing how your community interacts with at-risk families.

The community interaction survey guides your assessment of your community's strengths by asking you to rank evaluative statements with regard to characteristics of each of its ten principles. Ask a cross-section of your stakeholder crew to complete the survey. Not only does this task provide your

Figure 3.3. Community Interaction Survey *(continued)*

3. **Needed services should be available and accessible to all in a variety of settings, using a combination of public, private, community, and personal resources.**

High-quality education, health, social, family support, and other services are available to all who need them.	1	2	3	4	5
There has been an attempt to determine which services do not currently exist in the community, and action has been taken to make them available.	1	2	3	4	5
There is evidence of continuity of services. A family entering the service support system does not experience gaps in or barriers to services.	1	2	3	4	5

4. **Services should be culturally competent.**

Programs and staff are responsive to the needs of individuals with disabilities and of culturally, ethnically, linguistically, and economically diverse populations.	1	2	3	4	5

5. **Services should focus on primary prevention, early intervention, and strengthening the ability of children, youth, and families to help themselves.**

There is evidence of high-quality education; a variety of opportunities to accommodate different stages of growth and development; a comprehensive, consistent source of preventive and primary care; and early intervention activities designed around the concept of family support.	1	2	3	4	5

6. **Services should be comprehensive, and a continuum of services should be available.**

There is evidence of a comprehensive continuum of services ranging from prevention and early intervention to individualized, intensive family support services.	1	2	3	4	5
Round-the-clock coverage is available for emergency situations.	1	2	3	4	5
There are existing services that educate families and publicize resources and services.	1	2	3	4	5

stakeholders with input on community strengths and weaknesses but it also sparks community interest in your full-service school.

Strategy Five: Design a Unique Community Survey

A questionnaire you receive by mail asking which brand of pet food you buy is a survey. A phone call asking for your opinion about a political candidate is a survey. A television commercial claiming that "Four out of five dentists recommend . . ." is referring to the results of a survey. If you need to gather a particular kind of information from a particular population, but you cannot find a ready-made survey form, design your own.

The first thing to do is define its subject as concisely as possible. Ask yourself these questions:

1. Who are you surveying?
   - The service consumer?
   - The service provider?
   - Both?

2. What are your objectives? For example, you may need to determine the following:
   - Accessibility of services identified in the community service inventory
   - Perceived need for services, from consumer and nonconsumer perspectives
   - Adequacy of services to meet a specific population's needs
   - Quality of services that are available
   - Barriers to service delivery

If you and your stakeholders decide to create a unique survey (see the second part of Resource C for a sample "key informant survey," part of a larger community needs assessment), you should develop an understanding of some basic tenets of survey construction: question formulation, survey administration, sampling techniques, and data analysis.

Formulate Survey Questions

The questions you ask—and how you ask them—determine the quality of the response you receive. Careful consideration must be given to developing questions that are clear, to the point, at the appropriate language level, and jargon-free. Well-constructed questions elicit accurate and honest responses, and the resulting data are easy to summarize, analyze, and interpret.

The two most common types of survey questions are open-ended and closed.

Open-ended questions allow the subject to respond in his or her own words. The response is more complete and insightful than a simple yes-or-no answer, but it can also be more difficult to analyze. Though varying widely, responses must be forced into categories or classifications in order to summarize the results. Another drawback to open-ended questions is that the subject may perceive them as more time-consuming than closed questions and thus not take the time to answer. An example of a good open-ended question is "How would you describe your family's economic outlook for the next five years?"

Closed questions, or restricted items, ask the subject to choose an answer from a specified set of alternatives. Examples of closed questions follow.

1. Closed question with simple alternatives:

Which of the following services would you prefer? (Check one.)

_____ family counseling

_____ individual counseling

_____ group counseling

2. Closed question with ordered alternatives:

How often would you participate in family counseling if it were available at the school site? (Choose one.)

_____ never

_____ once per week

_____ once per month

_____ once every three months

3. Partially open-ended question:

Which services at this school site do you think families would use most frequently?

_____ counseling

_____ credit counseling

_____ recreational activities

_____ other (specify _____)

4. Another form of closed question uses a rating scale as the response alternative:

How important is it to this community to provide day care for adults who are working toward their high school diploma? (Circle one.)

1	2	3	4	5	6	7	8	9	10

Not Important   Very Important

You may use a scale with as few as three or as many as one hundred points, and you can label only the extremes or any points between. Some common scales are

from very poor to very well

from very weak to very strong

from strongly agree to strongly disagree

One of the advantages of rating scales is that the results are simple to analyze and summarize.

VERIFY THE QUALITY OF YOUR QUESTIONS BY USING THIS CHECKLIST.

☐ Make sure your questions are clearly worded. Test them on several other stakeholders or coworkers before asking them of the survey subjects.

☐ Decide whether you want to cover the widest range of alternatives possible or narrow the alternatives toward a definitive answer.

☐ Provide an *Other* category or a free-response space at the bottom of the survey form to allow for comments.

☐ Avoid offensive language. Be sensitive to your subjects.

☐ Do not use abbreviations or assume familiarity with terms you know. For example, PTA should be written out as "Parent/teacher association."

☐ If you ask questions with a time element, use a referent point or time period.

    POOR: How many times did you or a member of your family seek counseling last year?

    BETTER: How many times did you or your family see a social services counselor in 1994?

☐ Ask only one question at a time.

    POOR: Should the full-service school offer economic services or counseling services?

    BETTER: Should the full-service school offer counseling services?

☐ Avoid using negative words that may cause confusion.

    POOR: Should the school not offer economic assistance services on campus?

    BETTER: Should the school offer economic assistance services on campus?

Assemble the Survey

Simply placing a collection of questions on a piece of paper does not make a well-constructed survey. Consider the following points:

1. In what order should the questions be arranged? The survey should have continuity; related items should be placed together. Don't skip around between subjects. The survey should read like a book to encourage completion of the whole task.

2. Ask for demographic information last. Place the more interesting questions first to grab the reader's attention. Use short, transitional paragraphs to move the reader through the survey.

3. If some questions are potentially sensitive, place them after less objectionable ones. Try to spread sensitive issues—as examples, teen pregnancy and AIDS prevention awareness—throughout the survey instead of concentrating them in one section.

4. Within a given section of the survey, be consistent in the kind of response you request. Consistently ask for a checkmark, a check on a line, or a circle around a number.

5. Consider using color-coded response sheets or scanner sheets to facilitate tallying and analyzing the data.

6. Keep it short! Use more than one survey, over time, if necessary.

Select a Survey Sample

Without the proper sample, you cannot generalize your survey results to the population. For example, if you interview only agency and school personnel, the results may not accurately predict the feelings of the rest of your community. A *representative sample* reflects the community in which you live. Consider ethnicity, sex, occupation, and mitigating factors (such as migrant status of families) in your sample. If several languages are spoken in your community, consider translating the survey to broaden your representative sample.

A representative sample for a survey seeking to determine what services are needed to combat juvenile crime in a community might include law violators and their families; at-risk children and their families; providers of juvenile counseling or job services; judges, state's attorneys, and public defenders; law enforcement representatives; education representatives in administrative, instructional, and noninstructional roles; victims and their families; and the community at large.

An alternative to a representative sampling method is choosing a *random sample*. A computer program is one way of generating a table of random numbers. Then use the random numbers to select survey participants from a large list (such as a telephone book). Your sample size should be as large as possible yet practical.

Representative sample
a cross-section of a population, often used to provide a convenient estimate of some characteristic of the entire population

Random sample
sample selected so as to guarantee equal probability of selection to all same-size samples that could be formed from all members of the population involved

Administer the Survey

Your stakeholders need to choose a method or combination of methods for delivering the survey to a representative sample of your community. Here are several survey methods to consider.

Mail surveys are one efficient way to gather information from identified populations. There are several things to keep in mind about this option:

- Is there a way to piggyback your survey onto an existing mail service to your target population?

- Are you providing postage for returning the surveys?

- What about nonresponse bias? That is, what happens to accuracy if a significant portion of the sample does not respond?

- Which strategies will you use to increase response: cover letters, pre-contacting a percentage of the population by phone, or using follow-up letters?

Group administration, as an alternative to mailing individual surveys, means you solicit responses instead during regularly scheduled meetings of community groups. Discussion of confidentiality and the individual's right to refuse to participate, should take place before the survey is administered.

Telephone surveys may produce unreliable responses if survey personnel are insufficiently trained. Training should include techniques for accurate tabulation of responses, courtesy, clear speech, and response to hostile reactions. If the telephone survey is your chosen method, limit the length and number of questions. Ensure that adequate staffing and time are allotted to the task.

Personal interviews offer a high probability of obtaining insightful responses if you have sufficient staff and few time constraints. Anticipate having to train the interviewer(s), and construct a list of anticipated interviewee requests for additional information.

Other media also offer valuable data. Consider newspaper surveys, radio call-ins, local television shows, or town hall sessions as additional forums for information gathering.

Strategy Six: Use Computer-Based Mapping

Mapping
graphic representation of needs assessment information about the whole community or a portion of it

Mapping has an advantage because visual depiction of information gives that information greater impact than numerical presentation. For example, by linking the postal zip codes of people using a particular service with geographic depictions of the zip codes, you can generate community maps that show the distribution of service usage. The mapping aids attempts to understand social service information and how it is meaningful for the population. Advances in technology, including census data in a geographic format, allow very detailed information to be mapped. Here are examples of using computer-based mapping:

- Data from the juvenile justice system are mapped to zip code information in order to pinpoint where students involved in the system reside. Schools that serve those zip codes can then be targeted for delinquency programs (see Figure 3.4).

- Mapping the number of abuse-and-neglect reports generated in a geographic area helps to determine where in the community a caseworker and investigator should be stationed.

- Comparing current and previous maps of the number of individuals receiving economic assistance in a geographic area shows increase or decline in given locations. This information could justify moving the economic services office closer to the needy population.

If you do not have access to computer-based mapping and analysis, the same kind of conclusion can be drawn from a paper-and-pencil exercise. You may even choose to use both computer and paper methods of analysis for a more complete picture of your community.

The most important result of implementing a full-service school program is the gathering of information that provides possible reasons for certain student behaviors.

—George Dahlgren, middle school principal

Figure 3.4. Computer-Based Mapping

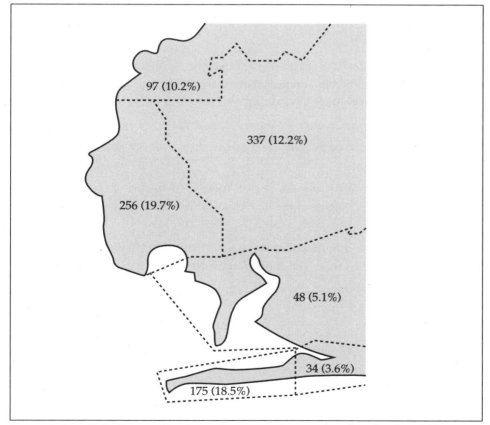

Increase in juvenile justice cases (number and percentage increase over 19___ , by zip code)

Strategy Seven: Conduct a Stakeholder Analysis

A stakeholder analysis enables your planning crew to compare the views and goals of its key players to the goals and design of your full-service school. Using this strategy helps to increase the involvement and commitment of your stakeholders. The concept of stakeholder analysis is really analogous to an ongoing needs assessment: during the program design phase, the stakeholders have an opportunity to shape the vision. As the program evolves, stakeholder input helps to foster communication and minimize barriers to implementation.

Set the stage for collaboration by presenting community needs assessment data to key stakeholders. A stakeholder analysis relies on good data. Once you collect the data (via a demographic, community services, community interaction, or unique communitywide survey), summarize the findings concisely for the stakeholders, using visual displays such as charts and graphs to reinforce the findings.

A stakeholder analysis takes place in one of two ways, depending on resources and time constraints. The first option is to interview individual stakeholders (see "Stakeholder Interview"). Or you can brainstorm the same issues in a group setting, with one person acting as a moderator. No matter

STAKEHOLDER INTERVIEW

(INTERVIEWER:) You have reviewed data that were gathered in an effort to initiate interagency collaboration in our community. The initiators of this data collection process believe strongly in these five guiding principles:

A. Human services in our community should be family focused.

B. Services should be available and accessible to as much of the community as possible.

C. We should look for ways to become more cost-effective and efficient and to use existing resources before soliciting funding for new resources.

D. We must plan *with* the community, not *for* the community. We believe in involving all members of the community in the planning process.

E. We are enthusiastic about improving our community's service delivery system. In order to measure our success, we must document results.

With these thoughts in mind, please answer the following questions:

1. What can our community do to improve family-focused services?

2. What are the major barriers to delivering family-focused services?

3. What are the greatest needs in our community?

4. How would you suggest measuring the program's success?

which approach you choose, the critical element is stakeholder involvement. Establishing your full-service school goals must involve people at all levels of the governance structure.

With the first option, the interview, distribute data reports (generated from a demographic survey, community service inventory, or community interaction survey) to each stakeholder, allowing time for review. Next, assign a two-person team to interview each stakeholder; one team member conducts the interview, and the other takes notes. Ask questions in a conversational style; doing so better elicits concerns about and vision of the proposed full-service school program.

Capture the stakeholders' input in a report that highlights the most frequently expressed issues and ideas, as well as other especially relevant or creative ideas. Share the summary report with all the stakeholders.

Remember that if stakeholders at all levels are not involved in the interview process, they are less likely to support changes in your community's service delivery system. By using the stakeholder analysis to determine your program's goals and objectives, the stakeholders clarify the community's critical needs. Here are some examples of critical needs:

- Improve interagency planning and referral systems, and coordinate eligibility determination

- Find ways to empower families, especially by involving parents and guardians in the process of assessing and improving service provision

- Emphasize alternative methods for financing programs, such as sharing the cost of caseworker positions or co-locating services

- Increase accessibility by using alternative forms of service delivery (for example, a service center collaborates with home-based services, mobile services, and transportation providers)

- Document success by establishing baseline data, sharing information from existing data systems, and creating a programwide data-collection design

Stakeholders may also use the report to expand the five guiding principles.

Option two for stakeholder analysis, brainstorming, is to prepare a written report containing information gathered from your needs assessment and present it to the stakeholder crew as a whole. This option saves time, but it also opens the door for individual personalities to dominate the crew's decisions.

The golden rule here is collaboration. If you choose option two, guard against one individual or agency becoming dominant. Ownership of your program's goals and design must belong to all stakeholders in order to build the foundation of trust necessary for program implementation.

Pointers

Use the report of stakeholders' interviews to reinforce the program's five guiding principles and to expand interagency collaboration:

- Build on the strengths of individual children, families, service providers, schools, and communities.

- Offer a variety of services tailored to the unique needs of individual students and families.

- Select prevention, intervention, and treatment services so as to reduce the number of students referred for crisis intervention services.

- Use natural support systems—family, friends, neighbors—to reduce the need for more intensive and expensive services.

- Share information and training across agencies, devoting time and effort to educating and retaining good staff.

- Safeguard confidentiality to ensure that there are no breaches of children's and families' rights, yet permit the sharing of information on a need-to-know basis.

Strategy Eight: Lead a Focus Group

A focus group is defined as a small group of individuals focused on a particular topic for a short period of time. The purpose is to gather information quickly and from a variety of perspectives. This approach saves time compared to a paper-and-pencil survey, and it helps you gain personal insight into community needs. Focus groups are also very useful as a training technique for expanding community awareness of available resources.

Depending on whether focus groups are carefully planned or not, there may be some disadvantages. The information gained is not as complete as the data from an extensive survey; also, depending on the comfort level of participants, responses within the focus group may be biased by the influence of dominant personalities.

You can pull together, for short and intense sessions, a full-service school focus group composed of key community agency personnel, workers in the front line of service provision, and representatives of families. The group assists your planning team in all six steps of program planning:

1. Identify target groups.

2. Identify significant problems facing families.

3. Identify services that families need and want.

4. Identify areas of duplication of effort and gaps in service among agencies.

5. Identify barriers to receiving services.

6. Develop an action plan.

The planning team may choose any number of participants for a focus group. A group of about twenty participants is relatively easy to work with and can break into four smaller groups of five members each. Invite two or three more members than you need, to compensate for no-shows. The focus group sessions should be scheduled at an hour convenient for the participants, and you may want to plan duplicate sessions in two locations to overcome transportation problems. Holding the focus group event in or near the proposed full-service school site helps set the stage to introduce the full-service school concept to your community.

Assign each workgroup a "family dilemma," a scenario typical of a family in your community, and give each workgroup member a typed copy of the scenario. (The planning team prepares the scenarios prior to the focus group session.) A simple way to write them is to ask a frontline caseworker to describe a typical family in his or her caseload. Alter enough of the story to protect the family's confidentiality. Two scenarios are given in the accompanying box.

You may decide to use the same or different scenarios for each workgroup. The facilitator for each workgroup reads the scenario aloud and guides the group through questions about the dilemma:

TWO EXAMPLES OF A FOCUS GROUP SCENARIO

The Whittakers (not their real name) have two small children. Dad is employed by a small business, and mom works part-time; their annual income is $24,000. Dad has a high school diploma and some vocational training. Mom left high school in tenth grade. Tommy, a third grader, has major problems in school—inattention, disruptive behavior, and falling grades—and the family's rising frustration with the school is causing strain in the marriage. Susan is only three but already beginning to act out.

The Millers (a pseudonym) have three children and income below the poverty level. Dad works for a construction firm, and the family struggles to make ends meet. Mom is unemployed. Daughter Nancy, sixteen, has a history of marijuana use and is mother to a six-month-old. The child's father is sexually active, may have been exposed to HIV, and does not provide financial support. Nancy did not receive medical care during pregnancy; neither has she received care since giving birth. Nathan is eight and is considered at risk because of poor retention ability, low family income, and academic underachievement. Susan, four, stays at home with Mrs. Miller, who shows signs of depression and alcohol abuse.

- What kinds of problems and need does this family have?
- What kinds of service does this family require to support its functioning?
- What do you see as the major barriers this family must overcome in order to get the support needed to function more effectively?
- What agencies or services are available in your community to help this family meet their needs?
- Is there any duplication of effort among the agencies and services that you mention?
- Are there any gaps in available community services that hinder progress for this family?

If time permits, ask participants to create additional scenarios based on their own real experiences with service delivery in the community.

Keep the focus group's operation as informal as possible. Serve refreshments, and make opening remarks very brief. Divide participants into four or five small workgroups. Aim for a mixture of participants in each workgroup, including agency personnel, frontline workers from all representative agencies, and family representatives. Designate a recorder or facilitator for each workgroup, and have the recorder document the workgroup's activities on a

---

FOCUS ON STAKEHOLDERS:

A Little Knowledge, a Lot of Action

Although Joan Adams is used to dealing with both tentative and aggressive behaviors that are manifestations of her sixth-grade students' development, she also knows that the start of any school year requires extra perseverance and commitment. This school year required even more from Joan: instead of having students feed into her class from just one elementary school, they came from three, one of which had been destroyed in a disastrous summer storm and was not even in Joan's own school district.

Several weeks into the term, most of Joan's students had settled into the school routine. Three students, however, were increasingly disruptive, bored, and inattentive. *What's causing this behavior?* Joan wondered. Then she noted that all three had come from the out-of-district school. Once she grasped what these students had in common, she found that they'd been classmates since kindergarten, had always made good grades, and hadn't previously shown behavior problems.

During one particularly trying class, Joan attempted to involve her three young troublemakers by asking them to draw a map of the southeast on the blackboard, writing in the name of each state's

capital. When they couldn't remember one name, Joan suggested they check their textbook. Two of the students returned to their desks to look. "We can't find it," they said. "Well, it's on page 64," Joan replied. There was a long pause while they turned the pages without stopping.

It was then that Joan noticed one more common trait: all three wore glasses. It was obvious that, for at least two of them, the glasses weren't working: they couldn't find the answer because they couldn't see the page numbers clearly.

Later, Joan discovered that although her full-service school offered annual vision screening conducted by an onsite health nurse, the district where these students attended elementary school had no such program. Digging deeper, she found that the students' glasses were considerably more than a year old. An immediate referral for vision screening resulted in new prescription glasses—and more attentive classroom behavior.

There was another outcome: at Joan's suggestion, services at all three elementary feeder schools were studied. The resulting data afford transitions that are far more successful for students and teachers.

---

flipchart. At the end of the session, arrange for these notes to be shared with the entire group, and incorporate them into session minutes so the planning team can analyze them later.

Action research
systematic reflection on practice, including (1) identifying a problem, (2) studying the problem by gathering data as a program continues, and (3) reflecting on the data in order to make decisions grounded in evidence

Strategy Nine: Take an Action Research Approach

The term *action research*, used to describe this strategy, is not intended to mean a scientific study using control groups and statistical analyses. The definition of a full-service school is to integrate "educational, medical, and/or social and human services for children and youth and their families on school grounds or in locations that are easily accessible."[4] A practical way to assess the needs of families that can potentially be served by a full-service school is to place a social worker or trained *case manager* at the proposed site of the full-service school; there they can collect information about and gain a better understanding of the community's needs.

Ask (or provide funding for) a community agency to assign a social worker or case manager to work actively with school-based personnel at the proposed full-service school site. The temporary assignment allows the worker to log extensive, firsthand observations that are sure to contribute information to the planning process.

The advantage of the action research approach is that one individual is dedicated to the information-gathering task for an established period of time, providing the planning team with access to specific, quality information. The disadvantage is that this approach provides only one person's viewpoint on service needs. If this approach is chosen, have the worker divide his or her time among representatives of schools, agencies, families, and the community. The worker may even choose to use some of the other strategies suggested in this chapter in an attempt to obtain detailed information. He or she should meet frequently with the planning team to provide updated information and generate new questions for assessment.

Case manager
person working directly with families to identify needs, coordinate resources, and assess progress toward families' goals

Strategy Ten: Conduct a Transition Study

Two pressing questions are usually asked once a full-service school program is in place: "What happens to students and families after they leave a full-service school site?" and "Aren't there services that can be provided to families before the child enters a school?" Just as there is danger in planning a program whose services are too diluted to make an impact, there is also danger in not offering support services to families for long enough periods of time to make a significant difference in their lives. Since families move in and out of crisis over time, no single age group benefits more than another from a full-service school program.

Use a transition study of services being provided to a target population over time to establish a continuum of services, to ensure that there are no gaps of time or support as they move from one age group to another or from one location to another. For example, students enrolled in a kindergarten class may be served by a host of prekindergarten programs and services designed specifically to identify developmental delays before a child enters school. A study of programs serving prekindergartners facilitates those pupils' smooth transition to kindergarten without interruption of family support services. Another example of a transition study is analysis of services across a school's feeder pattern. What happens to a targeted group of families as their children move from elementary to junior high, high school, and beyond?

The transition study helps ensure that support services are delivered over a longer period of time and without interruption. The transition study determines which service delivery approach is necessary and also provides a rich opportunity to collect longitudinal data about program outcomes.

Such a study is useful in both the original program design and the expansion plan of an existing full-service school program. Instead of looking at one site as the source of all services, assessment of the feeder patterns may indicate the need for service delivery across multiple school sites. Offering services at multiple sites can be a very cost-effective approach to service delivery, but beware of stretching personnel too thin, and diminishing service delivery, by moving them between sites.

Take the case of a registered nurse assigned to two school sites, where the ratio of students to nurse does not exceed 1,500 to 1 at either site. This ratio, frequently recommended, allows the nurse to successfully offer comprehensive health prevention, education, and intervention for two schools instead of one. If the student-to-nurse ratio is too high, however, the nurse is likely to be putting out fires and getting burned out as well; quality of service in both schools could deteriorate, defeating the purpose of your program.

A second example is a police officer assigned to offer drug and alcohol abuse prevention programs to intermediate-age students and to provide follow-up activities for middle school students. Assuming the high school these younger students feed into has a police officer on campus, early intervention and crime prevention services have now been continuous across nine grade levels. Students who stay in this feeder system benefit from prolonged exposure to prevention activities; students moving into or out of the system are exposed to some prevention activities whenever they enter.

Prioritizing the Issues

Prioritizing the issues is a matter of using data from the needs assessment strategies to answer the following questions:

- What significant health, social, and economic problems do families face?

- What services do families need and want?

- Is there duplication of effort or a gap in services offered by community agencies?

- What target group of children, youth, and families must be served based on the needs?

- What barriers to service delivery exist, from within families and from within the community agencies?

The greater the number of stakeholder crewmembers involved in prioritizing needs, the greater the number of people who support the decisions that create a shared vision for program success.

Nominal Group Process

The nominal group process is a decision-making method that enhances participation. Developed in President Lyndon Johnson's War on Poverty, it empowers community participants to vote on issues that are important to them. Each participant's vote carries equal weight. The nominal group process has these steps:

1. Presenting findings with regard to each issue (a summary of approaches to each of the first five steps in the planning process; see Figure 3.5 at the end of this chapter)

2. Answering any questions raised by the group

3. Voting on which issues are most important within each step

4. Tallying votes

5. Presenting results of votes

6. Categorizing each issue by "immediate," "short-term," or "long-term" action

Typically, each participant can use five votes (one for each issue) but only one vote for any one issue on the list. Votes are tallied and ranked in order of the number of votes received.

Tips for Reporting Results

No matter how thorough you think your needs assessment is, there will be some stakeholders who feel left out. Realize that you can't ask every question, and try to be open to suggestions for follow-up surveys.

Try to find neutral ground on which to disseminate the results, and include any community information networks.

Tailor presentation of results to your audience. For example, some groups want numbers, while others feel more comfortable with a philosophical approach. Use as many graphics and pictures as possible to capture the audience's attention and increase their understanding.

Whenever results reporting is well planned, the process builds a foundation for future efforts. The results help refocus on broad issues. For example, children's health data can be related to family support and preservation programs as well as school-based performance issues.

The needs assessment data is also a powerful tool to combat focusing on turf issues. When you can show statistically why you are restructuring and refocusing funding decisions, the central questions remained focused on what is best for children and families instead of what is best for the organizations involved in the full-service school program.

The Planning Process and Needs Assessment

In the design phase of constructing your full-service school, you need information in order to carry out the six steps of the planning process. Remember: the more information you have about your community, the better the decisions you and your stakeholder crew will make. Figure 3.5 shows how the information required by the first five planning process steps correlates with this chapter's needs assessment strategies. (Chapters Four and Five help you complete planning process step six, developing an action plan.)

The assessment strategies suggested in this chapter are not activities to be completed at the beginning of the planning effort and then abandoned as key stakeholders move on to implementation. The assessments provide baseline information for program goal setting and evaluation. Some of the strategies suggested (focus groups, surveys, interviews, computer-based mapping, and action research projects) are powerful tools for updating and assessing progress throughout the life of the program. The needs assessment is also your strongest source for completing supplemental funding applications. There will be continuous demand from stakeholders and community partners for current information about "how the families are doing."

Figure 3.5. Planning Process Steps and Corresponding Needs Assessment Strategies

Planning Process Step

1. Identify significant health, social, and economic problems facing families
   ① ⑤ ⑥ ⑦ ⑧ ⑨ ⑩

2. Identify services that families need and want.
   ① ⑤ ⑥ ⑦ ⑧ ⑨ ⑩

3. Identify duplication of effort and gaps in services offered by community agencies.
   ② ⑥ ⑦ ⑧ ⑨ ⑩

4. Identify a target group of children, youth, and families to be served based on need.
   ① ③ ⑥ ⑦ ⑩ ❹ optional

5. Identify barriers to service delivery, from within families and community agencies.
   ③ ④ ⑤ ⑦ ⑧ ⑨ ⑩

Key to Assessment Strategies

① Demographic survey
② Community services inventory
③ Physical facilities inventory
④ Community interaction survey
⑤ Community needs survey
⑥ Computer-based mapping
⑦ Stakeholder analysis
⑧ Focus groups
⑨ Action research
⑩ Transition study

Now you have ten new tools with which to pour a foundation of knowledge about your community, all designed to provide information for you and your stakeholder crew to use in ensuring that your goals are achievable, that your program design is responsive to the community's needs, and that all stakeholders have ownership in the program. In Chapter Four, you accumulate more new tools: those you need to obtain financing for construction of your full-service school.

Endnotes

1. Maslow, A. H. "A Theory of Human Motivation." *Psychological Review,* 1943, *50,* 370–396.

2. *Survey of Full-Service School Sites in Florida.* Tallahassee: University of South Florida Institute for At-Risk Children and Their Families, 1993.

3. Elders, J. *Principles to Link By. Integrating Education, Health and Human Services for Children, Youth, and Families: Systems That Are Community-Based and School-Linked.* (Centers for Disease Control and Prevention, Ewing Marion Kauffman Foundation, Maternal and Child Health Bureau, and Stuart Foundations.) Washington, D.C.: U.S. Department of Health and Human Services, 1994.

4. Florida Department of Education, Interagency Workgroup on Full-Service Schools. *Concept Paper.* Tallahassee: Florida Department of Education, 1992.

Chapter 4

Finance the Construction

Identifying Funding Approaches and Sources

Having available, ready, and trained personnel to handle daily crises is the most valuable aspect of a full-service school program. The effort is great, but more than worth the time. The easiest part of the program is the immediate success of services and providers. The hardest part is finding funding to start and continue the program.

—Barbara Reeves, elementary school counselor

Financing the construction of a full-service school often requires you to seek funding from multiple sources. Funding a full-service school program touches on more than meeting the needs of children and families; it also requires fulfilling the needs of *agencies* that are at risk! Because complex funding formulas can produce fragmented service delivery and costly, ineffective, or inefficient operating procedures, community agencies suffer from duplication of effort and ongoing funding crises. With each funding crisis, agencies are forced to reduce the number and quality of their services and to increase caseloads. They become like the families they serve: at risk.

Therefore if you want to build quality into your full-service school, you must find ways to coordinate service delivery and financing by working with, rather than in isolation from, other community stakeholders. Designing a solid financing plan now reduces risk and prevents the need for major remodeling later.

No single funding model is appropriate for all full-service schools, nor does remodeling your community's service delivery system solve everyone's problems. Trying to fund a full-service school large enough to solve everyone's problems may build not a "house" but a bureaucratic eyesore: a full-service school that cannot adequately solve anyone's problems. As your stakeholders develop an action plan for funding, remember Maslow's needs hierarchy and the medical triage model, where basic needs must be met first as well as prioritized by likelihood of success.

This chapter offers the funding tools you need to

- Overcome barriers to and develop effective strategies for successful funding

- Take a collaborative approach that guarantees effective use of existing funds and reveals the need for additional funds

- Understand the roles and politics of local, state, federal, and private funding sources

- Be able to choose funding sources whose goals are compatible with yours

Taken in its broadest context, funding strongly influences the scope, characteristics, and effectiveness of services and support available to children, youth, and families. As Kirst writes in *Education and Urban Society*, "The patchwork of funding strategies now used for school-linked services has resulted in small-scale, temporary programs rather than long-term programs that are systematically developed and funded."[1]

Your stakeholder crew must leap a major hurdle: ensuring adequate funding for implementation of the full-service school. Poorly constructed funding strategies may promise more than can be delivered. Stretching limited funds to meet program needs, and consequently hampering service delivery, is yet another danger of a poor funding strategy. Diluted services limit the impact of the program for children and families and cause stress and discouragement among staff.

Seeing Barriers to Funding as Opportunities

There are at least six major barriers to funding full-service schools. The barriers are often seen as obstacles to service delivery, but in a well-orchestrated collaborative effort, they actually become opportunities.

1. **Categorical or discrete definitions of funding.** *Categorical funding* barriers are policies that give one community agency the responsibility to address a single problem or population. Consequently, should families have multiple needs, they must contend with a separate agency for each problem. Eligibility requirements may also be defined in narrow terms. Children and families are often burdened by labels associated with the services they need—the "welfare family," the "at-risk population"—and the labels compound their problems.

   The opportunity presented by this funding barrier is to develop an integrated system of service delivery where labels and boundaries between programs disappear, the family unit is highly valued, and bureaucracy is reduced as much as possible within the constraints of the categorical mandates.

2. **Distinct eligibility criteria.** A large percentage of any service program's administrative costs is expended on screening applicants for eligibility. Families forced to meet the eligibility criteria of several separate agencies may receive overlapping or duplicated services, or no

Categorical funding
funding designated for specific services only, for example, funds for volunteer programs that cannot be used to purchase student supplies

Having a "Plan B" for Finances

The dreaded phone call comes. The major funding source for your full-service school initiative has been pulled. The steering committee advises you to proceed with your "zero-based budgeting plan." You're upset, but you know that most of the full-service school program will continue, and you're feeling smug. You know that your program will survive just fine without it.

Does this scenario make you a little uneasy? It should. In today's climate of funding cutbacks and lay-offs, it is often reality. How can you plan for a complete loss of funding? Here are "voices of experience."

"If you use a large grant source to initiate the program, spread the funding around! Don't concentrate all funds in one program that won't survive off other sources."

"Don't fund *any* personnel positions without local match dollars! For example, if you want to hire a person to recruit additional volunteers, use the grant dollars as match dollars with another funding source and pay 30–50 percent of the total position cost."

"Move people out from under the grant as quickly as possible. When opportunities present themselves to continue the program under a continuing or more stable funding source, don't hesitate to move people and resources around within the partnerships established as part of the effort. Build in the expectation that new programs will be expected to look for alternative funding!"

"Continuously seek out alternative sources of income. Consider Medicaid billing, family contributions, private donations, additional grant proposals, etc., as ongoing and mandatory parts of your program plan."

service at all. Endless paperwork, documentation, and administrative "safeguards" waste valuable time and divert funds from services.

The full-service school model offers the opportunity to develop flexible funding strategies that minimize overlapping eligibility criteria and create a single, common eligibility assessment for use by all agencies. Thus an application for free or reduced-cost lunch could also be used to apply for other programs such as health insurance or mental health counseling, with the same income eligibility guidelines for both. The only requirement is interagency dialogue and cooperation.

3. **Duplication and overlap of services.** While some desperately needed services go unfunded or underfunded, examples of duplicate funding and overlapping services are well documented. Many teen parents are considered at risk and thus are eligible for a variety of support services. Without coordination of the services, teen parents may discover they have three counselors but no transportation to the doctor's office for a physical exam.

The full-service school presents the opportunity to establish interagency collaboration, thus paving the way for cost sharing or

"Look for opportunities to match dollars from other program funds. More and more opportunities to fund new programs require that local commitment dollars be used to draw down additional funds. Be an entrepreneur. . . . Write an evaluation component in one program plan to match dollars in additional programs."

"Place priority on seed programs: those that need a one-time funding source to get started but have a mechanism for becoming self-sustaining. For example, one of our full-service school sites started a cadet program in collaboration with the local sheriff's department. With the purchase of a set of basic uniforms and equipment, the program has become self-perpetuating. The students contribute dues and participate in fundraisers to replace uniforms. The program is a valuable asset to both the students and the community."

"If program funds are lost, look for opportunities to adjust the working hours of other employees to maintain a level of service while new alternatives are explored."

"Use your evaluation component to readjust the levels and intensity of services so that funding priorities are based on program outcomes. Don't fund programs that don't get results!"

"Be sure to include your governance structure in all levels of decision making about funds! When partners participate in funding decisions, there is more ownership of program objectives. If funds disappear, the services that have become an integral part of partnership agreements will remain top priorities in budget decisions."

"Expand partnerships as quickly as possible. The more you give your program away to others, the more successful your program will be in the long run. Share the trials of program growth, but be especially careful to share every success with every member of your program!"

blended funding (discussed later in this chapter) as techniques for maximizing limited resources by reducing duplication.

4. **Lack of communication.** With each community agency specialized, there is very little communication within and across service providers—even among those who have the same basic goals for the same families.

   The opportunity and challenge is to build your full-service school's governance structure so that it lends itself to communication not only among service providers but also among families and the community at large. With improved communication, your stakeholders are better able to identify funding needs and develop appropriate strategies.

5. **Lack of clear documentation.** There is no shortage of statistics about the number of families who receive services from community agencies. But there is little documentation of the impact of these services. Does more and better service delivery prove that collaborating agencies make a difference in how well children perform in school? Data of this sort are not usually kept by individual agencies.

The program goals for full-service schools are long-term, which presents you with another opportunity: to develop a research model that tracks service delivery and cost-effectiveness and that shows whether you are making a positive change in your community. Stakeholders and taxpayers are more supportive of a program that documents effective, efficient use of tax dollars.

6. **The maze of funding resources.** Last but not least in the list of funding barriers is the difficulty of finding your way through the incredible maze of available funding sources. How monies travel from a funding source to a family is often referred to as a *funding stream*.

The opportunity here is for your stakeholder crew to travel through the maze, map the appropriate funding streams, and match those streams to the target population.

Funding stream
another term for categorical funds: targeted to a specific population and often having strict eligibility criteria

Funding Strategies

You may already have existing financial resources as the basis of your funding strategy. If that is the case, then as we have suggested earlier you can take steps to maximize use of those funds (reduce duplication, consolidate agency locations, share resources, and so on). But if you need additional funding, then we advise constructing an action plan using the eleven funding strategies that follow before you write any proposals to funding sources (Chapter Five).

The overall objective of any funding strategy for a full-service school program is to *seek stable and adequate funding*. Interagency collaboration requires long-term planning and funding, particularly in support of the infrastructure needed for effective service delivery. Invest in facilities and equipment, training, administrative support, technical assistance, and automated information systems to monitor and evaluate program success. *Soft money* is best used to start a pilot program or to fund a short-term project, not to fund your entire full-service school program.

Soft money
money that is accessible for only a limited time or for separate, discrete projects

Support What Has the Most Value

The first strategy we present is to *seek funding for services that have the most value*. In other words, services must be provided and paid for on the basis of appropriateness and effectiveness (as well as cost). If you increase efficiency and reduce expenditures in one area, reinvest the savings in expanded prevention and early intervention programs, as the next strategy suggests.

Second, *support front-end priorities*. Intervention and prevention services are more effective when they reach children at an early age; your funding strategy should direct monies especially to these priorities. Prevention is a better investment—and cheaper—than either treatment or rehabilitation. Unless you are committed to front-end priorities, specialized care and crisis intervention services will take a disproportionate amount of your total budget. A well-integrated system, capable of identifying troubled children and families at the first sign of problems, is the best and most effective prevention program.

Promote Collaboration and Flexibility

Strategy number three is to *collaborate.* The crew of stakeholders in the full-service school must seek the wisest ways to manage the community's resources. Collaborating agencies must look for the best mix of services that meet the community's needs.

Fourth, *plan* with *families, not for them.* All families have strengths to build on. They do not need handouts . . . only a hand.

Fifth, *be flexible* in specifying how dollars are to be used in your full-service school program. There are four basic kinds of funding sources: (1) local, (2) state, (3) federal, and (4) private. Greater flexibility in using categorical funds is found at the state and community levels. These more flexible funding sources allow for program administration that fosters pooling of funds, blending of resources, joint operation of programs, and service provision designed to meet the unique needs of families.

The sixth strategy is to *base your governance structure on collaborative decision making.* Develop funding policies that strongly encourage shared decision making about allocation of dollars to services and that seek collaboration among federal, state, and community funding sources.

Build on What You Have and What Is Good

Use existing resources before you solicit additional funds. The funding tenet of the full-service school is to supplement—not supplant—existing resources.

Strategy number eight is to *place high value on families.* Choose funding sources that seek to enhance the family's capabilities, not to spoon-feed so-called dysfunctional families. Advocate for funding that supports the view of the family as an active, intelligent consumer of services seeking necessary and appropriate care.

Focus on Results and the Long Run

Focus on achieving and documenting desired results. This ninth strategy means to be sure your program budget targets services that you are confident are going to achieve specified objectives. Regular and ongoing assessment of results is a critical part of interagency collaboration.

The tenth strategy is to *build in approaches to service delivery that survive and flourish* in spite of changes in community agencies. As an example, the public and private agencies that traditionally serve children with serious emotional disturbances must be ready to function within a system that is now being dramatically restructured by the dynamics of managed health care.

The final strategy is to *develop and expand your program through communication and training.* To expand awareness and understanding of children's and families' needs, stakeholders must take their message to policy makers and other local, state, and national audiences. Frontline workers, families, and administrators must participate in ongoing training to enhance the individual and collaborative skills that facilitate interagency planning.

Collaboration for an Effective Funding Plan

Keep these eleven funding strategies in mind as you take three steps toward guaranteeing effective use of existing funds and improving the likelihood of efficient use of additional funds: (1) identify common needs (hence funding requirements that are actually held in common), (2) streamline access to all services in order to maximize the use of funds for everyone, and (3) make service delivery information systems comprehensive and collaborative.

Step One: Identify Common Needs

Here is where the true spirit of collaboration and coordination in funding and planning a full-service school becomes manifest. Coordination occurs when agencies agree to refer families to each other; however, this is not the same as working together to solve the families' complex problems. Collaboration is a joint venture; it requires identifying common needs in a single, united effort. We all want the basic necessities for children: stable family support mechanisms, safety and survival, good physical and mental health, economic well-being, the best of academic opportunities, and preparedness to contribute to society as a working individual. We want essentially those same outcomes for families, along with adequate housing, employment, safe neighborhoods, and willingness as well as preparedness when it comes to contributing to the community.

Approaches to assessing what children and families need were discussed in Chapter Three; see in particular the use of focus groups. Our emphasis here is on improving the *funding* side of planning for the full-service school by forging agreement on what all stakeholders want to be able to afford.

Step Two: Streamline Access

Streamline access
improve cost-effectiveness and efficiency of service delivery through administrative change, better use of existing resources, and exploration of technological possibilities

Before seeking new funds, your stakeholder crew should analyze the community's service delivery system to see what aspects of your full-service school program can be delivered without any additional funding.

To take just one example, what is the effect on funding requirements of streamlining intake evaluations and eligibility assessments? *Streamlining access* keeps programs and services up-to-date with community needs, makes their delivery simpler and more efficient, eliminates unnecessary tasks for both families and service providers, reduces duplication of effort and information, and builds partnerships among agencies working toward common goals. In other words, streamlining access means improving services and lowering administrative expenses. Streamlining access makes your service delivery system more cost-effective and efficient. It also makes your funding plan less complex.

Enhanced use of funding streams is a golden opportunity for local agencies to consolidate resource and referral services for existing programs. For example, one agency may act as a referral service for all child care services in the area, while a second agency coordinates all transportation services. Often these efforts can be coordinated without any additional funding.

Here are three approaches to streamlining service access:

1. Make changes in administration

2. Put existing resources to better use

3. Explore the impact of technological changes[2]

Administrative Change

Streamlining access succeeds only if (1) the process is accompanied by changes in how services are administered, planned, organized, and delivered; (2) governance structures are restructured; (3) staff are trained and supported; and (4) accountability is ensured. Do not lose sight of the ultimate goal of all funding strategies: to create ongoing and reliable system change through collaboration that enables families to better access public and private services tailored to their special needs.

One technique for bypassing inflexible categorical funding is termed *wraparound funding*. This can be illustrated as follows. Each funding agency has limits to the amount or nature of its funds, as though applying a single Band-Aid to multiple wounds. However, several agencies can combine forces by adding their contributions, or Band-Aids, to form a larger bandage that wraps around the entire wound. These multiagency-source funds remain with the child over time, until healing is accomplished. For example, a child identified with a developmental delay at birth receives a continuum of services from birth to age five, using multiple funding resources, and ultimately is integrated into exceptional student services in public education. Developmental delays are minimized. Family support services build a foundation for the child to achieve optimal achievement at whatever level. The implication is clear that administrative change must take place to facilitate wraparound funding.

Funding consortia or clusters can also be arranged so that if no single agency has the resources to meet the needs of a population, a multiple-agency unit is formed. Each agency contributes its appropriate share. For example, an

Wraparound funding
a funding mechanism to provide all-inclusive services to a child, from a variety of sources, staying consistent over time

urban school setting is targeted for intensive crisis intervention and long-term prevention services. A funding consortium is established among a number of agencies to provide mental health counseling, drug and alcohol treatment and prevention programs, health services, transportation, day care, and academic tutoring. The funding consortium shares the cost of renting an existing facility, establishing office space, and staffing a twenty-four-hour resource center near the existing full-service school.

Another approach to administrative change is to establish a neighborhood development trust, a local funding organization specifically designed to identify, support, and invest in the local community. Such trusts often support the community's overall economic empowerment by including members of the local chamber of commerce or economic development committee. The trust acts likes a magnet to attract investment potential into the local economy, distributing money to stimulate community investment, drawing down additional dollars through matching amounts in community development grants, and providing a point of leadership in the community (in the form of a manager selected by local directors). Contributions are solicited from individuals, churches, local businesses, local organizations, local government, foundations, and state and federal funding sources. The trust supports the development of a large range of local initiatives that benefit families. The trust may, for instance, supply a loan for the cost of redesigning vacant facilities into a full-service school or for launching a community radio station, newspaper, or resource telephone line. Simultaneously, small grants or awards are made to create new alternatives to compensate for such community deficits as transportation, child care, recreational activities, youth employment, and so on.

Blended financing also streamlines access through administrative change. Several techniques ensure your success in this process. For one, a small proportion of funds are used as *hooks* or *glue money* to tie collaborative efforts together in a sort of blend. Blending entitlement dollars with *discretionary funds* makes services more accessible and places fewer restrictions on how funds are used. An example of blended funding is the state of Florida's capital outlay plan for building or renovating facilities at full-service school sites to house interagency efforts. The capital funding is dispersed to school boards based on evidence of community collaboration; service agencies agree to house programs and services at or near full-service schools that build the new facilities.

Many blended funding efforts can be described as maximizing federal funds. Using existing state and local expenditures to match federal funds, they increase federal financial participation in local service delivery. For example, some school boards choose to become Medicaid providers so that eligible services provided at the school site can actually be billed to Medicaid. Another example is a full-service school using federal employment funding to provide school-based child care. Using blended funds maximizes the effect of

Blended financing
melding federal and state funding to cut across historically separate service domains

Hooks
sums of money used in a program design to catch, hold, or pull other funding sources together

Glue money
a sum of money used to join or hold together different parts of programs

Discretionary funds
funds not specifically targeted for a special purpose

federal dollars in meeting local objectives, all the while streamlining program administration.

Use of Existing Resources

When families' needs are linked to existing services and resources, significant barriers to service delivery are minimized and local resources can be better organized via simple administrative changes:

Establishing toll-free telephone hot lines. Crisis counselors answer questions about availability, location, and eligibility requirements for specific services. In some communities, the hotline system is computerized; any person with access to a computer and modem can access a centralized directory of services that is continuously updated.

Designing joint eligibility application forms. Families requesting services fill out one application form for use by collaborating community agencies.

Co-locating or outstationing intake and eligibility staff. The concept of the full-service school is to streamline access to services by locating those services at or near a school site. But the same concept also applies to juvenile justice assessment centers, employability centers, and the like. Centrally locating all or most of the services related to a particular theme allows families easier and more cost-effective access to resources.

Taking a care coordination approach. A person or a team in the role of case manager assesses family needs and works with family dynamics to provide flexible coordination and access to services. In addition, care coordination builds family empowerment by writing a family care coordination plan with—not for—the family. (See Resource L for templates of a family needs assessment and a family care coordination plan.) By developing an interagency referral system using care coordination, new or additional funding may not be required if an existing job description can be changed to allow an employee of one agency to take on the task of interagency referral. This position might come from the school; it could be filled by a counselor, teacher, or assistant principal.

*Delegate **intake** authority for all agencies to onsite agencies.* If co-locating or outstationing staff is not practical or feasible, it may be possible to assign intake authority to other agencies whose staff are located at the full-service school site. For example, federal and state rules usually allow states or counties to delegate—through contracts and other agreements—virtually everything except making the actual eligibility decision. Therefore, other agencies can handle intake interviews, data collection, computer operations, and service delivery. Delegating Medicaid intake authority is particularly common. Hospitals, nursing homes, and health clinics take patient applications and forward them to Medicaid offices. If you plan to delegate intake authority, include in your action plan a detailed discussion of follow-up requirements

Intake
point at which a student or family first enters a program; process includes collecting basic demographic information in order to determine a family's eligibility for services

for program eligibility, shared intake authority, error rates and fraud, supervision, scheduling, paper-flow procedures, training, and dealing with problems in staff attitudes toward assuming increased responsibility.

Use the services of competing local resources. If several local organizations such as mental health providers or managed health care networks compete for business, work with these agencies to improve access for students and families at the full-service school location. Health facilities built as part of a full-service school can, for example, be accessed by several managed care networks, and health prevention services can thus be successfully offered on the campus.

Technological Change

Technological breakthroughs open doors to new automated information gathering and decision-making methods. As an example, *expert systems* for screening and intake programs automate eligibility decisions. Electronic tracking of family care coordination plans and services and automated access to community services information are just two further illustrations of what collaborating agencies are experimenting with. Consider these tools to streamline access to services at your full-service school:

Expert systems
computer systems designed to facilitate the decision-making process through use of extended database applications

- Advanced computer programming languages, which put more control in the hands of local planners. Communities can actually design new software that meets their needs and can interface with existing sources of electronic information.

Database
computer program designed to collect and store large numbers of facts, quantities, or conditions for further research or analysis

- Relational *databases,* which allow agencies to add new information (data elements) to their existing database without having to restructure it. This allows flexible definition of individual data elements, easier sorting and matching of information, and better security, in addition to improving access to the information stored in the database. Software advancements allow relational databases to communicate with each other across computer networks.

Computer network
a connection of computers that allows them to operate separately but communicate with each other

- *Computer networks,* which connect information systems within offices; among schools, communities, regions, and states; across the nation; and around the world using the Internet. These networks allow users to enter and access information stored in different locations.

- *Imaging technology,* which allows electronic capture and storage of all kinds of documents (photographs, medical records, birth certificates, immunization records, parental consent forms, etc.). Full-service school staff can use networks to input, retrieve, update, and view these images via their computer terminals, without having to reproduce and store hard copies.

- *Barcoding, touch-screen, voice-recognition, and voice-to-text conversion technologies,* all of which are revolutionizing data entry and retrieval. Touch screens and voice-recognition software allow community agency staff and the families they serve to listen to and read instructions from computer terminals and enter answers to questions directly into the computer system. The use of touch-tone telephone technology also opens the door to more creative and efficient data entry.

- *Electronic benefits transfer systems,* which use credit-card-type identification cards and networks to automate verification of eligibility and speed service delivery.

- *Portable computers and telecommunication links,* which use telephone lines to offer powerful and cost-effective intake and eligibility determination outside of agency offices and in locations convenient to families.

Step Three: Make Information Systems Comprehensive

The National Center for Service Integration (NCSI)[3] surveyed more than eighty family service initiatives similar to full-service schools. Many of the initiatives are looking for ways to exchange data among agencies and establish electronic communication networks. Based on the survey as well as telephone interviews, site visits, convening of an expert panel, and a symposium, the center proposes eleven functional requirements for a comprehensive service delivery system. The recommendations are valuable input in considering what funding needs center on the information systems that regulate and facilitate service delivery systems in your full-service school. Check your existing or proposed information system against this list.

☐ Common registration: at any point of entry, establishes an individual or family as a case, and collects and stores identifying and demographic information in a central location

☐ Comprehensive family assessment: identifies and comprehensively documents family needs and strengths

☐ Joint eligibility determination: establishes multiple services or benefits for which an individual or family is eligible

☐ Coordinated case planning: documents a plan for reaching individual or family outcome goals, encompassing activities and services from all relevant agencies and providers

☐ Comprehensive information and referral: provides data about and directions for obtaining services from agencies and organizations

☐ Cross-program client and service tracking: documents direct services and referrals for multiple programs, facilitating follow-up to ensure receipt of needed services

☐ Cross-program client outcomes tracking: documents results and interim indicators of individual or family progress toward goals

☐ Comprehensive community needs assessment: provides communitywide data on needs and available resources

☐ Multiprogram reporting: generates reports to meet a variety of internal and external administrative requirements

☐ Multisource financial management and billing: supports tracking and billing for services according to multiple funding sources

☐ Evaluation: uses data on program evaluation inputs and outcomes to assess program effectiveness and other evaluative criteria

The NCSI also recognizes that there are a variety of challenges associated with developing information systems; no one design addresses all of a community's issues. Some of the challenges facing system developers are these:

1. Reengineering the service delivery environment to correspond with the information system (or vice versa)

2. Creating a common vision around the development of the system

3. Linking existing systems

4. Creating organizational acceptance

5. Developing organizational capacity

6. Gaining consensus about who controls data input, use, and extraction

7. Balancing confidentiality and need for information

8. Mapping data across programs and agencies

9. Creating funding plans that are adequate and flexible enough to meet the vision

10. Identifying relevant models and expertise

11. Carrying out conversion, training, and implementation in an operational environment

12. Replicating the success of the program at other full-service school sites

The Politics of Financing a Full-Service School

Adopting a full-service school approach means changing the school's role. Critics argue that expanding the school's role to include social service functions interferes with traditional academic priorities. Proponents argue that collaboration with communities is necessary to meet the needs of students and families so that schools can do what they do best: educate. It is revealing that issues of financial collaboration often come to frame the central argument between these conflicting philosophical views. Nevertheless, the need for financing can also bring opposing sides together. The full-service school model advocates, as Kirst says, that "schools are overwhelmed with negative changes in children's conditions, and not likely to receive the funds to construct needed social services under the school's sole authority."[4]

Local Politics

If your community decides to advocate for a full-service school program, there are political issues on the local and state levels to be aware of. In your own community, there are three types of issues that affect your ability to collaborate on funding.

Control. Traditionally, each community agency has controlled its own funding, staffing, policies, and eligibility requirements for the clientele it serves. In a full-service school, some control is relinquished by each agency, yet overall someone must be accountable—which means, in control! Schools have elected boards with rule-making capabilities; the board is a legal entity that can vote on such things as millage rates (setting school taxes in mills per dollar); it has a system and staff in place for managing and auditing the budget. But what many school boards do not have is knowledge of or experience with funding programs that use a variety of funding sources. Somewhere along the line, your community's stakeholders must decide who controls the program's funds.

Cross-Training. Most community agencies are not experienced in the interagency collaborative process; therefore, their staff need training on how to work together and communicate across agency boundaries. For instance, there is the seemingly small example of agency jargon. Acronyms that make perfect sense in one agency are meaningless to another, or one acronym stands for two different things as two agencies use it. Creating a glossary of terms may be necessary to ensure that agencies communicate with each other.

Governance Structures. The two formalized governance structures proposed in Chapter Two (site-based and community-based) are necessary to keep the lines of communication open and all participants involved in decision making. Leaving stakeholders out of fiscal decisions causes irreparable damage to your action plan for financing a full-service school. Choose whichever governance structure better fits your community, or develop your own—but establish one. The structure lends consistency to your decision making and eliminates "political" inconsistencies.

Pointers

If your local school board is not ready for fiscal control of a full-service school program, explore a partnership within the community, as with a county commission, coalition, or social service agency.

State Politics

States play a critical role in pouring a foundation for interagency collaboration, the most obvious part of which is that they can provide funding for coordination among community agencies or for building physical facilities to house interagency efforts, while allowing communities the independence to design local programs. States may also set the stage for maintaining funding initiatives.

Federal Politics

The bulk of federal revenues for family support initiatives comes from four major programs: Medicaid's Early Periodic Screening, Diagnosis and Training Service (EPSDT); Title IV-F (the JOBS program); Title IV-E (Child Welfare Assistance); and the Family Support Act of 1988. In order to tap these funding sources, your program's planning team must understand each program's funding requirements and eligibility criteria and must be creative in designing a full-service school that meets federal requirements.

Funding Sources

The abiding message of this chapter is to use existing financial resources first, and then expand to supplemental funding sources as specific needs are identified for your full-service school. This section categorizes potential funding by local, state, federal, and private sources. The categories from which you select funding sources depend on your existing resources and the characteristics of your unique full-service school program. The number of sources is so great and changeable that we have not attempted to list them in the chapter text; a comparatively comprehensive list is located in Resource G.

Local Funding Sources

Local funding sources offer the most immediate financial resources for a full-service school. Those closest to the issues of their community have a personal stake in supporting interagency efforts. Here are some general categories of services that you may wish to explore within your community.

Government. *County governments.* In states where a system of county government exists, they have the power to dedicate county tax revenue to fund services or special projects that supplement state-supported and federal-supported programs. This is a particularly effective source of funds when grant requirements include local matching funds.

City governments. City councils can dedicate specific resources to be used for children's and family services.

Business. *Business organizations.* Many local businesses have access to corporate foundations. This provides an opportunity for the business to give back to the community in which it operates. Businesses may also contribute mentors, equipment, in-kind resources, or their products to your effort.

Community. *Children's services councils or child welfare boards.* Some states allow creation of special-purpose districts, boards with taxing authority, to be created by local ordinance and subject to voter approval by referendum. Revenues are raised by dedicated millage on local property taxes. Each board has broad representation from the community and collaborates with state and local, public and private agencies. A county may choose to establish a taxing authority dedicated to children's and family issues. Money generated through the taxing authority could, for instance, be used to directly fund a full-service school program in a high-risk neighborhood. In addition, generated funds can be used as cash match to bring in additional sources of revenue.

Community and civic organizations and associations. Do a complete inventory of organizations located in your community (refer to the inventory of Figure 3.2 and Resource C). Include groups such as the Jaycees; Kiwanis, Rotary, and Lions clubs; police chiefs and firefighters associations; college Greek associations; professional societies; and military groups. These organizations sponsor a variety of services and are always looking for new ideas to support.

Community organizations. Look to strong community organizations such as a chamber of commerce or the United Way to support your full-service school's activities. Don't forget that there are also other active groups affiliated with or focused on parks, libraries, schools, community colleges, universities, the police, and local hospitals that all have a stake in building strong families. Community organizations help connect you with the skills of individuals who can help families build on their own strengths. In approaching organizations, remember that you may also want to access the skills of individual members instead of asking for direct funding.

Interagency councils. If interagency networks already exist in your community, you have exciting resources for information, funding, and networking. These include special interest groups, such as an interagency council for preschool children, or groups that are broader in scope. Many funding sources require a local advisory and oversight committee to monitor your program's spending and its success. Ask school social workers, leaders in the community, administrators of social and human service programs, and school principals about committees or councils that already exist. Interagency groups are probably one of the strongest resources for your program. Make an appointment to meet with the group's chairperson to explain your program goals.

Not-for-profit boards or organizations. Explore the variety of not-for-profit organizations in your locale and their boards of directors. These independent groups provide wonderful technical expertise in program development and documentation. A relationship with a board member of one of these organizations may also provide an exciting opportunity to work with some creative funding strategies. To illustrate, suppose you have an opportunity to apply for a grant to develop a special program at the full-service school site. The grant funds a temporary position to get the program started, but it is difficult to establish short-term positions for program development and planning through the fiscal agent for the full-service school program (the school board). So a not-for-profit organization writes a cooperative agreement with the school board to submit the grant, hire a person, pay the person, and allow the full-service school's local oversight council to manage the program.

State Funding Sources

Every state has a variety of programs available under different categories of service. Some general categories you might want to explore are community development grants, departments of education and social and human services, mental health and substance abuse programs, juvenile justice, children's medical services, developmental and health services, community-based training programs, resource centers, multiagency networks, and departments of labor and employment. See Resource G for explanations of each category.

Federal Funding Sources

Federal sources can provide funding for a multitude of services in your full-service school.[5] To tap these sources, you must understand program requirements, be creative in designing your services to meet their requirements, grow accustomed to a different kind of school planning, and maintain accurate records and documentation to comply with federal billing and accountability standards.

Explore block grants for mental health, substance abuse, and maternal and child health programs; Medicaid; the Social Security Act for emergency assistance, foster care, and child welfare programs; jobs programs; the Public Health Service Act for community and migrant health centers; the Developmental Disabilities Assistance and Bill of Rights Act; and a variety of federal education acts. See Resource G for a comprehensive description of each category.

Private Funding Sources

Your local library probably has a large book entitled *The Foundation Directory*. It lists every private foundation in the United States. The directory also includes a brief background on each foundation, its funding priorities, geographic preferences, and time frames for proposal submission. Foundations usually prefer to invest their dollars in the community where they have a presence. Locate the major industries in your area for connections. If you are in a rural area, consider major companies in your state. Don't forget to include insurance companies. There are additional details on how to write a proposal for funding to foundations and other grant-making resources in Chapter Five.

Conclusion: Tips on Funding

We want to leave you with a collection of tips that highlight how you can use the financing tools offered in this chapter. Whether your full-service school's construction is financed by local, state, federal, or private funding sources, these tips give you firsthand guidance about how to pursue the dollars that will make your dream a reality. The tips fall into three categories: budgeting, grant writing, and political considerations.

Budgeting

Don't ignore infrastructure needs. A program manager position is critical, and you may need secretarial or data entry help. Consider the advantages of electronic information systems and computer technology from the very beginning.

Consider establishing a not-for-profit entity independent of personalities and organizations. Not-for-profit organizations maintain tax-exempt status, which allows the entity to apply for funding from foundations, corporations, and private individuals. These funding sources often allow greater flexibility in program implementation than is typically afforded by governmental sources.

Ask local organizations and foundations for funds, and point out the advantages their donations provide for the community and for the organization. Hospitals, for example, receive tax credits for donations.

Spread the cost of facilities among agencies that can pay rent. Do not leave one agency holding the bag.

Look for ways to provide one-time funding as opposed to ongoing program support. Programs that can be "institutionalized" after using start-up funds are very appealing to funding sources, and they provide stable, long-term support for families. Remember, every year is a crisis year in budget management.

Grant Writing

Set aside a small sum for grant match money to help you access additional dollars. Use local dollars to pull down other local, state, or federal funds.

When you submit a budget proposal, make sure the budget illustrates how your program crosses agency lines, thus demonstrating how the funder's investment will produce more for less. Document how you have maximized revenue by reinvesting budgets into services.

Be aware of what percentage of funding is dedicated to prevention and early intervention. If you are pursuing, say, juvenile justice intervention dollars and only 17 percent of the dollars are dedicated to prevention, your program plan may need to reflect a strong intervention model with prevention built in.

Pointers

In the Federal Register of Sept. 12, 1995, the Office of Elementary and Secondary Education, Education Department, invited applications for school districts to use a portion of their federal funds for coordinated services projects—projects that link agencies with schools to improve health and social services access. Up to 5 percent per fiscal year of discretionary Elementary and Secondary Education Act funds may be waived for coordinated services.

Resource G contains a list of funds eligible for these projects.

Political Considerations

Keep in mind what your fair share is. Rather than soliciting only legislatures and major funding sources, bring finances down to the community level. An individual community has individual needs. Look for areas to use resources where there is no existing collaboration.

Remember, the emphasis is not on how much you spend but on how you improve the lives of families. Make sure your evaluation plan reflects this issue.

If funding problems fuel the fire and personalities get hot, then back off, regroup, and reeducate. Don't force issues! Instead, in funding discussions within and outside your group of collaborators, emphasize local decision making and current success.

Hold a local, regional, or state conference for which representatives of organizations in the major funding streams set aside specific time to share information, work through "real" case scenarios, and develop action plans. Planning the event brings interested stakeholders together for creative discussions.

Have a community agency develop a resource notebook detailing funding sources for major problem areas. For example, an agency experienced with day care could provide information on all possible ways to pay for day care with existing funds.

Advocate for state-level interagency groups that model collaborative funding behaviors. The state-level group should focus on process, not events. The group can look for ways of easing the process of collaboration in support of families.

Plant little seeds. Talk about possibilities for collaboration with stakeholders, and then fertilize the idea over time. Sometimes ideas need time to grow. And sometimes you have to give your idea away in order to let it grow. When you develop program plans, be flexible, creative, brave, and passionately committed!

Funding streams shift like sand on a beach, so think in terms of change. Remember, trust between people lasts longer than money from any funding source. People are your major resource.

Remember that families learn best in the context of their own lives. As you set priorities for funding, look for unusual ways of providing family interventions that are adaptable. For example, you may want to provide an opportunity for a teenage parent to work in a child care center.

Don't get caught up in the fix-it scenario just because there is a funding source available. You may damage rather than help. Provide only services that are appropriate, and adequate for families at the point where the service is needed.

Endnotes

1. Kirst, M. W. "Financing School-Linked Services." *Education and Urban Society,* 1992, *25*(2), 166–174.

2. National Center for Service Integration. "Information Systems to Support Comprehensive Service Delivery." Symposium, Sept. 22–23, 1994, Washington, D.C.

3. National Center for Service Integration (1994).

4. Kirst (1992).

5. Kirst (1992).

Chapter 5

Frame the Funding Request

Writing Funding Proposals and Evaluation Plans

A full-service school not only offers the best of academic, mental health services and health education, but also enhances the lives of families by including adult education, parenting classes, and parent resource centers. Funding for these programs makes families, our state, and our nation the best they can be!

—Peggy Godwin, intergenerational specialist, Adult Learning Center

When the stakeholder crew gets down to the serious business of funding "construction" of your full-service school, a grant is likely to be one of the funding options they explore. The funding source that may potentially buy your full-service school house wants you to frame your funding request in a particular way. This description of your plan as well as specific documentation create a picture of the proposed project, so that potential funders can determine if the expenditure of their funds is a good investment—one that has a reasonable chance to succeed.

Grants are awarded by different sources: government agencies, private foundations, civic organizations, and others. Grants are awarded for a variety of purposes: research, construction, planning, implementation, equipment, training, and so on. They are awarded in different contractual forms, including cost-reimbursable or fixed-price. Think of the grant request, or proposal, as an opportunity to describe your program's framework to a potential buyer. One section describes your goals and objectives, another describes how you plan to meet those objectives, and yet another details which yardsticks you will use to measure your success. If you want to nail down a source of funds, you have to build your proposal to the funding source's specifications.

The contents of this chapter prepare you to frame your proposal and prove your program's worth, using tools that enable you to:

- Decide what grant funding will accomplish, based on your needs assessments
- Identify a proposal-writing team
- Develop a list of potential funding sources

- Write the proposal to source specifications
- Handle the results, whether or not your proposal is funded

Decide What Grant Funding Will Accomplish

Before you frame your request for *grant* funds, decide what you will accomplish if the funds are awarded to your full-service school. Here are some questions to help you pinpoint those goals:

- Does the *grant cycle* allow sufficient time for you to adequately design your program and write the *grant proposal?*

- Have you clearly identified a significant problem that cannot be resolved with existing programs or funds? Have you clearly identified a response to the problem that gets at its root causes, not just its symptoms?

- How important is the problem you seek to correct or the program you seek to fund? Do all of the community agencies involved in the project agree to a collaborative grant proposal? Is there a written interagency agreement that specifies the roles, responsibilities, and support of the collaborating agencies, as well as the program's purpose, staffing, and timetable, along with control of its funds?

- Does your proposal take a creative approach to solving the problem? Can you document previous, similar, successful efforts?

- Will a significant number of people benefit from your proposed project? Are populations in other communities likely to benefit from replicating your proposed project? In other words, will your proposed project produce a significant impact or have a multiplier effect?

- Is your proposal cost-effective? Can you show that the anticipated benefits outweigh the costs? Is there a significant bang for the buck?

Realize that grant funding is temporary or short-term in nature and intended for highly targeted missions. Be careful not to get hooked on the soft money: do not start a program that you may have to abandon in a year or two when those grant funds are no longer available. A critical part of any grant-writing effort is planning for your program's institutionalization: continuation of program services after the initial grant funding is gone.

Identify a Proposal-Writing Team

Select a proposal-writing team from the members of your stakeholder group who have the knowledge, experience, and skills to match your program objectives. One member might be an expert in the social service or education field

Grant
transfer or award of funds, power, or goods by deed or in writing

Grant cycle
time frame that includes receipt of the request for proposal, actual writing of the proposal, review of the proposal by the funding source, and notification of award or denial

Grant proposal
a written plan of action that forms the basis for a contract between the grantee and the funding source

▼ **Pointers**

Identify writing team members:

- Recruit university or community college faculty, staff, and students for their research skills (finding funding, establishing measurable objectives, writing proposals); for no-cost staffing by way of student internships, field studies, and volunteers; and for up-to-date technological, political, and legal information.

- Recruit members of community fundraising organizations and public radio and TV stations for their expertise in finding philanthropists and business donors, and for their public relations skills.

Designing a Grant Through Networking

When the project manager for the county's full-service schools wants to develop a new grant proposal, her first call is to a member of the stakeholder group, the director of the Educational Research and Development Center at the university. Why? Because the university has a wealth of resources to facilitate proposal writing, and because it is charged with providing community service—in other words, becoming a stakeholder in the full-service school program.

Universities and community colleges are also likely to have up-to-date technological, political, and legal data that can make for a better proposal.

The second call the project manager makes is to the manager of the university's public radio station for his knowledge of community affairs, his staff's expertise in public relations, and his station's ability to announce new programs or community meetings that address full-service school issues. Next, she calls on a business reporter for the *Press Gazette* for her familiarity with local business benefactors and other community resources. The director of the local branch of the retired senior volunteer program gets the next call for her ability to mobilize and train volunteers who help initially with proposal development and writing, and ultimately with implementing certain aspects of a particular program.

Don't overlook valuable resources, such as the ones this project manager draws on—they may be invaluable stakeholders in your full-service school.

---

in which your proposed program has an impact. Another may be experienced in designing realistic budgets for such programs. Ideally, at least one member of the team has proposal-writing experience; if not, you may need to seek an experienced person in the community to volunteer as a guide in the writing task.

Arrange for the team to review professional journals and periodicals for samples of successful programs funded by the federal government, state agencies, philanthropic foundations, and individuals. Ask community agency representatives who have written successful grant proposals to meet with your team to discuss the do's and don'ts of proposal writing.

Support the writing team's efforts in other ways: help set realistic deadlines for completing each section of the proposal; coordinate meeting times and places; arrange for such creature comforts as coffee or snacks; and provide paper, pens, flipcharts, markers, and other supplies.

Establish a write-edit-revise procedure that ensures review of each written section from two perspectives, content and coherence. You could, for instance, have a health care professional examine a program plan for immunizing all community preschoolers, or a budget analyst evaluate a financial plan for content. Have a technical writer or an English teacher read each section for coherence. The resulting edits or suggestions are then reviewed by your writing team and appropriate revisions made.

Develop a List of Potential Funding Sources

Remember that your program's objectives must fit those of the funding source. *Do not* waste time redesigning your program to fit a funding source's specifications. *Do* get a clear picture of what your community needs and then select funding sources that are responsive to those needs. The needs assessments described in Chapter Three help you not only establish the needs of your community but also clearly define your objectives and proposed solutions. See Chapter Four for types of funding sources and Resource G for lists of sources, to help narrow the field of potential funding sources:

- Government agencies: federal, state, and local

- Foundations

- Institutions such as universities, school districts, hospitals, and banks

- Unions and professional organizations

- Corporations that are located in your community

- Private parties interested in your efforts

Review professional journals and periodicals for descriptions of successful programs and their funding sources. Ask for proposal *guidelines* and copies of winning proposals from the sources you identify, or peruse the Educational Resources Information Center (ERIC) files through your local or university library. Search the Internet to find the most current information on funding, funding guidelines, and examples of successful programs across the country.

Write the Proposal to Source Specifications

The key to writing a proposal is preparation. Read and reread the funding source's request for proposal (*RFP*) or guidelines; establish a realistic time line for completion of writing tasks; and develop a plan for a needed, meaningful program.

Realize that most funding sources have their own unique funding missions and terms for funding. You must tailor your program plan and your written proposal to match those missions and terms. Here are some examples of common terminology in the grant-funding arena.

How Grant Funders Receive and Process Proposals

- *Solicited*: a funding source announces its intent to offer a grant for a purpose it has chosen and issues an RFP.

- *Unsolicited*: you initiate a request by proposing that a particular funding source support a program you have chosen.

- *Large and solicited*: a funding source issues a call for proposals or an RFP aimed at accomplishing a specific and large-scale or long-term objective.

Pointers

How to locate grants
  Documents:
- The Federal Register
- The Foundation Directory
- Grant alert periodicals
  Electronic sources:
- Electronic bulletin boards
- Educational Resources Information Center (ERIC)
  Other:
- Professional organization mailings
- State and federal departments of education
- Search the Internet

Guidelines
instructions or forms that define a funding source's requirements for grant proposals, including format, content, and length

RFP
request for proposal; contains the funding source's guidelines for format, content, length, and purpose of a solicited grant proposal

- *Small, usually solicited*: a funding source offers seed money for programs aimed at solving immediate problems or developing new methods.

- *Structured*: very specific guidelines are issued by the funding source, targeting programs that address a specific problem.

- *Unstructured*: very broad guidelines are issued by the funding source, and funding depends on your ability to propose a unique solution to problems.

How Grant Funds Are Given Out

- *Renewable*: once awarded, grant funding may be extended beyond the initial time frame, based on performance for subsequent time periods.

- *Nonrenewable*: funds are not extended beyond the initial time frame.

- *Cost-reimbursable*: you are allowed to expend forthcoming funds as identified in your proposal. Any changes in this budget must be approved in writing by the funding source. After a purchase is completed, you submit a cost-reporting form to the source, and your agency is reimbursed. You are limited to the approved budget amount.

- *Fixed price*: you are awarded the funds and can vary your expenditures without prior approval, so long as the funds are directed to completion of the project.

Understand that your first grant proposal is always the hardest. Familiarize yourself with the typical components of a funding proposal (the topics that follow in this section) and follow the guidelines offered in this chapter. In completing your first proposal, you gain experience that makes the next proposal much easier to prepare.

Parts of the Grant Proposal

Most RFPs and funding source guidelines describe a proposal format that must be strictly adhered to. They give detailed directions about what must be included in each section; be certain that you provide every piece of information requested. The typical proposal requires these sections:

- Cover letter

- Abstract

- Narrative, including mission statement, statement of the problem, goals and objectives, implementation plan, time line, personnel qualifications, resources, impact, evaluation, budget, and budget notes

- Required or supplemental appendixes

Cover Letter

Experienced grant writers recommend leaving the cover letter for last in the proposal writing process. This letter gives the funding source's reviewers their first—and perhaps lasting—impression of your proposal. It is important, therefore, that it be clearly written, jargon-free, and purposeful. Most funding sources require certain items in a cover letter (which should be printed on letterhead, if possible):

- Name and address of person submitting proposal
- Date submitted
- Name and address of individual and organization to which proposal is being submitted
- Subject of proposal and title of proposed program
- Short description of the target population
- Name of endorsing institution or organization submitting the proposal
- Summary of the problems, needs, objectives, and proposed solutions your program presents
- Name of person to contact for answers to questions about the proposal, and a statement of your willingness to provide further information
- Signature and title of individual submitting proposal

Abstract

The abstract appears at the beginning of the document and summarizes your proposal's significant points in a concise format of one page or less. Perhaps the most significant page of the entire document, the abstract expands the cover letter's first impression for the proposal's reviewers. The cover letter provides basic information; the abstract provides your program's most important details. Adhere strictly to the funding source's prescribed format for the abstract. Most require brief statements of need, goals and objectives, measurement methods, implementation plans, and definitions of key terms. Clarity and brevity are paramount.

Narrative

Each part of the proposal narrative can be likened to a puzzle piece: once fit together, the pieces illustrate the whole of your full-service school program. The needs statement explains why you are building your full-service school. The goals and objectives state what you seek to accomplish. The implementation plan is your step-by-step approach to how you will accomplish your goals. The time line keeps you on task. The qualifications of personnel and description of resources convince the reviewer that you have the right personnel and the right resources to do the job. The evaluation describes how you will know whether you have succeeded. The budget section is the price tag. As you can see, all of the pieces of the puzzle have to fit together to offer a complete picture of what you want funded and why.

The narrative is the lengthiest part of the proposal. It generally contains the following parts.

Vision and/or Mission Statement. Some grant proposals require both a vision statement and a mission statement (Figure 5.1). The former describes how your community's families will benefit, given adequate funding for the proposed program and ideal circumstances in which to operate. The latter describes how the proposed program supports the community's instructional, social, health, and financial needs. Remember to clearly match your program to the funding source's priorities.

Statement of the Problem or Need. Needs are gaps between what is and what should be. This is a chance to demonstrate which community needs your stakeholders have identified, how they were identified, and what will be done to fulfill them. To give credibility to your statement of the problem (also called

Figure 5.1. Sample Vision and Mission Statements

Vision Statement

The Families First Full-Service Schools Program is the philosophical basis for services to children and families in our county. This philosophy is based on the premise that the family is the constant in the child's life, while service systems fluctuate. In order to promote child well-being, it is the role of all individuals in the community, including the school system, in true collaboration with other public and nonprofit organizations, to provide assistance to families to enable them to be successful parents. It is not Families First's role to replace families and carry out the responsibilities of parents. It is our role to plan *with* families, not *for* them.

We believe that the status of children and families today in our county, as described in the March 1997 Kids Count Report, reflects a crisis situation both here and nationally. A greater crisis will develop in the future unless we meet and address the current situation. We seek to develop partnerships at the state and local levels with the business community; the religious community; the private, nonprofit, and voluntary sectors; civic and local governmental entities; and community schools to address the needs of children and families in our county.

Mission Statement

It is the mission of the Full-Service School Local Oversight Council to develop a program that adheres to these principles. Services should be:

- Family-focused
- Available and accessible
- More cost-effective and efficient
- Planned with, not for the community
- Focused on improving our community's service delivery

need statement or needs assessment), describe the process or techniques used for identifying the need (from Chapter Three), whether surveys, interviews, statistical data, or statements from experts. The needs statement documents why your program should be funded.

Including a review of pertinent literature demonstrates that you have developed your proposed program not only by assessing your own community's problems and needs but also by analyzing the efforts of others. This establishes the timeliness of the needs your program addresses and shows how your program's results can be generalized to other populations. If you have evidence of media coverage of the program, organization, or issue related to the program design, mention the coverage here (and provide copies of written materials in an appendix).

Define key terms as they appear in the narrative. For instance, if you mention *full-service school* or *integrated services,* define them with examples from your proposed program.

A statement of need should establish your program's significance, relevance, timeliness, generalizability to other populations, and contribution to the community.

Program Goals, Objectives, and Tasks. Flowing directly from the statement of need are the program goals and objectives, along with descriptions of the *tasks* that are entailed and indication of a method for measuring progress toward the goal. For example, if your statement of need includes statistics on the use of illicit drugs and alcohol among students in middle schools, then write a program goal to directly address that need.

Tasks
steps, activities, or procedures to accomplish objectives

A *goal* is an overall statement of your program's purpose. The goal should directly relate to the purpose and priorities of the granting agency and flow directly from the needs statement of your proposal. It is a statement of overall intent and outcome. A strong and clear goal statement indicates what you intend to accomplish—the final outcome. A goal should:

Goal
general statement of overall intent with a long-term perspective, sometimes referred to as an outcome measure

- Flow from needs
- Relate to the grant program's purpose
- Use the same vocabulary as the granting agency does
- Include outcomes expected when goals are met
- Define the target population

Just providing a service is not enough. *Objectives* help you specify, or quantify, the result of what you are trying to accomplish. Objectives must be achievable, and they must also lead to a changed condition. See Resource H for example goals, bases for measurable objectives, and suggested measurements for full-service school initiatives.

Objectives
statements that identify specific, concrete, and measurable ways in which goals will be fulfilled

Figure 5.2. Need, Goal, Objective Example

Need	Increased use of drugs and alcohol (as indicated by arrest records, agency logs of referral, student attitude survey, pretest of student knowledge of drugs and drug use). Always use statistical amounts in a needs statement.
Goal	Drug, alcohol, and tobacco use reduction among targeted middle school students
Objectives	Decrease the rates of drug, alcohol, and tobacco usage among 120 sixth graders during the 1998–99 school year, measured by:

1. A decrease in arrest records for targeted students for at least six months following the program activity time line to the target benchmark rate set by the state Department of Juvenile Justice

2. A reduction of at least 25 percent in logs of referrals at agencies currently serving students referred for drug, alcohol, and/or tobacco use

3. An increase in test scores for at least 80 percent of students participating in the program reflecting student knowledge related to drug and alcohol use; scores will be tabulated using a normed pretest and posttest survey method

Each goal may have several objectives. (Figure 5.2 shows how quantifiable objectives are derived from the qualitative goal being realized.) Each objective must be time-bound; note, too, that statements of objective do not include methods. Each objective should:

- Flow logically from needs
- State what will be done
- State by whom it will be done
- State to whom it will be done
- State when it will be done
- State the results of its accomplishment
- Lead to quantitative and/or qualitative measures

Objectives can be used to show four different categories of change: in process, product, behavior, and performance. Describe your objectives in terms of the appropriate category.

See Resource H for examples of a student evaluation checklist for use by the teacher to assess program objectives before and after program activities. Be sure that all your proposal's stated objectives are attainable and not trivial. Specify completion dates; define expected results in concrete terms; and confirm that the results can be measured.

Ultimately, your list of objectives serves as the design for evaluating your program by documenting whether or not each objective is achieved.

Tasks and Time Line. To carry out an objective, you define one or more *tasks*, specifying activities that must be accomplished to complete the objective. Together, these tasks define all the steps that occur in satisfying the objective. A task should:

- Show what is to be accomplished
- Provide a time frame
- Designate the responsibility for accomplishment
- Designate the resources that must be used
- Designate the steps necessary to accomplish the task (unless the task is so simple and straightforward that individual steps are unnecessary)

Figure 5.3 offers an objective and then illustrates one way in which task statements can be presented in this section of your grant proposal: a project task chart.

Implementation Plan. The implementation plan is a detailed, systematic explanation of how your goals and objectives will be put into practice. It begins with a statement detailing your overall approach:

- A brief description of the program's target population (who the program will serve)
- The selection criteria for the target population
- An explanation of your program's intent (for example, training, service integration, service co-location)
- A plan or strategy for ensuring that your program will continue after the initial funding period expires

Following the statement of approach, list the series of tasks necessary to implement your plan. You make the plan easy for the proposal's reviewers to interpret if you support your key points with visuals such as charts and tables. In any case, summarize how each task or step relates to the goal and objective (as in Figure 5.3). Include a time line for implementation of tasks.

Qualifications of Key Personnel. Funding sources, particularly those at the federal level, consider personnel qualifications paramount to a program's success. One way to effectively document the qualifications of your program manager and other key personnel is to prepare a short paragraph about each position, including the staff member's name (if you have already selected the person to fill the position), title, responsibilities, and qualifications. Present vitae or résumés of key personnel in an appendix. Clarify how your

For me, the most important aspect of full-service schools is their ability to serve the multiple needs of students and their families. The hardest part is bringing everyone together to work toward the same goal.

—Lori Lanier, community facilitator, Family Support and Preservation Program

Pointers

Here are some tips for documenting personnel resources for implementation of your plan:

- If a proposal requires submitting vitae, have them written in the same format, restrict length of each one to two pages, and use a desktop publishing program to polish their look.
- Specify the full-time equivalent (FTE) status for each staff person, indicate the duties to be performed and discuss each person's job-specific qualifications.

(continued)

program's staff interacts by including an organizational chart in either the narrative or an appendix; diagram who conducts the program, who is responsible for what, and who reports to whom. A project staff task chart (Figure 5.4) supports distribution of tasks among key personnel.

Pointers

(continued)

•For larger RFPs, an affirmative action and equal opportunity statement is often required; it usually belongs in the personnel component of the proposal.

•Some RFPs ask for a chart of organizational capability that illustrates local resources available to your program: community organizations, libraries, research facilities, universities, media, office space, computer facilities, etc. Focus on resources that directly relate to your program and on a few specific examples of why your program suits the purposes of the funding source.

Figure 5.3. Project Task Chart

Objective: Decrease the rates of drug, alcohol, and tobacco usage among 120 sixth-grade students during the 1999–2000 school year, as measured by an increase in test scores for at least 80 percent of students participating in program activities reflecting student and parent knowledge related to drug and alcohol use. Scores will be tabulated using a normal pretest and posttest survey method.

Task	Steps	Staff	Success Criteria	Time Line
1. Collect baseline data	1.1 Administer pretest to targeted students	CC, BH, ED	Report on summative info.	9/1/99–10/1/99
2. Research student curriculum	2.1 Literature review	ALL	6–8 page report	9/1/99–10/1/99
	2.2 Interview students	LC	Summary report	9/1/99–10/1/99
	2.3 Curriculum search	CC, BH	3–5 samples	9/1/99–10/1/99
3. Design curriculum for students and parents	3.1 Develop and/or modify lessons	ALL	6 lessons, 2 hours each–student plan	10/1/99–11/1/99
	3.2 Prepare handouts		2-hour presentation for parents	
4. Implement curriculum	4.1 Make necessary schedule changes	ALL	All students scheduled for participation	11/1/99–12/1/99
	4.2 Lesson plans for students	ALL	All students receive training	1/1/00–3/1/00
	4.3 Evening education session for parents	CC, EH	Parent attendance log	2/1/00
5. Posttest	5.1 Posttest all participants	ALL	Comparison scores for all students and parents	4/1/00

Figure 5.4. Project Staff Task Chart

Activity #3 Task #	Staff Members, FTE, and Time in Days				Total Days for Task
	CC .50 FTE	BH .30 FTE	EH .50 FTE	LC .25 FTE	
1.1	3	2	2		6
2.1	5	5	5	5	25
2.2				15	15
2.3	5	5			10
3.1	10	10	10	10	40
3.2	2	2	2	2	8
4.1	1	1	1	1	4
4.2	6	6	6	6	24
4.3	9		9		18
5.1	2	2	2	2	8
Total days/staff	42	33	37	41	158

Resources. The resources section of a proposal includes a list of facilities, equipment, supplies, and *in-kind* donations that are readily available to your proposed program. The goal of this section is to convince the funding source that you have adequate resources and facilities to accomplish its objectives. If your program will use facilities or equipment belonging to a community agency other than your own, be sure to include a letter of commitment or authorization from that agency in an appendix.

Impact. Sometimes a subsection called "Impact" is added to the resources section of a proposal. It discusses your program's potential impact on the world, the nation, a state, a school district, a special population, and so on. The question is, if the project is funded and carried out successfully, what will be the short-term and long-term residual impacts of the program?

Proposals that use product objectives (such as dissemination of materials as a program task; see Figure 5.3) should include details about impact for the specific groups of people who will receive products. Remember the new opportunities that technology presents for dissemination of program materials and outcomes. For example, details of the program can be placed on a World Wide Web (or other) server for global distribution. Details of how this is to be done, with analysis of the specific tasks for the person responsible, demonstrate that the personnel requesting funds have knowledge of the technology and how to use it.

Evaluation. It is not enough to feel good about a full-service school program. Competition for funding dictates that you have a well-defined, focused, and powerful plan for evaluating your program outcomes. The evaluation plan

In-kind

products or services offered within or in association with an organization and having cash value; used to demonstrate stability and self-sufficiency through community support

Pointers

Review these questions to help shape proposed evaluation of the program's eventual impact:

• Will the population with the greatest need be served?

• What is the program's long-term goal?

• How will the services offered make a difference?

• How is the program likely to be accepted in the community?

• How well will the program be integrated with existing community resources?

• Is funding being redirected toward prevention and early intervention?

• What barriers to and opportunities for complete program implementation can be identified?

SOME EXAMPLES OF HOW TO CALCULATE IN-KIND RESOURCES

Building or Space

Condition One: Donor Retains Title to the Space

Calculate the fair rental value. This number can be substantiated in the provider's records by having qualified individuals write confirmation of fair rental value. Helpful people to consult are real estate agents or property managers to give an estimate of that value. The calculation should include the established fair monthly rental of the space times the number of months donated during a contract year.

Condition Two: Donor Passes Title to the Provider

The value of a building space passed to a provider is calculated by this formula:

1. Fair market value (FMV) at acquisition (excluding the land): $ _____

2. Estimated useful life at the date of acquisition: _____ years

3. Annual depreciation (item 1/item 2): $ _____

4. Total square footage: _____ sq. ft.

5. Number of square feet to be used on contract: _____ sq. ft.

6. Proportion of time during contract period the project will occupy the building/space: _____ percent

7. Value of building to project (divide item 5 by item 4; multiply the result by item 3, and then by item 6): $ _____

Use Allowance

If a depreciation schedule is not used (that is, if the item is not normally depreciated in the provider's accounting records), a use allowance can be calculated by estimating the value of the space and adding the normal cost of upkeep, such as repairs and maintenance, insurance, etc.

Equipment

Condition One: Donor Retains Title to Equipment

Consult local companies that rent equipment for an estimate of the fair rental value.

Condition Two: Donor Passes Title to Provider

Either calculate the fair market value of the donation or calculate the annual value to the project. (Most federal guidelines suggest claiming no more than 6.67 percent of the fair market value.)

Goods and Supplies

Calculate the fair market value at the time of the donation.

(continued)

SOME EXAMPLES OF HOW TO CALCULATE IN-KIND RESOURCES *(continued)*

> **Personnel Services**
>
> Calculate the value of the staff that another agency contributes as in-kind service by dividing the annual salary by 2,080 (the number of hours in a fifty-two-week year) to obtain the hourly rate; then multiply the hourly rate times the number of hours to be provided. The result is the value of the in-kind service.
>
> Calculate the value of volunteer hours in one of two ways. For nonprofessional volunteers, multiply the number of volunteer hours by the minimum wage. For professional volunteers, calculate as for in-kind services.

describes the process by which you gather, analyze, and interpret data to assess the program's overall effectiveness. The information gleaned from an evaluation serves to enhance the program's credibility by assessing its effectiveness, as well as providing insight for future improvement or expansion.

A well-written evaluation plan contains both formative and summative evaluations. A *formative evaluation* measures movement toward achieving objectives while the project is in progress. Because it evaluates both progress toward completion and effectiveness of the process, this evaluation sets the stage for any changes that need to take place no later than midway through the program and has checkpoints along the way to gauge progress. If your proposal has, say, an objective of reducing the number of interagency referrals for alcohol, drug, or tobacco use, then the formative evaluation includes collection of data about halfway through the grant period so as to assess progress toward this objective.

Summative evaluation builds on what is learned in the formative evaluation; its intent is to produce a final analysis of the program's progress. It makes use of data gathered both during the program and upon completion. It can also include information on the effectiveness of the process.

As more information about full-service school programs is published, consensus is building about what the evaluation plan for these organizationally complex programs should look like. The items in the checklist of Resource I, "Characteristics of an Effective Evaluation Plan," if incorporated into your evaluation plan, can successfully adapt conventional wisdom to meeting your full-service school's objectives.

Budget and Budget Notes. A proposal's budget must be realistic, reasonable, well researched, and within the guidelines of the RFP. It must also be tied directly to the needs, objectives, and activities described in the narrative. Misunderstandings on budget items are often the fatal flaw in getting funds. Present your budget by category (salaries, expenses, equipment, and so on). Explain budget items (in short paragraph form) to clarify or justify dollar

Formative evaluation
measurement of progress in achieving objectives while the project is ongoing; thus assessment of both progress toward completion and effectiveness of the process

Summative evaluation
evaluation built on information from the ongoing formative evaluation, to produce final analysis of program progress

amounts, to show how your program's design promotes fiscal continuity, and to emphasize cost-effective features. If your proposal contains a substantial amount of in-kind contributions and resources, refer to the dollar amounts in the budget. It is common practice to add a column to a budget spreadsheet that reflects local-commitment dollars.

Use a budget note—a short paragraph of explanation—for every line in the budget. Though short, budget notes should be as detailed as possible: "Dr. H.'s full twelve-month salary is $31,780, or 1.0 FTE; .50 FTE of his current salary is $15,890, including salary, workmen's compensation, social security tax, and retirement benefits." Or: "Staff will need to travel to conduct interviews at local community centers. Centers are located within 35 miles of the full-service school site. Travel will be reimbursed at the current state rate of $0.29 per mile times an estimated 200 miles of travel over the period of grant activities."

Grant reviewers often read the proposal abstract first and then turn to the budget page before reading the entire proposal. Make sure your budget requests are tied directly to your program needs, implementation plan, and evaluation plan as defined in the abstract.

Appendixes. An appendix contains information that is essential to or supportive of the funding source but is not required to be part of the narrative. Because funders often place limits on the number of pages that can be included in a narrative, you can move tables and charts to an appendix if necessary. Just be sure each visual is referred to in the narrative. Here is a list of items that might appear in an appendix to a grant proposal:

- Summary tables of needs assessments, statistics, and so on.
- Figures, charts, visuals
- IRS tax-exempt determination letter of the nonprofit agency that serves as the project's fiscal agent
- Fiscal agent's most recent audited financial statement
- Fiscal agent's total annual budget
- Vitae or résumés of key personnel or short narratives of staff members' qualifications
- Letters of endorsement or commitment, with specific details of program support
- Samples of measurement instruments used in the evaluation plan
- Evidence of media coverage of the program or organization, or of issues directly related to the program's design
- Capability statement, describing the resources and credibility of the organization submitting the proposal, including accreditation or achievement of other standards, endorsements, commendations from officials or community groups, and media reports

• Organizational history: when your organization was founded; the source of its funds; guiding philosophy, mission, or goals; and significant programs or other funded grant achievements

Writing the Grant Proposal

To write successful grant proposals, follow these tips.

Read and reread the RFP or guidelines! Many proposals are eliminated from consideration because they simply do not meet the goals or formatting requirements of the funding source. Similarly, insist that someone other than the proposal's writers edit it for both typos and clarity. Although grants are awarded on the basis of merit, those merits may be obscured by errors in grammar, punctuation, or spelling—or by language that is perfectly clear to you but wholly unclear to someone not on intimate terms with your proposed program. Therefore beware of jargon, acronyms, or labels peculiar to your community, agencies, or program. Assume that you should explain or define each term when it first appears in the proposal.

Establish a writing timetable. This ensures that you meet the deadline for proposal submission. Allocate an adequate number of people and sufficient resources to the writing process. Assign specific tasks to specific people with specific deadlines—and put the assignments in writing. Be sure to allow ample time for editing.

Keep the language *clear, direct, and succinct.* If more than one writer authors sections of the proposal, edit the final manuscript to ensure consistency of style and a natural flow.

As for the *mechanics of production,* use word processing software to compose, edit, and revise. Keep each section in a separate computer file for easy editing. Use an easily readable typeface and size, preferably a serif font in 10 or 12 points for body text. Resist the temptation to reduce the type size in order to squeeze more information onto the page. (Doing so may make reading your document difficult, and the proposal's reader could react accordingly.) Use boldface or italic type to highlight key words or concepts, or to set off headings and subheadings. But be selective about what you highlight; overusing boldface and italics affects impact adversely.

Organize headings and subheadings so that sections are easy to find and refer to. Most RFPs or guidelines are subdivided in ways similar or identical to the requirements for the proposal. Use bullets, numbers, or letters to organize and highlight related items or lists. Provide a table of contents and an index. The former helps the reader know at a glance whether you've responded appropriately, and the latter helps the reader find, evaluate, and rate the key elements of the proposal.

Get help. Most RFPs contain a section on how reviewers "grade" proposals. Ask someone outside your project to evaluate your proposal using the funding source's guidelines; having your proposal graded helps you fine-tune its organization and emphasis. Ask members of your stakeholder crew to apply to become proposal reviewers—to give you valuable perspective—or locate someone in your community who has been a reviewer and ask the person to evaluate your proposal. Also, locate previous recipients of awards from the funding source, and ask them to share proposal-writing tips.

Establish a contact at the funding source by phone, by letter, or in person. This is someone who will answer questions during the writing and after submitting the proposal. Ask for a list of others who requested the RFP so you will know who you're competing with. If there are two hundred applicants for two pilot-project awards, then you know not to be too disappointed if you don't get the award. You also know that your time might be better spent on writing a proposal for a grant that has fifty applicants for ten awards.

Finally, *print the entire package* with a laser or inkjet printer. Dot matrix printers generally do not provide high-quality, easily readable output.

The better your evaluation plan is designed, the more likely you are to "successfully document success." This high level of preparation is your best insurance of getting a fair hearing for your proposal. Making such preparation habitual is also the key to obtaining funds for other projects or from other sources as your full-service school program changes and expands.

The Completed Proposal

Even after the proposal is written, read the entire RFP *again* to make sure that you have included all required documentation. Check for forms and signatures, proper sequence of information, and spelling and grammatical errors. Have someone else review the completed proposal—before making the required number of copies. Then verify that all final copies are complete and correctly collated.

Mail the proposal early enough to be received at the funding source by the deadline date. When you mail the proposal, ask for a return receipt; by doing so, you have a record of the date on which the funding source received it. Late proposals are automatically rejected—with no exceptions.

The review process typically takes six to eight weeks. Many funding sources notify applicants periodically of the proposal's status during the review process.

Handle the Results: Funded or Not Funded

If one of every ten proposals that you write are eventually funded, your writing team is effective. If your program is not funded, don't throw the proposal away. Grant proposal writing is an evolutionary process. Request feedback from the funding source reviewers; this helps you revise and refine future proposals. The same proposal, with only minor revisions, may be acceptable to more than one funding source; even if this is not the case, much of the substance for other proposals has already been crafted in preparing the unsuccessful one. Write a brief letter to the funding source thanking them for considering your proposal; doing so paves the way for increased communication when you next submit a proposal to them.

Most of all, learn from the experience. Here are twelve common reasons why funding is not granted:

1. The deadline for submitting the proposal was not met.

2. The guidelines for content, format, and length were not followed exactly.

3. The proposal was not original enough; the ideas presented were "more of the same."

4. The proposed program was not among the funding source's priorities for the funding year.

5. The proposal was not written clearly; the reviewers were confused about program design.

6. The proposal was not complete as specified in the RFP or guidelines.

7. The writer did not seem to know the territory; there was evidence of lack of expertise.

8. The proposal seemed beyond the capability of the writers. The writers lacked training, experience, or resources.

9. The evaluation design or the measurement techniques were either not clear or not rigorous enough to document the program's intended objectives.

10. The budget was unrealistic. Too much money or too little money was requested to meet the program's objectives.

11. The cost of the program was greater than its potential benefit.

12. The writer took a highly partisan position and was vulnerable to the prejudices of the reviewers.

If your program is funded, do not spend any money until you receive official, written confirmation with an authorized signature. Notification that your program has been funded often comes with a request for additional information, adjustment in specific budget items, or other requirements and restrictions. Remember that approved funding basically turns your proposal into a contract with the funding source. Grant funds may be monitored or audited to ensure progress is being made and funds are expended according to the budget approved by the funding agency.

Along with funding notification, you are likely to receive information about implementation dates the funding source considers critical, such as when interim and final reports are due, and when spending or billing must be terminated.

Once your program is implemented, you must seek approval from the funding source before making any significant changes in your plan, goals, or budget. If you want to make changes in personnel, the target populations, or program outcomes, be sure to ask the funding source what the proper procedures are for obtaining their official approval before changes are implemented.

Keep the communication flowing. Successfully funded programs often receive and spend funds independently of any further communication with the funding source. Even if the funding source does not require reports from you, send them. More problems are created from a lack of communication than from a surplus. Though there is no guarantee that your program will receive additional funds because you share information and products with the funding source, making the source aware of your program's results and your community's support may mean stronger consideration for future funding requests.

After you have successfully written funding proposals that meet your buyer's specifications, you have completed construction of your full-service school house. Now it needs furnishings. Chapter Six offers to equip your full-service school with confidentiality and interagency agreements, family care coordination plans, and topics for cross-training, all of which also come in handy as you "remodel" your growing and changing program.

Chapter 6

Furnish the House

Sharing Information, Publicity, and Training

As you know, reaching the point of raising the roof for your full-service school means drawing a blueprint for collaboration, pouring a foundation of knowledge about your community's assets and needs, financing your program's construction, developing a framework, and building to stakeholder specifications.

Although construction of your full-service school now seems complete, your program might not pass inspection year after year unless you top off your school house with these communication tools:

- Confidentiality and information-sharing guidelines

- Interagency agreements

- Family care coordination plans

- Public relations

- Cross-training

In this chapter, we describe how you can develop these tools, offer examples that show how you can adapt them to meet your program's needs, and provide tips for using the tools creatively. With these additions to your weighty toolbox, you signal the success of your collaborative building and ongoing remodeling efforts: to community agencies, the families who live and work in your community, the students who fill your classrooms, the organizations that offer funding, and all of your school's stakeholders.

Students and families at our full-service school center have a great opportunity to be successful. We coordinate twelve onsite services, including career counseling and assessment, job referrals and placement, employability skills training, health care, child care, and more.

—Shirley Parker, teen parenting program coordinator

Confidentiality and Information-Sharing Guidelines

Confidentiality guidelines
written or verbal practices designed to keep spoken and written information about individuals private and available only to certain designated individuals or agencies

A commonly cited barrier to interagency collaboration is the existence of *confidentiality guidelines* that restrict, rather than promote, information sharing among agencies working with the same families. Confidentiality need not be a barrier to interagency collaboration if agencies agree on how much and when information can legitimately be shared. Ask yourself and your collaborators, Why protect information? Why share information?

Based on state and federal law, pertinent literature, and interviews with public officials and community agency personnel, Soler and Peters[1] suggest seven major reasons information should be kept confidential:

1. To protect embarrassing personal information from disclosure. This includes history of emotional instability, marital conflict, medical problems, physical or sexual abuse, alcohol and drug use, limited education, erratic employment, and so on.

2. To prevent possible discrimination. This can result from improper release of potentially harmful information about children and families: HIV status, mental health history, drug use, charges of child abuse, and so on.

3. To protect personal security. Domestic violence is an obvious example, should law enforcement personnel disclose the new whereabouts of a woman who leaves home.

4. To protect family security. As an example, immigrant families may avoid public health clinics and social services for fear of action by the Immigration and Naturalization Service.

5. To protect job security. A history of mental health treatment—regardless of job performance—could, if known, affect promotion or even continuation of employment, as well as prospects for finding another job.

6. To avoid prejudice or differential treatment. Teachers might lower expectations if they know that a child's family is eligible for food stamps (or free school lunch); the effect on performance could indeed become self-fulfilling.

7. To encourage individuals to use services designed to help them. Adolescents might not avail themselves of mental health services or medical consultation on HIV or birth control if they fear that teachers, peers, or parents will find out.

Although it is critically important to protect confidentiality, appropriate information sharing does foster more effective service delivery and less duplication of effort, which benefit both families and service providers. Soler and Peters also offer seven reasons for sharing information:

Pointers

In general, there are four checkpoints to consider when you develop confidentiality guidelines. Look for places or situations in your program where:

1. Information is gathered
2. Participation is altered (that is, when a service or program is added or deleted)
3. Information is shared
4. Treatment is provided

1. To conduct comprehensive assessments. Although most agencies are geared to offering limited services, children and families at risk usually have multiple needs. This argues for making use of information from a number of agencies.

2. To provide all necessary services. Once again, it is in the interest of both agency and client to provide all services of value to children and families.

3. To coordinate service plans and avoid duplication. Even with their varying missions, agencies find services overlapping or making conflicting demands on clients. Coordination thus frees up resources that are otherwise wasted.

4. To facilitate monitoring of services. With information sharing, agencies are better able to ensure that needed services are provided and that mandated services are properly reimbursed.

5. To make services more family focused. This fundamental goal of the full-service school is promoted through sharing information, which enlarges the perspective of a given service provider, as when a young person's delinquent behavior is seen in the context of a parent's chronic unemployment or emotional instability or the family's inadequate housing. When the larger picture is seen, an agency can take steps to make other, appropriate services available.

6. To serve the needs of the broader community. Statistical analysis may clarify effectiveness of programs, unmet and projected needs in the community, and ways to allocate limited resources.

7. To promote public safety. For example, the community could be assured that an individual applying for a license to operate a child residential facility has never been the subject of a confirmed child-abuse report.

How do collaborating agencies establish a policy for information sharing that respects confidentiality? We recommend Soler and Peters's five-step approach (Figure 6.1).

Step One: Learn each agency's requirements for confidentiality and information sharing. The first step in collaborating on information sharing is for each agency to share its confidentiality requirements. Federal and state regulations and statutes, community agency and school board policies, and professional codes of ethics all contribute necessary components to an interagency policy. Make time for each of your stakeholder agencies to share its confidentiality requirements in this standard format:

- What information about families is legally deemed confidential? Consider how a provider of mental health services is governed by very specific laws, regulations, and guidelines about what information may be shared, with whom, and under what circumstances; these

Figure 6.1. Soler and Peters's Five-Step Approach

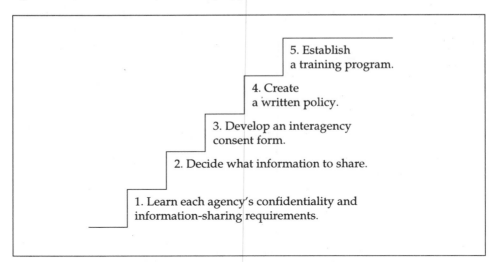

guidelines are significantly different from those for a provider of emergency food services.

• What information is not confidential? Each community agency probably collects some information that is considered public.

• Are there exceptions to confidentiality rules? Under what special circumstances can confidential information be shared: in certain emergencies? in developing a family care coordination plan? in other instances?

• What information sharing is authorized, and under what conditions?

• To what extent can information be shared based on the service recipient's consent? What are the requirements for consent? Who can consent for a minor?

• What provisions for information sharing are already in place, such as interagency agreements and memoranda of understanding?

Conduct collaborative discussions of confidentiality and information sharing in small-group or large-group settings or as a panel discussion. Distribute printed copies of each agency's guidelines to the stakeholders. Identify and document what these policies have in common; you may discover fewer barriers than you expect.

Step Two: Decide what information to share. Adopting a *need-to-know* policy emphasizes the importance of children's and families' confidentiality rights. In other words, collaborating agencies should agree to collect only the information that they need to know for adequate service provision. For example, a teacher may need to know that a child has had an upsetting night and deserves extra attention during class. The teacher does not need to know that

Need-to-know
a policy that answers three questions:

• What information is needed?

• Under what circumstances and to whom may this information be released?

• What is the intended use of the information?

the child's parent was removed from the home and placed in a drug and alcohol treatment center for observation. If the parent is going to remain at the center for an extended period of time, however, the teacher may need to know that the child's parent will not be at home.

Realize that a need-to-know policy also helps to limit the use of excessive or irrelevant information, which has significant cost and liability implications. Unnecessary information sharing also increases the danger of inappropriate or damaging disclosure of personal information; it defeats cost-effectiveness by increasing paperwork, administrative costs, and the likelihood that inaccurate or unreliable information is used for decision making.

Step Three: Develop an interagency consent form. Most community agencies already have specialized forms, perhaps titled Consent to Participate, or Authorization for Services to Minors, or Consent to Monitor, or Authorization to Receive and Exchange Information. If a common confidentiality and information-sharing form has not already been developed by the partners in your full-service school program, create one to replace existing single-agency forms (see Resource J for a sample interagency consent form).

Step Four: Create a written confidentiality and information-sharing policy. Answer these questions to create your written policy regarding use of the interagency consent form:

- Under what circumstances must a consent form be used?

- Given that multiple agencies are involved with your full-service school, who is responsible for obtaining written consent?

- How and when should the consent form be presented to an individual?

- What are the guidelines for handling situations where consent is difficult or impossible to obtain?

- What else can you do to protect confidentiality in your full-service school? One possible action is to draft a code of ethics and have each community agency's staff sign it.

- What restrictions apply to use of information? For example, under federal regulations, the recipient of information about an individual may use that information only for the purpose for which disclosure was made.

- How is re-release of information to be handled? If a family consents to release of information in order to receive one service, is that same consent valid should the family apply for another service at a later date?

- When and how is it acceptable to modify the consent form? Can it be modified before signing it? Can the standard form be modified to meet the unique needs of a particular child or family?

FOCUS ON STAKEHOLDERS:

Process for Developing Confidentiality Guidelines

It took one year to write an interagency agreement to establish juvenile justice confidentiality and information-sharing guidelines for our county. Why? Well, the process was complicated by a number of factors.

Although new state law reflected needed information-sharing changes, it took local action to actually effect those changes. The full-service schools director suggested developing a local agreement, at a meeting of the local juvenile justice council, which took it under advisement. Both the council and the school system realized that developing the agreement would require input from other affected parties, and law enforcement and court personnel were contacted.

But before they could take concrete action toward developing a confidentiality agreement, agency representatives discovered that they didn't speak the same language—at least when it came to juvenile justice terminology. School system representatives said "sent to court"; court representatives said "adjudicated." A glossary of terms was developed, and agencies were soon able to translate each other's communications accurately.

The next stumbling block: each agency had its own method of recording information about juveniles. Before they could decide how to share information, then, agency representatives had to document who had what information and how it was stored and accessed.

Then: who would lead the process of writing guidelines? In this case, the school system volunteered to take the lead, and other agency representatives breathed a sigh of relief as the process got under way.

Why are agency representatives happy with the results, despite the lengthy development time? For one thing, existing professional relationships helped establish and increase the level of trust that is so important to any change-related process: two police chiefs, the county sheriff, the state's attorney, the clerk of the court, the school superintendent, and the director of the juvenile justice department all signed the resulting document. For another thing, the agency representatives shared goals: they were all committed to preventing juveniles from becoming at risk and to intervening when necessary to promote the community's safety and security. They were also committed to sharing resources, eliminating duplication of effort, and involving their members in cross-training efforts.

The results? An agreement that ensures local compliance with state law regarding confidentiality and information sharing about juveniles, protocols on how to share information, guidelines on who shares information with whom, and training outlines for each agency's staff. And a fresh look at some old problems by virtue of bringing these stakeholders together. Before the agreement, juveniles who had been adjudicated (sent to court) were automatically expelled from school; after the agreement, expulsion is no longer automatic. Parent involvement is greater as well, and the county is justifiably proud of the improved juvenile justice system derived from this model of collaboration.

You may find it advantageous to create an informational flyer that reinforces your written policy while simplifying distribution. Service providers can then easily explain the meaning of confidentiality and release of information to service recipients (see Resource J for a sample informational flyer).

SCENARIOS FOR TRAINING AGENCY STAFF ON CONFIDENTIALITY AND INFORMATION SHARING

Suppose a multiagency *staffing* is conducted with family members present, but under pressure of time constraints agency representatives also discuss a second family's situation. What are the dangers in doing so? How can such occurrences be prevented?

You are eating lunch in a local restaurant with a coworker, who starts discussing a family receiving services at your full-service school. What should you do or say?

After she enrolls in a teen parenting program, a pregnant teen's name is given to a local coalition that deals with high-risk pregnancies. Should a consent form be completed? If so, who should sign it?

The parents of an eighth-grade student refuse to sign a consent form. You suspect the parents are hesitant because their children were once taken from them on the basis of a child-abuse-and-neglect complaint. Should you modify the consent form to exclude release of information to the agency that removed the children?

Staffing

meeting of family members, social and human service agency representatives, and education system representatives to arrive at a common understanding of the strengths and issues facing a family, and to develop a unified family care coordination plan outlining action to be taken

Step Five: Establish training for community agency staff. Distribute written materials and provide ongoing training on confidentiality to employees. One of the most effective ways to conduct such training is by using real-life (but pseudonymous) scenarios to provoke discussion about confidentiality and information sharing (see "Scenarios for Training Agency Staff on Confidentiality and Information Sharing").

Confidentiality is a difficult issue, so deal with it early in the process of building your full-service school. Accept the fact that both agencies and families have concerns about sharing information, and then work out practical ways to deal with those concerns.

Interagency Agreements

Developing and negotiating agreements among community agencies fosters collaboration. Such agreements facilitate goal accomplishment and ward off misunderstandings that could become significant barriers to implementing your full-service school program. Successful agreements document how agencies collaborate by addressing three basic topics:

1. Where are we? (What is the current state of collaboration?)

2. Where do we want to go? (What do we want to accomplish?)

3. How do we get there? (What are the specific details that need to be worked through?)

Developing such agreements does not happen by chance. Timing is critical. If a formal interagency agreement is proposed too early in a collaborative

Pointers

Confidentiality considerations:

- Find out what information sharing your state statutes allow.

- Lock files; record who accesses, files, or destroys confidential records.

- Negotiate electronic information exchange protocols (as with fax transmissions).

- Plan for extraordinary situations, such as when parents forget to sign a consent form.

- Adopt a need-to-know policy.

- Use realistic scenarios to provoke discussion, or convene a panel of experts to answer questions.

- Document guidelines in handbooks prepared for students, parents, and agencies.

(continued)

Pointers

(continued)

- Consult a risk manager for feedback on the adequacy of your guidelines.
- Ask community agencies' legal counsel to review your consent form and guidelines.
- Develop a Parent's Bill of Rights; post it in waiting areas and hallways.
- Ask parents to read the parental consent information flyer and then summarize it in their own words.
- Address confidentiality violations at the lowest possible level.
- Include a confidentiality oath in new-staff orientation.
- Model confidentiality by holding private conversations behind closed doors.

relationship, the agreement may be more difficult to negotiate and less effective than your stakeholders want it to be. On the other hand, if you wait until collaboration is firmly established, mistakes or omissions that are difficult to undo may already have been made; also, in such a case the agreement is not seen as making good on its promise of innovative change in existing practices. We suggest developing interagency agreements sooner rather than later; they can always be renegotiated as circumstances change.

Involve the Stakeholders

All stakeholders should participate in each stage of planning, developing, implementing, and evaluating an interagency agreement. Remember that families are key stakeholders. Too often, schools and other community agencies interpret family involvement to mean that the service provider gets families to support the established mission after the fact; avoid repeating this mistake by involving families from the start. Involving stakeholders also means creating a data collection, feedback, and evaluation process that ensures agreements are developed and updated on the basis of valid, current information.

Develop an Agreement

We present two types of interagency agreements for your consideration. The first, called a school-based agreement, is a formal approach to negotiating exchange of funds or establishment of liability among collaborating agencies. It is a useful guide for providing specific services at a school-based location. Use the descriptions for each section of the figure to decide which details you want to include in your own agreement, and modify the suggested wording to meet your needs. (Figure 6.2 illustrates the opening portion of a sample school-based interagency agreement; see Resource K for a complete version.) The community-based interagency agreement (Figure 6.3 and Resource K) documents agencies' collaboration, but without the exchange of funds or liabilities included in the school-based agreement. The directions given in Resource K for developing the form help you first to decide which parts of the agreement apply to your program, and then to modify the wording to meet your needs.

Neither of the interagency agreements suggested here constitutes a legal contract. All final agreements (especially those involving exchange of funds) should be reviewed by attorneys for the collaborating agencies. But keep in mind that an interagency agreement goes beyond the legalities of funds and liabilities: such an agreement establishes a framework of trust among collaborating partners and answer the questions: Where are we? Where do we want to go? How do we get there?

Figure 6.2. Interagency Agreement, School-Based

INTERAGENCY AGREEMENT
between

_____

and

_____

1. Partners, initiation date, duration, and renewal: This AGREEMENT made and entered in this _____ day of _____ , _____ by and between _____ , hereinafter called PURCHASING AGENCY, and _____ , hereinafter called the PROVIDER, shall end on _____ , _____ . This AGREEMENT may be renewed each year upon mutual agreement by both parties.

WITNESSETH:

2. WHEREAS, the Full-Service Schools Program exists to stimulate the creation of collaborative partnerships among education, health, and human services providing agencies to more effectively and efficiently meet the needs of children, youth, and their families in support of children's success in school; and

   WHEREAS, the PROVIDER desires to provide appropriate educational and early-intervention opportunities at selected schools (list names) through provision of a prevention specialist to students who may be experiencing family problems related to substance abuse or indications of personal substance abuse;

   Now, therefore, in consideration of the foregoing, the parties agree as follows:

3. Services:

   Note: If there is not exchange of money involved, this section may be included to ensure a reporting schedule for data collection and evaluation of program outcomes.

The maximum amount reimbursable to the PROVIDER by PURCHASING AGENCY under this AGREEMENT shall be forty thousand dollars ($40,000.00).

   A. Level of expertise: PROVIDER agrees to provide a counselor with qualifications as follows: master's-level education, experienced licensed preferred, but an individual with a bachelor's-level education with appropriate training and experience may fill the position. A particular criterion will be thorough knowledge of community resources.

   B. Types of service: Any one of the following mental health and related services may be provided: individual, group and family counseling, classroom presentations, case management.

   (continued)

Pointers

When funds change hands among agencies, the auditing requirements of the funding agency must be carefully adhered to. Therefore:

- Review the interagency agreement carefully with the full-service school's finance department. Its representatives need to understand the mutually beneficial nature of fiscal arrangements established by the agreement.

- Risk managers and facility supervisors may have legitimate concerns about liability, safety, and the use of school or agency facilities during extended hours.

- Other key stakeholders may have needs and concerns of their own that vary according to the circumstances of your full-service school programs.

- Have as many stakeholders read the agreement as possible, to minimize chances of misunderstanding.

Figure 6.2. Interagency Agreement, School-Based *(continued)*

C. Hours, locations: Services will be provided twelve months per year at _____ School on school grounds, in family homes, in community centers, or at appropriate "summer camp" settings. Individual will provide forty hours per week of service with at least five hours scheduled during evening hours convenient for parents. Attendance at Full-Service Schools scheduled meetings may be billed toward weekly hours.

D. It is agreed that Full-Service Schools grant funds shall not be utilized for any service covered by any other funding source. In addition, the PROVIDER shall assess Full-Service Schools clients for fees on the sliding scale as per agency policy. Provider shall keep accurate and complete records of any fee, reimbursement, or compensation of any kind, assessed against or collected from any client or other third party, for any service covered by this AGREEMENT, and shall make all such records available upon demand. PROVIDER shall report such fee, reimbursement, compensation, and funding to PURCHASING AGENCY for such payments received for each unit from all sources to the extent such payments exceed the actual cost per service. This reimbursement may be deducted from PROVIDER's invoices.

Family Care Coordination Plan

The family care coordination plan is a tool designed to guide families through answering a series of critical questions:

- What are our family's strengths? What resources do we have at home? in our extended family? in our community?
- What are our children's needs?
- What are our family's needs?
- What short-term and long-term goals do we have as a family?
- What services do we need? in what order of priority? with which delivery methods?
- How do we decide whether our goals are being met or whether our plan needs to be changed?
- How do we decide if we are benefiting from the family care coordination plan process?

A family care coordination plan results from a family-centered process involving the family and community agency professionals. The process has four steps (see p. 120).

Figure 6.3. Interagency Agreement, Community-Based

FULL-SERVICE SCHOOLS PROGRAM

INTERAGENCY AGREEMENT

Collaborating Partners:

Children's Medical Services   Children's Learning Place   Public Health Unit

_____ School District   Retired Senior Volunteer Program

Head Start   Family Network

PURPOSE

The Full-Service Schools Program exists to stimulate creation of collaborative partnerships among education, health, and human services providing agencies to more effectively and efficiently meet the needs of children, youth, and their families in support of children's success in school. The intent of this agreement is to document an interagency planning process to identify target groups of children, youth, and families to be served based on need; identify significant health, social, and economic problems facing families; identify services that families need and want; identify areas of duplication of effort and gaps between services among agencies; and identify barriers to receiving services within the families and within the agencies providing services.

The intent of this agreement is to clarify agency roles and responsibilities in the process of streamlining access to services in the areas of screening, referral, assessment, family support planning, service delivery, and transition planning for children from birth through age seven and their families.

SCREENING AND REFERRAL

Together we will:

- Develop and update an interagency Consent to Share Information form with accompanying parental informational pamphlet for the purpose of obtaining consent from parents or guardians to exchange information between service agencies.

- Collaborate to determine developmentally appropriate screening tools and procedures, train our individual staff members in administering the screening, decide on mutually agreeable dates and procedures for screenings, conduct the screenings as appropriate, obtain parental consent with the use of the interagency Consent to Share Information form, and share screening results among agencies. (See Resource J for a sample of the Consent to Share Information form.)

The Public Health Unit will:

Conduct early and periodic screening, diagnosis, and treatment (EPSDT) screenings on Medicaid-eligible children to include a health and developmental history; physical examination; nutritional and developmental assessment; routine immunizations; laboratory tests; health education; and vision, dental,

(continued)

Figure 6.3. Interagency Agreement, Community-Based *(continued)*

and hearing screenings. If a problem is identified, Medicaid providers can arrange for treatment. With parental permission, screening results will be reported to other appropriate collaborating agencies. (For example, if the child is 2½ to 5 years of age, results will be reported to Children's Medical Services.)

Children's Medical Services will:

Conduct developmental screenings for children 2½ to 5 years of age using the Dial-R or other instruments as appropriate. These will include vision and audiometric screenings and will be documented year-round with the exception of July, dependent on continued funding. Screenings will be conducted in the agency's office, on school campuses, and/or in homes. With parental permission, results will be reported to other appropriate collaborating agencies.

Note: Collaborating partners may wish to add language to clarify interagency sharing of information and confidentiality guidelines.

1. *Risk assessment* gathers baseline information regarding the family's medical, nutritional, educational, developmental, and psychosocial needs.
2. *Planning* establishes priorities among the identified needs.
3. *Linking* identifies service providers and coordinates care.
4. *Follow-up and monitoring* establishes checks to ensure the family actually receives services, keeps appointments, and benefits from the process.

The family care coordination plan process may be initiated in a variety of ways, depending on the methods you choose for identifying, screening, and determining eligibility for particular services (see Chapter Two).

Regardless of how the family care coordination plan is initiated, it is usually necessary first to address the family's immediate needs (food, clothing, shelter, emergency medical treatment, child care). Then the real work with the family begins; programs that stop at satisfying only immediate needs are least effective. (See Resource L for a sample family needs assessment survey.)

During the risk-assessment step, the family begins the process of identifying its strengths and resources, concerns and priorities. To accomplish this, one or more survey tools may be necessary, and families with literacy or language barriers may need your assistance to complete the surveys. One agency or individual should ensure completion of the surveys and the initial information sheet that accompanies the family care coordination plan. We recommend acquiring risk-assessment information in this order:

1. Collect the initial family information (name, address, phone numbers, social security numbers, etc.) that is needed for the plan.

2. Identify the family's strengths. The family support scale in Resource L helps to begin this process.

3. Assess the family's needs (see the family needs scale in the same Resource).

4. Based on the services identified by the needs assessment, assemble a team of service providers to work with the family to complete the plan.

5. Arrange for the team members and the family to meet and write the family care coordination plan.

Whenever possible, use existing sources of information, such as forms that have already been completed by the family or computerized database systems, as the basis for writing the family care coordination plan (Resource L). For those families dealing with multiple agencies, it is especially frustrating to give the same information over and over again.

Ideally, the family care coordination plan is entered into a computer-automated system so that all authorized community agencies can access the most current information.

Public Relations

There is an ongoing need for public relations in a full-service school. Any positive program should consider a solid public relations program as a tool to disseminate information, build support in the community, and expand the excitement of the program's success. How can you get started? What do you tell? Whom, and how?

First, ask yourself some important questions about what makes news. Does your story:

- Affect many people?

- Have a local or community angle?

- Mention prominent people?

- Have immediacy (timeliness)?

- Have a human-interest angle?

- Focus on something extraordinary?

If all of these statements are true, then you have information that the community is interested in hearing. Now you must decide how you want to transmit your message. You have a number of options, as the next sections reveal. Your full-service school's stakeholders have the job of agreeing on which types of public relations to use and when. We provide you with a brief description of each type and a list of pointers for your public relations strategy.

Pointers

Consider asking members
of the local press to attend
planning meetings or to
participate as members of
governance structure
teams.

Written Materials

No matter how much you *talk* about full-service schools, there is always a
need for written materials. The problem with written materials is keeping
information current as your program changes and expands. Choose a standard format, use a word processor or desktop publishing program, and
update materials continuously. As a possible format, recall the service
matrix in Chapter One (Figure 1.5). It has proven to be an excellent communication tool, since interested persons can see at a glance what types of service are provided, where the service is located, and the funding source for
the service.

You can produce written materials that define your full-service school
program. Illustrate outcome measures, goals, and mission statement; list collaborating agencies and sites; and name a contact person. Always date written
materials.

Local Networking

Local networking usually occurs in one of two forms: face-to-face meetings or
newsletters. Never miss an opportunity to talk with people in interagency or
business meetings, during special-interest group sessions, and at civic functions. Ask to be placed on the agenda of local meetings that are well attended.
Distribute written materials to interested parties. Publish your own newsletter; if sufficient funding is not available to do that, submit articles about your
program to newsletters published by other organizations.

Press Releases

A press release is a formal statement, written for publication, about an event
or relevant information. Here are some hints about using press releases:

- Use formal press releases sparingly. Decide if your news item is better
  served through a news release than with an article, letter to the editor,
  or feature.

- Follow the format shown in "Sample Press Release" to be sure it is correctly written.

- Do not use releases as propaganda. They are meant for legitimate news
  items that interest the community. One poorly written news release can
  damage your program's reputation with the press.

- Distribute news releases fairly, to all local media sources instead of a
  select few.

News Conferences

A news conference is an excellent way to ensure that your story receives balanced presentation in the media. But reserve news conferences for significant
stories only. An effective conference requires thorough preparation:

SAMPLE PRESS RELEASE

Press Release

For Immediate Release

Date: July 11, 19__

Contact: Carol Calfee, project manager for full-service schools

Phone:

Fax:

Santa Rosa Healthy Kids Detailed

Milton, Fla.—Affordable health insurance will soon be available to all Santa Rosa County students! Details of the Santa Rosa Healthy Kids program will be announced July 13, 19__, during a press conference at the [location], Gulf Breeze, Florida.

Healthy Kids, a private nonprofit effort created by the 1990 Florida legislature, was designed to offer low-cost health insurance to students not covered by any other health insurance program.

School Superintendent Bennett C. Russell will officially announce the start of the first open enrollment for students enrolled in Santa Rosa County Schools. Rose Naff, executive director, Healthy Kids Corp., will also be present to launch the program. In Florida, Santa Rosa County becomes only the third county selected to pilot the Healthy Kids program. Superintendent Russell will reveal the efforts of the local public-private partnership that formed to win approval for Santa Rosa's selection as a Healthy Kids pilot site. The press conference will be held in the [restaurant] and will begin promptly at 3:30 P.M.

(END)

- Set the time and place.
- Announce the news conference via a press release distributed to all media (radio, television, newspaper, special-interest magazines, etc.). Because press releases tend to get filed away if they are sent too soon, release them less than one week before the conference. Two days prior to the conference, follow up personally with each media representative.
- Prepare a press kit for every participant. The press kit should include:

    A copy of the press release

    Cover letter focusing on the purpose of the conference and thanking those in attendance

    Formal agenda

    Historical perspective on the program

    Background data on the lead agency

    List of key stakeholders

Pointers

To build good public relations:

- Be sensitive to community values; deal with non-threatening issues first and delicate issues later. At the same time, do not duck the tough issues; be proactive and send a positive message before someone else sends a negative one.

- Match the message to the medium: don't cram a description of your entire program into a three-minute broadcast.

- Know your subject; keep written material handy for support and accuracy. Don't rush your answers; consider the question, and answer clearly and deliberately. Avoid jargon.

- Sound confident—even if you don't feel confident. If information cannot be released or if you don't have an answer, say so.

- Be relaxed and sincere, but not joking; don't express personal opinions. Don't talk off the record.

- Tailor your delivery to the audience. If you speak to senior citizens, for example, stress the role they can play as volunteers.

- Let community agencies preview material that mentions them. Choose one spokesperson for your program, who will develop a personal relationship with members of the media. Keep a scrapbook of all media coverage and send copies to collaborating agencies.

Pertinent background materials such as sample newspaper articles
Journal articles on the topic being presented

- On the day of the conference, have a key stakeholder deliver welcoming remarks. A second stakeholder can clarify program goals with brief explanatory comments. Other stakeholders may speak for two to three minutes, each giving a perspective on the benefits to families in the program (topics can be assigned ahead of time to guarantee adequate coverage of the subject). Reserve five minutes for questions from the press before making closing remarks.

Editorial Conferences

If your program does not receive enough positive attention—or if you receive too much negative attention on a particular aspect of your program—consider talking with the media editors responsible for those features. The purpose of the editorial conference is usually to provide an introduction to the concept of full-service schools. What you want from the editors is a commitment for long-term coverage. Be prepared: know the particular media organization's position (on and off the record), and suggest possible editorials on your program.

Letters to the Editor

Letters to the editor can effectively educate the community about your program. Make letters short and to the point. Always have someone else proofread and react to the letter before you submit it. Balance criticism with compliments. Consider submitting a series of letters to broaden the community's understanding of your full-service school.

Feature Stories

Many newspapers, radio stations, and TV stations produce longer feature stories or programs on topics that they feel have considerable human interest. If an editor does not feel that your program qualifies as hard news, suggest a feature story as an alternative. Working with an editor or reporter on feature stories also helps to create relationships with news agencies for the future.

Electronic Media

Local television stations may consider a short news story on your full-service school or a series of shorter features over a period of one week. Radio stations frequently host guest speakers. If a radio or TV station is affiliated with a public broadcasting network, it may be required to provide thirty-second-to-one-minute public service announcements. For details, guidelines, or procedures, contact your local public broadcasting station (radio or TV).

Paid Advertising

Do not ignore the possibility of recruiting a business partner or sponsor to provide commercial advertising in local newspapers, on television, or on radio. This strategy is particularly effective to announce limited enrollment periods, publicize special events, or provide a forum for public discussion of, say, teenage parenting rates in your community.

Local Conference on Collaboration

Pull collaborators together to sponsor a local conference. Not only does this provide a training opportunity but the conference also offers a forum for highlighting individual services. Include a display area where collaborators can hand out information on their agencies, and invite guest speakers from the community. Advertising for the event, in addition to news coverage during the event, provides a positive format for communication with the community.

Other Conferences

Look for local, state, regional, and national conferences related to full-service schools, collaboration, community empowerment, capacity building for families, dropout prevention, and similar topics. Apply to present information about your program at the conference. Conferences offer the opportunity to share your ideas with others, while your program benefits from the ideas you receive in turn.

Speakers Bureau

Recruit a small group of skilled stakeholders to act as speakers for special events. Speakers bureau members appreciate receiving a package, including handouts, overhead transparencies, or an electronic presentation.

Creative Messages

Don't limit your program presentations to conventional approaches. Look for creative ways to get your ideas across:

- Create run-time computer programs using presentation tools. The end product is a computer disk that can be used in a compatible computer. The recipient puts the disk in the machine and types in a simple command to start the program.
- Create a three-minute videotape telling the story of an imaginary family in your program. Walk the viewer through the family's problems and explain how the full-service school program is designed to meet family members' needs.
- Contact a nearby university to see if students in a marketing class can work with your program. Students gain experience from developing

Rarely—except for Christmas, perhaps—do children and adults come together with such hope and excitement (and a tinge of anxiety) as when they meet in a classroom. We adults owe children these gifts: dedication, preparation, observation, and congratulation—wrapped in the expectation that the best is yet to be. Full-service schools offer a collaborative "Christmas" that brings children and adults together for a glorious school year. The wonder of it shows on our faces.

**—Cynthia Descher,
family builder**

press releases, writing public service announcements, creating video-tapes, and preparing written materials; your program benefits from fresh public relations ideas.

Cross-Training

In order to cope with the changes that the full-service school experience brings, creative and innovative training strategies are needed that enable providers to be more responsive to families' needs. Change can only take place with an increase in individual capability. Human experience consists of balancing capability against challenge. Status quo is maintained when our capabilities (in the dual form of ability and willingness) are equal to the challenges we face. Change shifts this balance and disrupts the status quo. If our capability is greater than what the challenge requires, positive change results. If our capability is less than what the challenge requires, negative change takes place.

The key word here is capability. Instituting a full-service school program stresses the relationship between capability and challenge. *Cross-training* is the tool that increases individual capability to deal positively with change. The purpose of any training program in a full-service school is to build each individual's capability to develop collaborative relationships. Cross-training must include as many collaborators as possible: caregivers, families, teachers, principals, community agency personnel, educational and civic leaders, and so on. Cross-training must be an ongoing part of your program; as the program grows, training nurtures growth of both the program and the individual.

Cross-training

process by which interagency partners in a full-service school program share experience, expertise, and information in an effort to build the collaborative skills necessary to meet the complex and diverse needs of students and families

What to Train

Training is most effective if it meets the participants' needs. Ask participants in the full-service school program to suggest categories of thought and need in which to pursue training. Some possible training topics and approaches follow:

- *Why build a full-service school?* Provide information on your full-service school model, the importance of the program to the community, and the benefits of collaboration (Chapter One).

- *Effective teamwork strategies.* Draft a mission statement, set goals and objectives, define team members' roles and functions, set guidelines for effective meetings, discuss trust and rapport, explore decision making and open communication, and provide tips on conflict resolution.

- *Examples of collaboration* in your community and beyond. Ask stakeholders to provide examples of the collaborative process within your community and the results that have been attained. Provide information on full-service school programs from other areas of the country.

- *Community resources for families.* Share information from needs assessment (Chapter Three). One product of this training could be a community resource guide.

- *Grant proposal writing and funding sources.* Review the basics of proposal writing (Chapter Five), and provide information about funding sources. One goal could be to establish an interagency grant proposal writing team.

- *Needs assessment.* Provide information on different strategies for assessing community needs (Chapter Three). Ask experienced participants to bring results of needs assessments they have conducted. Develop a community profile.

- *Program evaluation.* Provide information and exercises on how to write a comprehensive evaluation plan that measures your program's success (Chapter Five). Include methods for evaluating families' satisfaction with service delivery; then use the information to plan change toward a more family-friendly full-service school.

- *How to write an interagency agreement.* Provide guidelines for a comprehensive interagency agreement (discussed earlier in this chapter), and have participants draft an agreement.

- *How to write a family care coordination plan.* Provide information on family care coordination plans (also in this chapter). Designate part of the training session to focus on the relationship between a family's life goals and the role that your program can play in helping them realize those goals.

- *Positive public relations.* Ask participants to develop a one-year public relations plan (based on information in this chapter).

- *Confidentiality.* Convene a panel of parents and representatives from school family service agencies. Pose questions about confidentiality to each panel member. Ask a moderator to emphasize points of consensus.

- *Cultural sensitivity.* Offer exercises in cultural sensitivity to heighten awareness among program participants.

- *The special challenges of service providers.* Ask members to vote their interest in a series of short discussions on the topics listed in Resource M. The discussions allow participants to share their expertise.

- *Low-literacy populations.* Ask providers who work with low-literacy adults to provide insight on how to communicate with and teach low-literacy persons.

- *Customer relations.* Many private businesses develop training programs based on the idea that the customer is always right. Look for ways to adapt such a training program to the notion that "the family is always right." Include basic customer relations principles and methods for managing conflict between providers and "customer" families.

How to Train

Nontraditional forms can provide a spark to your training program. Consider group activities, but also explore creative alternatives:

- Develop methods to individualize programs. Use smaller modules of reading materials and study questions, videotapes of presentations, and computer-assisted conferences with professionals from other parts of the country.

- Collect real-life family scenarios for brainstorming sessions.

- Suggest team-building exercises.

- Distribute reviews of literature and research.

- Organize a conference highlighting the full-service school program and its stakeholders.

- Provide adequate time for networking among partners.

- Publish a newsletter.

- Write a weekly column for a local newspaper.

- Look for computer software programs on training topics.

- Develop multimedia presentations from publishers of materials on at-risk youth to spark interest and enthusiasm.

- Explore options through distance learning (satellite transmission, computer networking, e-mail, teleconferencing, and so on).

- Attend conferences and interagency meetings.

Conclusion

Now your toolbox is as filled as we can help you make it. But this does not mean that it is filled to capacity. Consult the Annotated Bibliography for myriad sources of valuable information; review the Resources for adaptable forms, assessments, and examples; and return to previous chapters or the Glossary, whenever advisable, to reinforce what you have learned.

Construction of a full-service school does not have a completion date. Rather, it is an ongoing program of building and remodeling that requires the skill of both master and apprentice stakeholder crews. Remember to keep your stakeholders involved, be open to creative and innovative ideas, remain flexible, and be responsive to both supporters and detractors. Develop interagency agreements, information-sharing guidelines, and cross-training programs. Work with families to write care coordination plans that make change possible. Initiate valuable media relationships. All these tools help signal your program's successful collaborations, now and in the future.

Endnote

1.   Soler, M. I., and Peters, C. M. *Who Should Know What? Confidentiality and Information Sharing in Service Integration.* New York: National Center for Services Integration Information Clearinghouse, National Center for Children in Poverty, Columbia University, 1993.

Conclusion

As you now know, a full-service school integrates educational, medical, social, and other human services into an effective service delivery network that reaches children, youths, and their families. Service delivery can be accomplished by co-locating service providers on school grounds or at easily accessible sites. In the construction industry, a neighborhood of tract houses places families in nearly identical homes. In the construction of a full-service school, however, each community develops its own model "house," one that is custom-built to fit the community's families. The quality of your community's model house depends on the effectiveness of services your full-service school offers, the timeliness of service delivery, and the minimization of duplicate efforts, cost, and bureaucracy.

Every construction project, great or small, begins with the project manager taking the first step: comparing models and evaluating needs. By choosing to read *Building a Full-Service School,* you have already taken the first leadership step. You understand the conceptual model for a full-service school, you know why your community can benefit from a full-service school, you recognize the differences between full-service and traditional schools, and you realize that certain myths must be overcome. You are able to imagine how a "real" full-service school works for your community.

As a leader, you must construct a blueprint for collaboration that involves planning and decision making with stakeholders. Your leadership role requires identifying key stakeholders and their roles, deciding where the full-service school will be based, identifying what services are needed, and determining how and when those services are delivered.

In order to draw the most effective, most collaborative blueprint, however, you must thoroughly assess your community's needs. You can pour a solid foundation of knowledge about your community by evaluating the depth and breadth of existing resources and discovering the gaps between resources and needs. Inventory existing community services and physical facilities; compile demographics and mapping data; assess community interaction and stakeholder commitment; and analyze the outcomes of focus

Full-service schools are indeed the wave of the future. They are responsive to today's problems. They are potentially cost-effective. And they are well received by students, parents, and school people.

—Joy Dryfoos, author of
Full-Service Schools:
A Revolution in Health
and Social Services
for Children, Youth,
and Families

131

groups, action research, and transition studies. Remember that you're building a custom school house, and feel free to design a survey that combines these strategies or initiates new ones.

Any discussion of new ideas or improved services brings home the reality of financing your full-service school's construction. One of your leadership tasks is to clarify funding barriers and transform them into funding opportunities. Financing your full-service school's construction also requires collaboration if the result is to be an effective plan that identifies funding approaches and sources. Developing an astute knowledge of politics at the local, state, and federal levels enables you to take advantage of multiple funding solutions.

When your stakeholders are ready for the serious business of financing construction, framing the funding request requires you to write proposals and develop evaluation plans. You must decide what you want to accomplish with the funds, identify a proposal-writing team, develop a list of potential funding sources, and write the proposal to the source's specifications. Whether a proposal is funded or not funded, you must prepare to take appropriate action.

As you move into your full-service school house, you'll want to share information and prepare plans for publicity and training. If you're to furnish your house with ongoing community involvement, stakeholders need to know about confidentiality and information-sharing guidelines, interagency agreements, family care coordination plans, public relations strategies, and cross-training topics.

The tools in *Building a Full-Service School* afford you a step-by-step guide to your school's construction, but you can find the nuts and bolts in the Resources, many of which are available in electronic format on a companion diskette available through Jossey-Bass Publishers. Because facilitating communication is so important to a successful construction process, the Glossary translates some familiar and some not-so-familiar terminology. The Annotated Bibliography gives you the opportunity to browse through current designs and explore others' experiences with the full-service school concept.

The state of Florida proves that it can be done. For the 1997–98 school year, Florida's Bureau of Instructional Support and Community Services lists 327 full-service schools in sixty-six districts, serving almost three hundred thousand students and fifty-five thousand families. An investment of $11 million at the state level yielded more than $13 million in in-kind services that support full-service schools.

Be patient. Be flexible. Keep your sense of humor. Building a full-service school can be challenging and rewarding, and we know you can do it.

Resources

🖫 *Note:* Resources marked with this icon are available in electronic format on a separately purchased companion diskette. See page 228 for details.

Resource A

💾 Matching Full-Service Goals and Services

Part One: Typical Goals and Corresponding Services

Educational accountability challenges public schools to "recognize fundamental economic and societal changes and restructure schooling for the next century."[1]

A full-service school is the ideal tool for constructing programs that respond to such challenges. The following matrix shows how "rooms" in your full-service school can be combined to build a complete "house"—one that responds to the demands of educational accountability.

Goal	Corresponding Services
Readiness to start school Communities and schools collaborate to prepare children and families for children's success in school.	Mental health counseling Child study or student assistance teams Health services Insurance programs Children and families services Intergenerational programs Parent workshops and education Head Start, First Start, Even Start programs Before- and after-school child care programs Nutrition programs Economic services Early intervention programs Transportation Family literacy and family counseling Child care Health care Extended reading programs Prekindergarten initiatives
Graduation rate and readiness for postsecondary education and employment Students graduate and are prepared to enter the workforce and postsecondary education.	Mental health counseling Guidance services Tutoring and mentoring programs Adult literacy ESOL programs (English speakers of other languages) Child study or student assistance teams Teen parenting programs Family counseling Teacher or peer adoption programs Dropout prevention programs Children and family services Intergenerational programs Job services Employability and career counseling Volunteer programs

Goal	Corresponding Services
Student performance Students successfully compete at the highest levels nationally and internationally and are prepared to make well-reasoned, thoughtful, and healthy lifelong decisions.	Mental health counseling Competence-based curriculum Child study or student assistance teams Teen parenting programs Tutoring and mentoring Resource officer programs Career counseling Dropout prevention programs Study skills and habits Health insurance programs Children and families services Intergenerational programs Parent workshops Volunteer programs Youth programs (4-H, Boy Scouts, Girl Scouts, special interest clubs, etc.) Substance abuse counseling Attendance initiatives Academic programs Student behavior incentives
Learning environment School boards provide a learning environment conducive to teaching and learning.	Increased use of technology Business partnerships Adult education classes Child study or student assistance teams Community use of facilities Professionalization programs Time-on-task activities School climate programs Expectation and performance programs Teacher, parent, student participation Teacher morale and attitude programs Violence prevention
School safety and environment Communities provide an environment that is drug-free and protects students' health, safety, and civil rights.	Mental health counseling Delinquency services Child study or student assistance teams Safety education Teen parenting programs Resource officer programs and law enforcement Before- and after-school child care Community use of facilities

(continued)

Goal	Corresponding Services
School safety and environment *(continued)*	Health services
	Health insurance programs
	Children and families services
	Graffiti control
	Building and grounds beautification programs
	Guardian ad litem services
	Legal services
	Business partnerships
	Parent workshops and family counseling
	Nutrition programs
	Youth gang intervention
Teachers and staff	Staff wellness programs
The schools, district, and state ensure professionalism of teachers and staff.	Professionalization programs
	Child study or student assistance teams
	In-service training on available community resources to support families
	Peer teacher programs
	Technology initiatives
	In-service training from the community on identifying and referring students with special needs
	Increased participation of instructional and noninstructional staff in community support service training opportunities
Adult literacy	Adult literacy classes
Adults are literate and have the knowledge and skills needed to compete in a global economy and exercise the rights and responsibilities of citizenship.	GED preparation classes (General Educational Development) and ABE (Adult Basic Education)
	Extended school day
	Community education
	Junior college and university coursework
	Legal services
	Employment services
	Elderly services
	Housing assistance
	Foster care
	Adult health care
	Economic services
	Nutrition programs
	Budgeting programs
	Voter registration programs
	Business partnerships

(continued)

Goal	Corresponding Services
Adult literacy *(continued)*	Parent workshops and seminars through community sponsors
	Parent use of technology equipment
	Tutoring and mentoring programs
Parent involvement Communities, school boards, and schools provide opportunities for involving parents and guardians as active partners in achieving school improvement and education accountability.	Volunteer services
	Tutoring and mentoring
	Parent workshops
	Special events
	Family involvement centers
	Make-and-take workshops

Endnote

1. Florida Commission on Education Reform and Accountability. *Blueprint 2000: A System of School Improvement and Accountability for 1994–95 School Improvement Plans*. Tallahassee: Florida Department of Education, 1994.

▣ Part Two: Service Matrix for a Full-Service School

Service	Description/Clientele	Location and Hours	Funding Sources
Assessment			
Child Welfare			
Educational			

Service Matrix for a Full-Service School *(continued)*

Service	Description/Clientele	Location and Hours	Funding Sources
Health			
Juvenile Justice			
Mental Health			
Operational			

Service Matrix for a Full-Service School *(continued)*

Service	Description/Clientele	Location and Hours	Funding Sources
Prevention			
Recreational			
Vocational			
Community			

See Resource A for template listing suggested services.

Resource B

💾 Job Description: Full-Service Schools Program Manager

An individual recruited, selected, and employed by a host agency to coordinate the collaborative process and development of the full-service schools program.

TITLE

Program manager (or coordinator)

QUALIFICATIONS

1. Master's degree or higher from an accredited institution
2. Currently hold or eligible for certificate in at least one area of education, and certification in administration, supervision, or educational leadership
3. Five years of experience in education

OR

Comparable experience in social or human services if host agency is other than a school system

REPORTS TO

Host agency designee and local governance structure body

SUPERVISES

As assigned

JOB GOALS

- To provide leadership for, coordinate, and direct planning, developing, implementing, and evaluating of the functions and services of the full-service schools program.
- To collaborate with key community leaders and other people to maximize existing resources by building an infrastructure supporting the mission of a continuum of service for children and families at full-service school sites and within the community.

ESSENTIAL FUNCTIONS

General

- Assists in interpreting and implementing applicable district, state, and federal policies, laws, and regulations to staff personnel, agencies, and school sites
- Provides appropriate information to the assistant superintendent or other personnel
- Develops, recommends, and administers assigned department budget
- Recommends and directs committees as needed or assigned
- Assists in planning and implementing staff development programs
- Prepares appropriate administrative reports
- Provides own method of transportation when required to reach various locations
- Prepares and presents oral and written reports to the public and the school system
- Keeps systematically abreast of new trends and publications
- Participates in appropriate activities for continued professional growth
- Assumes responsibility to maintain a valid teacher's certificate
- Facilitates alliances and partnerships with state, county, and city agencies and private organizations to establish a continuum of services for students and families at full-service school sites
- Serves as liaison with state, county, city, community, and neighborhood governing bodies
- Establishes linkages with faith communities, community agencies (health, social, financial, etc.), and educational institutions (elementary through high school, community colleges, universities)
- Establishes linkages with local policy makers, legislators, businesses, etc.

ESSENTIAL FUNCTIONS *(continued)*

- Establishes linkages with health providers (hospitals, clinics, other health care settings, long-term, home, preventive, and wellness)
- Performs other duties as assigned

Specific responsibilities

- Initiates, evaluates, and coordinates development and implementation of the district full-service schools program
- Serves as liaison and maintains organizational responsibilities with community agencies
- Develops procedures and policies for the full-service schools department
- Prepares additional proposals for supplemental funding
- Maintains records of program development
- Advises on development of the computerized database system
- Develops, analyzes, and evaluates assessment instruments
- Advises on job announcements, job descriptions, selection criteria, and placement of personnel
- Participates on local and state committees related to the full-service schools initiative

LENGTH OF EMPLOYMENT

Twelve-month contract

SALARY

Based on the adopted salary schedule for administrative personnel

EVALUATION

Annual evaluation by the assistant superintendent for instruction in accordance with local policies and state laws

ENVIRONMENT

Activities occur inside and outside; subject to indoor and outdoor environmental conditions

EQUIPMENT

Audiovisual equipment, instructional computers, multimedia presentation tools

SUPERVISION AND CONTROL

Is personally responsible for satisfying all of the above essential functions with minimal supervision

Resource C
Community Needs Assessment

🖫 Part One: Community Service Inventory

1. **Assessment services** may be defined as diagnostic and evaluative. Assessments usually involve professional determination of the nature of a child's or family's problems and consideration of the strengths and weaknesses of the child and his or her family environment. Assessments may be conducted to determine eligibility for a particular program and/or to develop a plan of services to be provided. These may be conducted for a single program or in a multiprogram environment.

Service Available?		Category	Source (e.g., agency, school, program, or support group)
Yes	No		
		Behavioral	
		Psychiatric	
		Psychological educational	
		Psychological	
		Social	
		Social and family	
		Other	

2. **Child welfare services** are provided to students and their families to assist and support the family unit. Supportive services, such as financial assistance and protective supervision, assist the child to remain within the home. If the family is so stressed that it cannot remain intact, substitute services may be provided. Respite care may be considered a child welfare service or a mental health service, depending on the level of focus of the service provided.

Service Available?		Category	Source
Yes	No		
		Supportive services Child advocacy	
		Crisis intervention	
		Flexible funding, e.g., housing deposits	
		Food and clothing banks	
		Home services, e.g., homemaker, housekeeper	
		Housing	
		Interagency case management	
		Nonresidential runaway services	
		Parent effectiveness training and support groups	

Service Available?

Yes	No	Category	Source

Supportive services *(continued)*

Yes	No	Category	Source
		Parent training	
		Protective supervision for child abuse and neglect cases	
		Voluntary family services	

Substitute care services

Yes	No	Category	Source
		Adoption services	
		Economic services (e.g., food stamps, AFDC)	
		Emergency shelter services	
		Family group homes	
		Foster care	
		Independent living services	
		Pregnancy and parenting for teenage students	
		Runaway shelter	
		Other	

3. **Educational services** are intended to provide knowledge and socialization skills development for students. By law, all students are entitled to free and appropriate public education. Students with emotional and behavioral problems may require special services to help them obtain an education.

Service Available?

Yes	No	Category	Source
		Adult basic education	
		Adult GED classes (general equivalency diploma)	
		Alternative schools and programs	
		Child care, extended day (before, after school)	
		Child care, prekindergarten disadvantaged	
		Child care, prekindergarten handicapped	
		Child care, weekends, intersessions, summer	
		Child care for adults sessions	
		Community education	
		Community service programs	
		Computerized literacy center	
		Curriculum development and improvement	
		Dropout prevention programs	
		Educational guidance counseling	
		Educational homework help	
		Exceptional education	

Service Available?

Yes	No	Category	Source
		Educational services *(continued)*	
		Field trips	
		Guest speakers	
		Head Start or prekindergarten program	
		Homebound instruction	
		Hospital instruction	
		In-service training for agency personnel	
		In-service training for school personnel	
		Integration of technology into the curriculum	
		Intergenerational programs	
		Mentoring	
		Migrant education	
		Parents as teachers programs	
		Participation incentives	
		Resource rooms with checkout educational materials	
		Scholarships	
		Self-contained classrooms for exceptional students	
		Special day school	
		Summer camps	
		Support and training for child care staff	
		Teenage parenting programs	
		Tutoring	
		University and community college coursework	
		Other	

4. **Health services** are those activities that involve detection and treatment of physical impairments or damage to the body. Included are routine physical examinations and follow-up care as well as prenatal and postnatal care of pregnant teenagers and treatment of sexually transmitted diseases.

Service Available?

Yes	No	Category	Source
		Acute care (spinal cord and head injury)	
		Birth control	
		Chronic disease	
		Dental checkups	
		Dental services	
		EPSDT screening and assessment (early periodic screening, diagnosis, and treatment required for Medicaid)	

Yes	No	Category	Source
		Health services *(continued)*	
		Health counseling	
		Health education	
		Health support aide services	
		Laboratory services	
		Learning disability assessment	
		Medical and physical examinations	
		Neurological testing	
		Nursing and advanced registered nurse practitioner (ARNP) services	
		Nutrition counseling and services	
		Physical disability testing	
		Physical restoration	
		Physician services	
		Pregnancy screening	
		Prenatal and postpartum care	
		Primary care	
		Program eligibility for additional health service	
		Screening and treatment of sexually transmitted diseases	
		Speech and language assessment	
		Substance abuse screening	
		Treatment for drug and alcohol abuse	
		Treatment of eating disorders	
		Vision and auditory evaluation	
		Other	

5. **Juvenile justice services** include a range of service options in response to offenses committed by juveniles. The services described here fall into two general categories: diversionary and nonresidential. Other services provided that are not listed here range from supervision within the geographic area to detention and other residential programs. Residential and nonresidential services may be provided at the discretion of a staff member; most are stipulated by a court.

Yes	No	Category	Source
		Diversionary services	
		After-school programs	
		Alternative education programs	
		Child care	
		Counseling, individual, family, and group	

Service Available?		Category	Source
Yes	No		

Diversionary services *(continued)*

Yes	No	Category	Source
		Counseling, in-home	
		Credit counseling	
		Crisis line	
		Dropout prevention programs	
		Drug prevention	
		Drug treatment	
		Educational and vocational financial assistance	
		Health services	
		In-school suspension	
		Job counseling	
		Job placement	
		Job training	
		Literacy programs	
		Parent information and education programs	
		Pregnancy prevention programs	
		Public transportation	
		Recreational programs	
		Resource directories	
		Respite care	
		Runaway services	
		Teen parenting programs	
		Teenline services	
		Truancy intervention	
		Tutoring	
		Other	

Nonresidential services

Yes	No	Category	Source
		Assessment centers (dropoff sites for law enforcement officers; processing; evaluation for psychological, education, and other services)	
		Delinquency intervention services	
		Halfway house	
		Nonjudicial diversion—alternative to judicial system involving some form of community control	
		Nonsecure detention	
		Postcommitment services—transitionand support services	

Residential services

Yes	No	Category	Source
		Secure detention	
		Special intensive group prevention services	

Service Available?

Yes	No	Category	Source

Residential services *(continued)*

Yes	No	Category	Source
		Students reentering society from judicial system	
		Training school	
		Other	

6. **Mental health services** encompass a broad range of residential and nonresidential programs and services directed toward treating and resolving students' and family members' emotional problems. Mental health services can be divided into seven major categories: (1) early identification and intervention; (2) community-based therapeutic services; (3) emergency services; (4) independent residential services; (5) therapeutic residential camp services; (6) camp residential services; and (7) inpatient hospitalization.

Service Available?

Yes	No	Category	Source

Early identification and intervention services

Yes	No	Category	Source
		Family counseling	
		Guidance counseling	
		Mental health counseling through licensed clinical social workers	
		Peer counseling	
		Screening services	
		Self-help and support groups	
		Student assistance teams	
		Other	

Community-based therapeutic services

Yes	No	Category	Source
		Contracted behavioral support	
		Day treatment programs	
		Home-based services	
		Out-of-home respite care	
		Outpatient therapy services, adult	
		Outpatient therapy services, family	
		Outpatient therapy services, student	
		Purchased individual services	
		Purchased therapy services	
		Respite care in home	
		Specialized treatment, office	
		Therapeutic after-school care	
		Other	

Service Available?

Yes	No	Category	Source
		Emergency services	
		Crisis intervention in the home	
		Crisis telephone lines	
		Developmental services, adult	
		Developmental services, student	
		Emergency services	
		Psychiatric emergency response services	
		Other	
		Independent residential services	
		Independent residential home	
		Semi-independent living	
		Therapeutic foster care	
		Therapeutic group care	
		Other	
		Therapeutic residential camp services	
		Residential treatment centers	
		Wilderness camps	
		Other	
		Crisis residential services	
		Crisis stabilization	
		Other	
		Inpatient hospitalization	
		Forensic hospital	
		Inpatient hospitalization	
		Short-term inpatient hospitalization	
		Specialty hospital	
		Other	

7. **Operational services** include those that are the infrastructure of the full-service school. These services span the boundaries of other domains. Included in this domain are case management, advocacy, self-help and support, transportation, legal, and volunteer services.

Service Available?

Yes	No	Category	Source
		Planning	
		Bureaucratic changes	
		District or region-based coordinators	

Service Available?		Category	Source
Yes	No		

Operational services *(continued)*

		Evaluation coordinator	
		Family resource coordinator	
		Family services planning teams	
		Individual education plan (IEP) committee	
		School-based child care teams (multiagency intervention teams)	
		School-based coordinator	
		Transition case-planning committee	
		Other	

Case management

		Coordination of health services	
		Coordination with delinquency services	
		Coordination with mental health services	
		Family services planning team	
		Medically complex staffing	
		Multidisciplinary full team staffing	
		Multiple handicap assessment	
		Service plan assessment	
		Targeted case management	
		Other	

Other support

		Advocacy	
		Baby-sitting co-ops	
		Community advisory group	
		Hotline (information referral)	
		Information dissemination	
		Legal services	
		Self-help and support	
		Transportation	
		Volunteer services	
		Other	

8. **Prevention services** include those actions taken to prevent mental illness and health or education problems. Prevention services include activities and education efforts that promote physical health and positive mental health or reduce the incidence of illness. Early identification of problems and early intervention are also considered prevention services.

Service Available?

Yes	No	Category	Source
		Prevention services *(continued)*	
		Abuse and neglect prevention	
		Delinquency prevention	
		Dropout prevention	
		Health education and disease prevention	
		Injury prevention	
		Intergenerational programs	
		Runaway prevention screening	
		School-based substance abuse prevention	
		Supplementary services to classroom education	
		Training and consultation by health professionals	
		Other	

9. **Recreational services** for students and adults include age-appropriate formal and informal interactions or amusement activities with peers and adults. Recreational activities provide youngsters and adults with important social skills and interpersonal activities.

Service Available?

Yes	No	Category	Source
		Child care, extended day (before and after school)	
		Child care, weekends, intersessions, summer	
		Enrichment and talent development, family	
		Enrichment and talent development, parent	
		Enrichment and talent development, student	
		Special projects	
		Summer camps	
		Teen activity club	
		Youth center	
		Other	

10. **Vocational services** are services designed to assist youths and their families, with or without disabilities, to move from education to employment. These services include development of skills in career selection, job finding, job retention, and specific technical skills needed for job accomplishment.

Service Available?

Yes	No	Category	Source
		Agricultural education, adult	
		Agricultural education, student	

Yes	No	Category	Source
		Vocational services *(continued)*	
		Business education, adult	
		Business education, student	
		Career education, adult	
		Career education, student	
		Home economics, adult	
		Home economics, student	
		Job find, placement, and retention, adult	
		Job find, placement, and retention, student	
		Job-seeking skills training, adult	
		Job-seeking skills training, student	
		Life skills training, adult	
		Life skills training, student	
		Occupational testing, adult	
		Occupational testing, student	
		Part-time job development	
		Summer employment	
		Supported employment, adult	
		Supported employment, student	
		Technological education, adult	
		Technological education, student	
		Vocational skills training, adult	
		Vocational skills training, student	
		Vocational adjustment, adult	
		Vocational adjustment, student	
		Vocational testing, adult	
		Vocational testing, student	
		Work experience, student	
		Other	

11. **Community resources** are those local institutions found within a community setting that are already established and providing services to the general public. Linkages with the resources may provide opportunities for families, such as educational and recreational activities, family educational experiences, and additional support services on or near the school site.

Yes	No	Category	From Agency
		Business organizations (list):	

Service Available?		Category	From Agency
Yes	**No**		
		Community resources *(continued)*	
		Children's services councils (list):	
		City government	
		Civic organizations (list):	
		Community colleges	
		Community organizations (Kiwanis, Optimists, Lions, American Legion, etc.) (list):	
		County government	
		Creative resources (artists, musicians, architects, historical society, Audubon Society, etc.) (list):	
		Hospitals	
		Libraries	
		Parks	
		Police	
		Special populations (youth groups, senior groups, people with disabilities, welfare recipients) (list):	
		Universities	

Part Two: Key Informant Survey[1]

Please complete and return within five days.

A. Needs

Keeping in mind both the need itself and the degree to which that need is being met, please CIRCLE ONE NUMBER IN EACH ROW to indicate how serious you feel each need is in your community.

Basic Material and Financial Needs	Not Serious	Not Very Serious	Somewhat Serious	Very Serious	Don't Know
1. Housing payment assistance	1	2	3	4	9
2. Food	1	2	3	4	9
3. Clothing or furniture	1	2	3	4	9
4. Utility assistance	1	2	3	4	9

Housing	Not Serious	Not Very Serious	Somewhat Serious	Very Serious	Don't Know
5. Available housing $300 per month or less	1	2	3	4	9
6. Low- or no-cost repair (elderly)	1	2	3	4	9
7. Low- or no-cost repair (other)	1	2	3	4	9

Employment	Not Serious	Not Very Serious	Somewhat Serious	Very Serious	Don't Know
8. Basic skills for employability	1	2	3	4	9
9. Employment training and placement	1	2	3	4	9
10. Availability of full-time jobs	1	2	3	4	9
11. Availability of day labor	1	2	3	4	9
12. Sheltered workshops	1	2	3	4	9
13. Vocational skills	1	2	3	4	9

Child Care	Not Serious	Not Very Serious	Somewhat Serious	Very Serious	Don't Know
14. Infant and preschool all day	1	2	3	4	9
15. After school	1	2	3	4	9
16. Weekends and off hours	1	2	3	4	9
17. Sliding scale fee pay	1	2	3	4	9

Recreational and Cultural Activities	Not Serious	Not Very Serious	Somewhat Serious	Very Serious	Don't Know
18. Low- or no-cost family activities	1	2	3	4	9
19. Youth enrichment or development	1	2	3	4	9
20. Neighborhood-available programs	1	2	3	4	9

Education	Not Serious	Not Very Serious	Somewhat Serious	Very Serious	Don't Know
21. Achievement of basic high school competency	1	2	3	4	9
22. Adult literacy	1	2	3	4	9
23. Vocational training (schools)	1	2	3	4	9
24. Truancy and dropout prevention	1	2	3	4	9

Physical Health	Not Serious	Not Very Serious	Somewhat Serious	Very Serious	Don't Know
25. Affordable dental care	1	2	3	4	9
26. Affordable outpatient sick care	1	2	3	4	9
27. Short-term inpatient care for physical illness	1	2	3	4	9
28. Long-term nursing home care	1	2	3	4	9
29. Home health care (skilled)	1	2	3	4	9
30. Homemaker or companion service	1	2	3	4	9
31. Congregate or home-delivered meals	1	2	3	4	9
32. General health care or nutrition education	1	2	3	4	9
33. Respite for caregiver	1	2	3	4	9
34. Day care for physically disabled or elderly	1	2	3	4	9
35. Family planning	1	2	3	4	9
36. Teen pregnancy prevention and services	1	2	3	4	9
37. AIDS and HIV-related services	1	2	3	4	9
38. Prenatal health care	1	2	3	4	9
39. Independent living skills for blind, deaf, or handicapped	1	2	3	4	9

40. Means to obtain medication	1	2	3	4	9
41. Adequate health insurance	1	2	3	4	9

Mental Health	Not Serious	Not Very Serious	Somewhat Serious	Very Serious	Don't Know
42. Affordable outpatient individual and family counseling	1	2	3	4	9
43. Parenting education	1	2	3	4	9
44. Short-term inpatient care for mental illness	1	2	3	4	9
45. Long-term residential, group home, or nursing home care for mentally disabled	1	2	3	4	9
46. Coping skills for family responsibilities	1	2	3	4	9
47. Skills for responsible personal behavior	1	2	3	4	9

Substance Abuse	Not Serious	Not Very Serious	Somewhat Serious	Very Serious	Don't Know
48. Drug and alcohol abuse prevention services	1	2	3	4	9
49. Drug abuse outpatient treatment	1	2	3	4	9
50. Alcohol abuse outpatient treatment	1	2	3	4	9
51. Inpatient treatment for alcohol or drug abuse	1	2	3	4	9

Household Violence and Related Issues	Not Serious	Not Very Serious	Somewhat Serious	Very Serious	Don't Know
52. Child protection services	1	2	3	4	9
53. Adult protection services	1	2	3	4	9
54. Services for victims of rape or sexual asault	1	2	3	4	9
55. Services for victims of domestic assault or sexual abuse	1	2	3	4	9
56. Foster care for children and adolescents	1	2	3	4	9
57. Adoption	1	2	3	4	9
58. Services for children and youth with behavior or emotional problems	1	2	3	4	9

Public Safety and Legal Services	Not Serious	Not Very Serious	Somewhat Serious	Very Serious	Don't Know
59. Delinquency prevention	1	2	3	4	9
60. Crime prevention	1	2	3	4	9
61. Social readjustment after conviction	1	2	3	4	9
62. Relief following fire or disaster	1	2	3	4	9
63. Low- or no-cost legal services	1	2	3	4	9
64. Tax-preparation assistance	1	2	3	4	9
65. Budget and credit counseling	1	2	3	4	9
66. Services to reduce noise, air and water pollution	1	2	3	4	9
67. Legal guardianship	1	2	3	4	9
68. Racial or ethnic discrimination	1	2	3	4	9
69. Public accommodation for deaf, blind, or handicapped	1	2	3	4	9

Transportation	Not Serious	Not Very Serious	Somewhat Serious	Very Serious	Don't Know
70. Accessible public transportation	1	2	3	4	9
71. Adequate transportation for disabled or elderly	1	2	3	4	9
72. Reliable transportation for work, medical, or necessary trips	1	2	3	4	9

Systemwide Issues	Not Serious	Not Very Serious	Somewhat Serious	Very Serious	Don't Know
73. Information and referral services	1	2	3	4	9
74. Planning and coordination of health and human services	1	2	3	4	9
75. Coordination of community development	1	2	3	4	9
76. Public recognition of community strengths	1	2	3	4	9
77. Other (any category)_____	1	2	3	4	9

B. Priorities

1. (WRITE IN THE APPLICABLE ITEM NUMBER FROM THE LEFT MARGIN ABOVE.)

   Which of the above unmet needs do you believe is the most serious in our community? _____

   Which of the above unmet needs do you believe is the second most serious? _____

   Which of the above unmet needs do you believe is the third most serious? _____

2. Describing your community, generally what kind of place is it to live: (CIRCLE ONE NUMBER.)

   1. Excellent   2. Good   3. Fair   4. Poor

C. Barriers to Services

For each of the following barriers that might prevent people from using existing services, please indicate your view of how serious this barrier is for people in our community. (CIRCLE ONE NUMBER IN EACH ROW.)

	Not Serious	Not Very Serious	Somewhat Serious	Very Serious	Don't Know
1. People's dislike of service environment	1	2	3	4	9
2. Eligibility restrictions	1	2	3	4	9
3. Cost of services	1	2	3	4	9
4. Lack of information about available services	1	2	3	4	9
5. Lack of transportation	1	2	3	4	9
6. Inconvenient locations	1	2	3	4	9
7. Lack of child care	1	2	3	4	9
8. Communication barriers	1	2	3	4	9
9. Perception of costs as excessive	1	2	3	4	9
10. Inconvenient hour or days	1	2	3	4	9
11. Concerns about confidentiality	1	2	3	4	9
12. Perceptions concerning quality of services	1	2	3	4	9
13. Prior bad experience	1	2	3	4	9
14. Reluctance to go outside family and friends for help	1	2	3	4	9
15. Wait for service too long	1	2	3	4	9
16. Lack of handicap access	1	2	3	4	9
17. Other_____	1	2	3	4	9

D. Groups in Need

How serious are the service needs for the following population groups?

	Not Serious	Not Very Serious	Somewhat Serious	Very Serious	Don't Know
1. Ethnic minority	1	2	3	4	9
2. Elderly	1	2	3	4	9
3. Children and youth	1	2	3	4	9
4. Working poor	1	2	3	4	9
5. Handicapped	1	2	3	4	9
6. Women	1	2	3	4	9
7. Other _____	1	2	3	4	9

E. Groups Providing Services

In your opinion, how effective are the following organizations in meeting their stated mission or function?

	Not Effective	Not Very Effective	Somewhat Effective	Very Effective	Don't Know
1. Churches	1	2	3	4	9
2. Department of Health and Rehabilitative Services	1	2	3	4	9
3. Public schools	1	2	3	4	9
4. United Way	1	2	3	4	9
5. Public health	1	2	3	4	9
6. Other service organizations _____	1	2	3	4	9

F.   Given that there will never be enough resources to meet all human service needs, please share your suggestions concerning current community resources. (ATTACH ADDITIONAL SHEETS IF NECESSARY.)

1. Are there any services for which the need has diminished? If so, please describe.

_____ Yes   _____ No   _____ Don't know

_____

_____

_____

2. Are there any areas **over**served relative to their needs? If so, please explain.

_____ Yes   _____ No   _____ Don't know

_____

_____

3. How can resources or services be shifted or redirected to be more effective? Please explain.

_____

_____

4. Which of the following best describe your role and the populations with whom you most frequently come into contact? (CIRCLE ALL THAT APPLY.)

Males	Black	Business
Females	White	Schools
Children (0–17)	Disabled	Service providers
Elderly (over 59)	Chronically ill	Government
Family units	Low income	Clergy
Other:		

_____

5. What is the zip code where you live? _____

6. What is the zip code where you work? _____

Thank you for helping identify health and human service needs in your community; please complete and return your responses in the enclosed envelope. Your additional comments or suggestions are welcomed.

Endnote

1. Koppich, J. E., and Kirst, M. W. "Editor's Introduction." *Education and Urban Society*, 1993, 25(2), 123–128. Copyright © 1993 by Sage Publications. Reprinted by permission of Sage Publications.

Resource D
💾 Demographic Survey

Data	Source and Date

A. Community Status: rural, urban, suburban, mixture

_____   _____

B. Geographic Barriers: describe physical barriers to service delivery (such as isolated farmlands, two large bodies of water that create transportation barriers, thirty miles to existing social services, dense population, and so on.)

_____   _____
_____   _____
_____   _____
_____   _____

C. Key Facts About Children

1. Number of children younger than eighteen

2. Percentage of total population younger than eighteen

3. Percentage of children living in
   - two-parent households
   - single-parent households
   - households headed by someone other than a parent

4. Ethnicity:
   - percentage of children who are white
   - percentage of children who are black
   - percentage of children who are of mixed race
   - percentage of children who are of Asian heritage
   - other significant groups

5. Ages
   - number of children under one year of age
   - number of children between one and five
   - number of children between five and ten
   - number of children in other significant age groups

D. Community Descriptors

1. Population (number)
   Political description (e.g., 80,000, in urban county)

Data		Source and Date

2. Percentage at or below poverty level as determined by latest census or other reliable source _____ _____

3. Principal employers (include names, types of industry, number of employed in each)

_____ _____
_____ _____
_____ _____
_____ _____

4. Percentage of unemployed _____ _____

5. Crime rate:
   - felonies per thousand adult population _____ _____
   - misdemeanors per thousand adult population _____ _____
   - felonies per thousand juvenile population _____ _____
   - misdemeanors per thousand juvenile population _____ _____
   - other relevant data_____

6. Divorce rate _____ _____
   Number of single heads-of-household _____ _____

7. Number of runaways _____ _____

8. Evidence of domestic violence
   - number of abuse complaints involving domestic violence _____ _____
   - number of arrests for domestic violence _____ _____

9. Number of low-income single parents (families earning less than $ _____ per year) _____ _____

10. Identity of interagency councils already in place _____ _____

_____ _____ _____
_____ _____ _____
_____ _____ _____
_____ _____ _____

11. Evidence of special programs designed to meet the needs of families

_____ _____
_____ _____
_____ _____

12. Evidence of community collaboration

_____ _____
_____ _____
_____ _____

Data	Source and Date

E. Specific Information on Population

1. Rate of incidence for at-risk behaviors, e.g., alcohol or drug abuse, smoking, percentage of children younger than eighteen who indicate use of alcohol or cigarettes in the last eighteen months   _____   _____

2. Infant deaths (number per thousand)   _____   _____
   Low birthweight babies (number per thousand)   _____

3. Juvenile crime statistics, particularly early onset numbers

   _____   _____
   _____   _____
   _____   _____

4. Availability of services provided by social service agencies (Target specific agencies and request caseload information)
   - number of families receiving abuse or neglect intervention services   _____   _____
   - number of families receiving economic assistance   _____ _____   _____
   - _____ _____   _____
   - _____ _____   _____

5. Number of single heads-of-household   _____   _____

6. Health problems (list most prevalent problems)

   _____   _____
   _____   _____
   _____   _____
   _____   _____

7. Mental health statistics

   _____   _____
   _____   _____
   _____

8. Teen pregnancy rate (live births for teens 13–18 divided by total live births)   _____   _____

9. Criminal activity of parents
   - number of parents of students from a school site arrested for a misdemeanor or felony during the previous year   _____   _____
   - _____ _____   _____
   - _____ _____   _____

Data		Source and Date

10. Behavioral survey information such as violence and suicide indicators, levels of physical activity, substance abuse, diet and weight indicators, sexual activity, accidents and injuries

   _____   _____

   _____   _____

   _____   _____

F. School-Based Information

1. Dropout rate

2. Rate of suspension and expulsion

3. Absentee rate

4. Rate of in-school suspensions

5. Percentage of students on free or reduced lunch

6. Percentage of students in counseling services

7. Behavioral problems at school that persist in spite of normal interventions (description of problems persisting, with any relevant numbers)

   • _____

   • _____

   • _____

8. Number of students retained in one or more grade levels

9. Number of students who are academically underachieving (may be based on teacher perception)

10. Number of students who are limited-English-proficient (have difficulty communicating effectively in the English language)

11. Learning and behavior problems (what types are common, and how many students are served in special programs dealing with each classification)

   • _____

   • _____

   • _____

Data	Source and Date

12. Number of students with handicapping conditions:
    physical   _____   _____
    emotional   _____   _____
    learning   _____   _____

    _____   _____   _____

13. Rate of parental involvement (measured by parent
    attendance at parent-teacher conferences, parent
    organization roles, volunteer hours, etc.)
    - _____ _____   _____
    - _____ _____   _____
    - _____ _____   _____

14. Evidence of community involvement (such as business
    partnerships, mentors or tutors, etc.)

    _____   _____
    _____   _____
    _____

15. Evidence of special programs in place to meet needs of
    targeted groups of students and/or families

    _____
    _____   _____
    _____   _____

16. Evidence of problem-solving teams in place for joint decision
    making to deal with special problems the school is facing,
    e.g., gang intervention programs, suicide prevention team

    _____   _____
    _____   _____
    _____   _____

G. Mitigating Factors That Influence Major Decisions

1. Population growth   _____   _____
2. Rate of migration   _____   _____
3. Immigration   _____   _____
4. Homelessness   _____   _____
5. Other societal factors   _____   _____

Resource E
Full-Service School Facilities

Part One: Suggested Facilities Size and Design Criteria[1]

Space type: School Health Room

Square footage

Minimum .70 net square feet per FTE capacity, excluding storage, restrooms, and nurse's work room.

For each professional staff member, there should be 120 square feet of office space.

Each file cabinet should be provided 12 square feet.

A computer terminal will require 40 square feet (includes room for a printer) plus proper ventilation and an access point for the cable.

Add 20 percent of the total space generated for internal circulation space, for hall space, restrooms, etc.

Components of clinic space

The space should provide at least the following functional areas:

- reception and waiting room
- exam and treatment room
- restrooms
- recovery and sick room
- nurse's and aide's work room
- private counseling room
- lockable storage and filing room
- laundry area (optional)
- health education room (optional)
- dispensary (pharmacy area)

Number of beds

There should be a minimum of three beds in the sick room of elementary and middle schools with a student capacity of under 500, and a minimum of four beds in the sick room of elementary schools and middle schools with a student population over 500. High schools of any size should have a minimum of three beds. Each bed should be separated by at least a curtain for privacy. There needs to be some portable and private way to isolate the sick students.

Program description

Floor surface should be tile, or any nonskid surface that is able to be cleaned and disinfected regularly.

Clinic entrance and egress should ensure privacy.

Telephone line for direct connection of a telecommunications device for the deaf (to accommodate deaf students as well as deaf parents). If school is already TDD-accessible, this is optional.

Emergency line to school administrative office.

Modem or fax line. Necessary only if there is a computer terminal or fax machine.

If there is more than one computer terminal, there will need to be a controller. The controller will have to be placed in the school's "telephone closet." The controller requires a dedicated 125 volt, 20 amp electrical circuit. The telephone closet must be dry; it must not be a combination phone and mop closet. (Water and computers do not mix.) In the telephone closet, there must be at least a 4' × 4' piece of 3/4" plywood over 5/8" firerock drywall for mounting wiring blocks and connectors for computer terminals.

Windows (very strong recommendation), especially in sick room, work room, and any office. There must be means to cover the windows with blinds or curtains, so that light can be eliminated (for indicated reasons, such as migraine headaches) or privacy assured.

All rooms must be adequately lighted, even though there will be windows. This will assure proper lighting on cloudy days and during nonschool hours.

Central heat and air for proper ventilation; with a thermostat in each exam room to control temperature.

Frost-free refrigerator for ice and medicine storage; electrical outlet and plumbing for ice-making connection for refrigerator. Refrigerator may be standard or under-the-counter size.

The *waiting room* should accommodate fifteen to twenty persons if the health room is to be used to serve the community.

The *nurse's or aide's work room* should be equipped with a telephone, lockable cabinets, and shelving.

The *exam room* should be equipped with an exam table with a paper roll to cover, two rolling exam chairs, an exam light, high-intensity light (to remove slivers, look at rashes, head lice, etc.), height and weight scales, shelving, a lockable supply cabinet, and a sink. Equipment available for exam rooms to include an otoscope, an ophthalmoscope, a stethoscope, and a blood pressure cuff.

The *sick room* must be situated to allow direct sight supervision of sick students, either through line-of-sight or observation window.

The *laundry area* should be equipped with a washer and dryer, electrical outlet for washer and dryer, and drainage for washer (optional).

The *counseling room* should afford visual and acoustical privacy. Although it does not need to be soundproof, it should be designed with sufficient sound absorption materials such as carpets, acoustic tile ceilings, and walls and doors of appropriate thickness. Electrical outlets should be available for vision and hearing testing apparatus. If the counseling room is not to be used for hearing screening, then the *nurse's work room* must also be sufficiently soundproofed in order to perform hearing screenings and must have sufficient electrical outlets for vision and hearing testing apparatus.

The *storage area* should be equipped with lockable filing cabinets and shelving. This area should also accommodate vision and hearing machines and used clean clothing.

The *dispensary and pharmacy area* should be equipped with shelving and lockable cabinets and have easy access to water fountain, cooler, or sink.

Private toileting space, one in elementary school clinics and two (male and female) in middle and high school clinics, with doorways in excess of 30" to allow wheelchair access (5 feet is necessary for turnaround). There must be enough space *and light* to perform a catheterization. There must be a shower. A tub will be necessary only in schools where

provision of physical therapy requires a tub. The shower must be equipped with a hose-type sprayer with a flexible extended nozzle. The shower area must be large enough to accommodate a wheelchair and another person. There must be hot and cold running water at the main sink and in the shower. An exam or procedure table should be located in the bathroom area, for such procedures as urinary catheterization.

Location

If the clinic space is designed to be a component of a larger design of co-located services, the facility should be located to accommodate this design. However, because co-location of health and human services at school sites is intended to support teachers in their work with students, as well as provide direct services to students, the location of the facilities that house these services should be easily accessible to the teachers and other school personnel. It is essential that the clinic staff be perceived by the school faculty as colleagues and part of the professional school team.

Therefore, the clinic space should be adjacent to the student services area and readily accessible to students, teachers, and staff. Ideally, there will be a direct exit to a parking lot, where sick students can be received by their parents or, if the clinic serves the community, where people can enter and exit via the parking lot.

If there are additional services provided in the collaborative, the school health rooms should be adjacent to or near the other social services, because many of the students using the social services will also need health care.

The clinic itself must be in a handicapped-accessible location in the school, preferably on the first floor. If the clinic must be on the second floor, give strong consideration to installing an elevator to transport the sick or injured.

Other

If there are laboratory functions, additional space

and equipment needs will have to be addressed separately.

If there are any built-in shelving or desk units, the remaining space must be sufficient for handicapped accessibility.

Space type: Reading Resource Room

Purpose
Central reading and resource material storage and browsing areas

Size
Minimum 8' × 8'

Requirements
Ample shelving for reading and lending materials

Doorway must accommodate wheelchair access. Interior must allow for turnaround space after shelving is installed.

Lighting should be controllable from within the room.

Space should be equipped with small desk or table, chair, and reading light.

Other
If a reading room cannot be accommodated, the shelving for reading and lending materials should be placed in the meeting and training room.

Space type: Waiting Room

Purpose
Reception area for students, family members, and visitors for scheduled or unscheduled appointments or meetings

Size
There should be a minimum of 100 square feet, with an additional 25 square feet per person times the number of persons to be accommodated in the waiting room at any given time.

Requirements
There should be a comfortable area for students and families waiting to be served in schools offering multiple services. This area may need to accommodate families with infants and young children and the accompanying paraphernalia (baby carriers, diaper bags, toys, etc.).

Changing areas for infants, as needed.

Playroom for young children of families or teen parents receiving services, as needed.

Doorway must accommodate wheelchair access; interior must accommodate wheelchair turnaround.

Lighting should be controllable from within the room.

Comfortable chairs or other seating arrangements.

Part Two: Sample Floor Plans

Elementary School Health Room

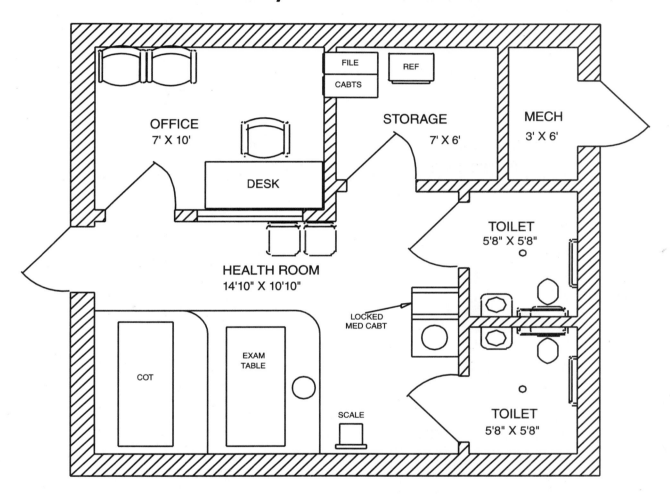

468 sq. ft.

Amspacher & Amspacher • Architects

2003 N. Ninth Avenue

Pensacola, FL 32503

(850) 434-0123

digitized by William Christopher Bruner

Office Building for School Campus

Plan #1

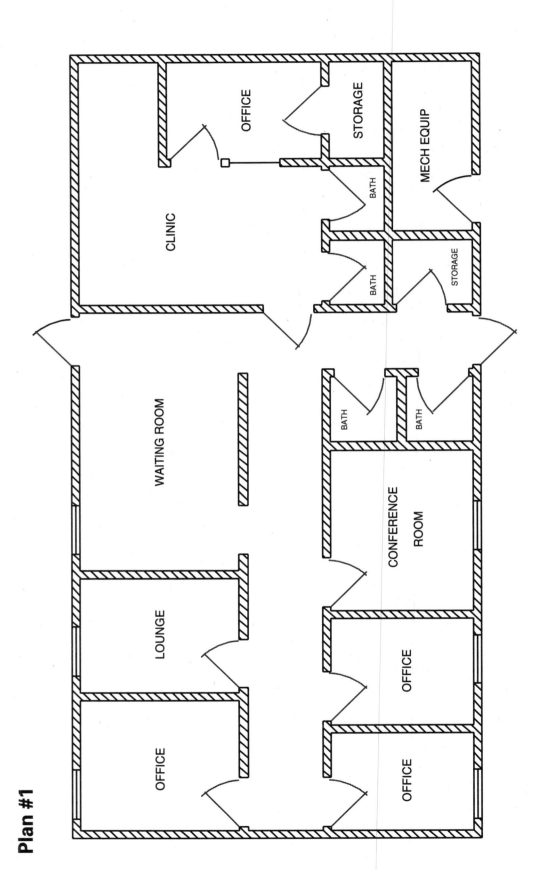

OFFICE

CLINIC

STORAGE

MECH EQUIP

BATH

BATH

STORAGE

WAITING ROOM

LOUNGE

OFFICE

BATH

BATH

CONFERENCE ROOM

OFFICE

OFFICE

Amspacher & Amspacher • Architects
2003 N. Ninth Avenue
Pensacola, FL 32503
(850) 434-0123
digitized by William Christopher Bruner

Office Building for School Campus

Plan #2

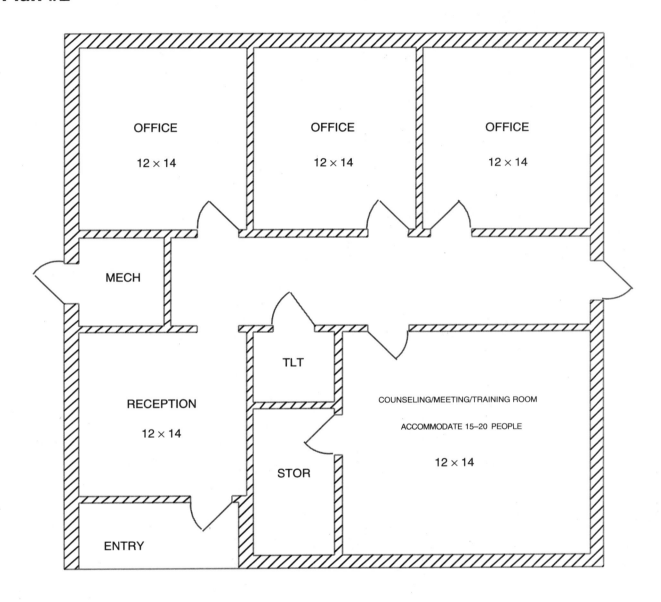

1,400 sq. ft.
Amspacher & Amspacher • Architects
2003 N. Ninth Avenue
Pensacola, FL 32503
(850) 434-0123
digitized by William Christopher Bruner

Office Building for School Campus

Plan #3

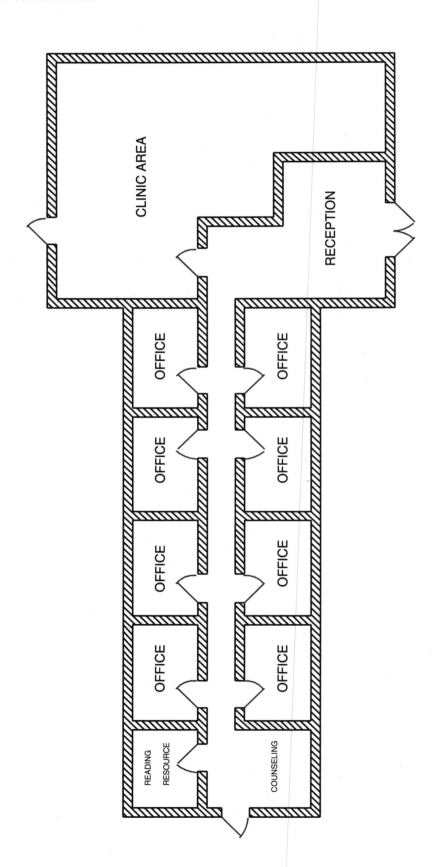

3,000 sq. ft.

designed by Locklin Technical School staff, Santa Rosa County Schools, Florida

digitized by William Christopher Bruner

Office Building/Day Care Center
for School Campus

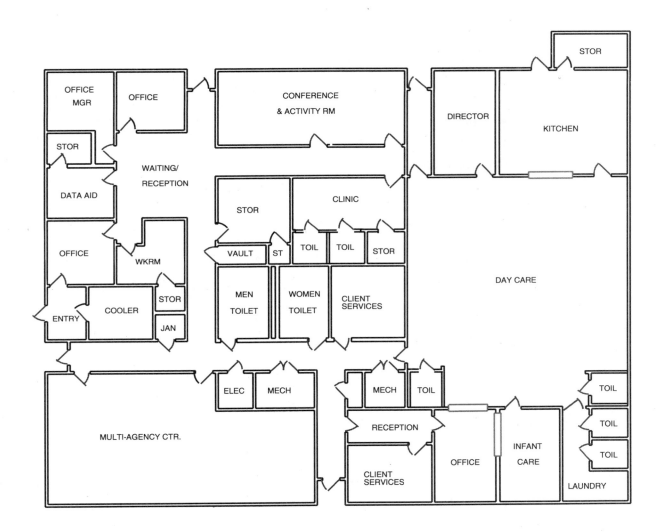

9,116 sq. ft.

Amspacher & Amspacher • Architects

2003 N. Ninth Avenue

Pensacola, FL 32503

(850) 434-0123

digitized by William Christopher Bruner

Satellite Clinic Offices

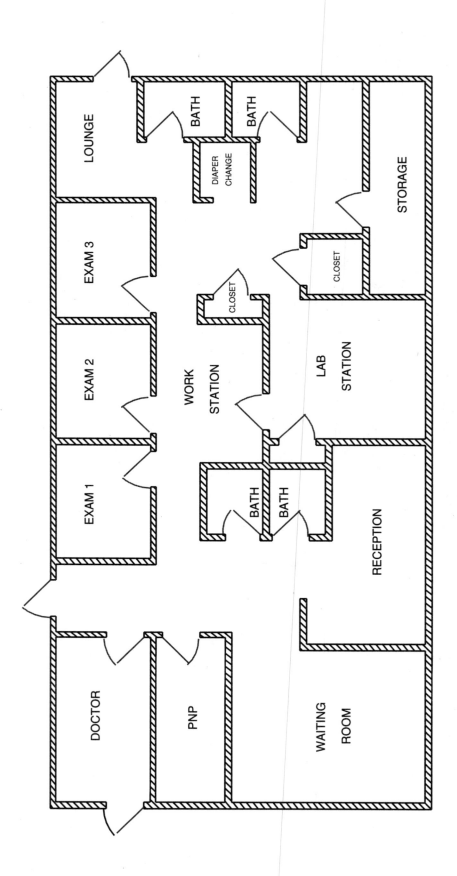

1,800 sq. ft.

digitized by William Christopher Bruner

💾 Part Three: Sample Facilities Agreement

This agreement made between the _____ School Board (hereinafter referred to as the "Board") and _____ (hereinafter referred to as "User");

In consideration of the following mutual promises and conditions, the Board and User agree as follows:

1. The Board grants to the User the temporary use of the facilities described in Exhibit "B," attached hereto and made a part hereof for the purposes, dates, and times set forth on said exhibit. Such use shall be in conformance with and subject to the Board's Use of Facilities Policy and to any Administrative Regulations developed pursuant to such policy.

2. Prior to use of Board's facilities, User shall pay to Board fees set forth in Exhibit "B."

3. User shall conform to the general conditions of use set forth in Exhibit "A" and the additional conditions of use, and other matters, if any, set forth in Exhibit "B."

4. User warrants that all information, including the information set forth in any application for temporary use of the Board's facilities, which User may have given the Board in connection with the use of the facilities described on Exhibit "B," is true, complete, and correct.

5. The agreement shall be deemed dated, and become effective, as of the date on which a duly authorized representative of the Board executes this Agreement, provided such date of execution is later than the date on which the User executes this Agreement.

6. This agreement shall not be assignable or transferable in any manner without the express written consent of the Board.

7. This agreement shall be binding upon the heirs, executors, administrators, successors and assigns of the Board and the User.

Exhibit "A": SPECIAL CONDITIONS

1. The User agrees to provide at its expense public liability and property damage insurance with limits of at least $5,000,000 for injury to any person or persons, including death, and $1,000,000 for damage to property covering the occupancy and use of the demised premises with the Board as an additional named insured, said insurance to be placed in an insurance company authorized to conduct business in the State of _____ and having a Best's Rating of A:VI or better. User shall furnish Board with a certificate or duplicate of such policy or policies attached to the request for facility use. Said insurance certificate shall contain a statement stating that the Board is an additional named insured and that the insurance is not cancelable without first giving twenty (20) days written notice to the Board.

2. All organizations using school facilities shall covenant and agree at all times to save, hold, and keep harmless the Board and indemnify it against any and all claims, demands, penalties, judgements, court costs, attorney's fees, and liabilities of every kind and nature whatever in connection with any injury to or from the use of the premises by anyone occupying or using the same, or arising out of any activity of the User, or due to the installation, operation, or maintenance by the User of any fixtures or equipment in or upon the demised premises or that may be incurred by reason of any default or failure of the User to comply in any respect with the provisions of this Agreement.

3. Risk of any loss to User's property shall be entirely upon User. User may not store any equipment, material, or other matter in Board's facilities without express written approval from the Board.

4. No equipment, material, or other matter that presents a health or safety hazard to persons

or property may be brought upon the Board's facility. The use of open flames, makeshift electrical wiring, flammable, and/or caustic materials and the like is prohibited.

5. All persons using the Board's facility pursuant to this agreement shall confine themselves to the area of the facility for which temporary use has been granted to User.

6. The use of any forms of tobacco, illegal drugs, liquor, profane language, obscene materials or acts, gambling, or violence is prohibited.

7. Food or beverages may not be used without express written approval from the Board.

8. Equipment, material, or other matter owned by the Board may not be used or moved without express written approval from the Board.

9. Prior to the termination of the temporary use, unless other arrangements are expressly approved in writing by the Board, all equipment and material brought upon the facility by User shall be removed and the facility cleaned up and restored to the condition in which it was provided.

10. User shall at all times provide sufficient supervision of its activities to ensure compliance with this Agreement. The Board may, but has no duty to, require additional supervision, including police supervision, as it deems appropriate for protection of the facility and other Board property and to determine User's compliance with this Agreement.

11. Electrical equipment shall not be operated without express written approval from the Board.

12 Use of a facility may be terminated by the Board in the event of any emergency, and breach of this Agreement, or in the event that the facility is required for any Board program that cannot reasonably be held at another time and place.

13. The maximum capacity of the facility, as set forth in this Agreement or as otherwise set forth by the Board, shall not be exceeded.

Exhibit "B"

1. Description of use of facilities: Room #42 in Bldg. 86 may be used during the hours of 7:30 A.M. – 9:30 P.M., Monday through Friday, from July 1, 199_, to June 30, 2002, for the purposes of:

    Parent education classes
    Client interviews, etc.

2. Any fees charged: User will contribute $ _____ per month or assume the cost of the following support expenses: telephones, long-distance calls, paper supplies, office consumables, copy machine maintenance, postage, maintenance, janitorial expenses, etc. (itemized expenses).

3. Additional conditions of use (other than in Exhibit "A"):

Copies of this agreement are on file in:

1. The full-service schools program office
2. Building maintenance department
3. User agency

Signatures (with titles) and addresses

(Include an attorney, signatures of highest-ranking administrative officials, signature of chairperson of interagency group.)

IN WITNESS WHEREOF, the parties hereto, by the undersigned, do bind said parties, set their hands and seal on this _____ day of _____, _____.

NAME OF ORGANIZATION

By:_____

Title:_____

Address:_____

Witness:_____

NAME OF ORGANIZATION

By:_____

Title:_____

Address:_____

Witness:_____

Endnote

1. Interagency Workgroups on Full-Service Schools. *Size of Space and Design Criteria for Facility Spaces Associated with School Health Rooms and the Concept of Full-Service Schools.* Departments of Education; Health and Rehabilitative Services; and Labor and Employment Security, Florida Department of Education, 1992.

Resource F

💾 Community Interaction Survey[1]

Rank the following in order of their effectiveness within your community setting.

1	2	3	4	5
no evidence	in existence but not effective	moderately successful	successful but needs improvement	strength of the community

1. Services should be community-based and community-delivered.

Services and support programs are locally planned, operated, and evaluated with broad public and private community involvement.	1	2	3	4	5
Families and youth are essential partners with professionals in planning and implementing services and programs.	1	2	3	4	5

2. Services should be family-centered; driven by the needs of children, youth, and families; and built on strengths.

Families and providers (and whenever possible, young people themselves) are involved in planning and implementing services that support family independence and strengthen community ties.	1	2	3	4	5
There are current family assessment initiatives in place.	1	2	3	4	5
There are current family-focused initiatives, including programs offering home development specialists or in-the-home services.	1	2	3	4	5
Parent and family involvement is encouraged in all settings.	1	2	3	4	5
Professionals believe in family support planning and the concept of interagency collaboration to meet the needs of students and families.	1	2	3	4	5
Parents take an active role in educational and support activities.	1	2	3	4	5
There is a single point of intake for families to receive information, complete paperwork, and participate in a family-focused plan of delivery for services.	1	2	3	4	5

3. **Needed services should be available and accessible to all in a variety of settings, using a combination of public, private, community, and personal resources.**

High-quality education, health, social, family support, and other services are available to all who need them.	1	2	3	4	5
There has been an attempt to determine which services do not currently exist in the community, and action has been taken to make them available.	1	2	3	4	5
There is evidence of continuity of services. A family entering the service support system does not experience gaps in or barriers to services.	1	2	3	4	5

4. **Services should be culturally competent.**

Programs and staff are responsive to the needs of individuals with disabilities and of culturally, ethnically, linguistically, and economically diverse populations.	1	2	3	4	5

5. **Services should focus on primary prevention, early intervention, and strengthening the ability of children, youth, and families to help themselves.**

There is evidence of high-quality education; a variety of opportunities to accommodate different stages of growth and development; a comprehensive, consistent source of preventive and primary care; and early intervention activities designed around the concept of family support.	1	2	3	4	5

6. **Services should be comprehensive, and a continuum of services should be available.**

There is evidence of a comprehensive continuum of services ranging from prevention and early intervention to individualized, intensive family support services.	1	2	3	4	5
Round-the-clock coverage is available for emergency situations.	1	2	3	4	5
There are existing services that educate families and publicize resources and services.	1	2	3	4	5
There is a centralized information and referral source: a phone line, person, or agency.	1	2	3	4	5

7. **Services should be flexible.**

Services can be adapted to individual circumstances and are provided at convenient times and places.	1	2	3	4	5

Agency personnel in direct contact with children and families are permitted increased flexibility.	1	2	3	4	5
With evidence of increased flexibility, there is also increased accountability for outcome-based results.	1	2	3	4	5

8. Public, private, and community services should be coordinated, integrated, and collaboratively delivered.

There is good interaction among education, health, and human services.	1	2	3	4	5
Does communication exist between the local agencies? (Communication might take place in the form of interagency councils, collaborative funding efforts, attempts to streamline paperwork, etc.)	1	2	3	4	5
There are existing universal data such as screenings, health examinations, and needs assessments available from other sources.	1	2	3	4	5
Contacts with the business community are strong.	1	2	3	4	5
The challenges being faced in the community are leading to creative thinking and cooperation among agencies to solve service coordination problems.	1	2	3	4	5

9. Services should be of high quality and developmentally appropriate.

Staff training is in place to ensure that individuals are fully qualified and know how to work collaboratively to meet the needs of children, youth, and families.	1	2	3	4	5
There is a procedure for periodic reevaluation of services and delivery plans.	1	2	3	4	5
This procedure may be requested by families.	1	2	3	4	5
An evaluation system is in place to ensure the highest standards of service and a focus on desired outcomes.	1	2	3	4	5

10. Services should be cost-effective.

Program accountability and evaluation are focused on the "value" of each service in the delivery system that is effective and efficient.	1	2	3	4	5
There is evidence of streamlining among agencies to promote cost-effectiveness, that is, there are opportunities to conduct referrals between community agencies that will not require	1	2	3	4	5

additional funding; there are collaborative efforts among agencies to provide specialized services such as dental, medical, or mental health services; there are consolidated eligibility criteria set up between agencies to eliminate duplicate paperwork, wasted resources, and duplicate services.

Endnote

1. *Survey of Full-Service School Sites in Florida.* Tallahassee: Florida Department of Education, University of South Florida Institute for At-Risk Children and Their Families, 1993.

Resource G

Funding Sources

Part One: Federal Funding Sources

There are several federal funding sources that could be used to provide funding for a large variety of services on a school site. To tap these sources requires understanding program requirements, creative design of the services to meet requirements, a different kind of school planning, and accurate recordkeeping and documentation to comply with federal billing and accountability standards.

Federal funds come and go with the political wind. The list that follows may give you some general guidelines on where to ask questions about federal funds. Keep in mind that at the time this book was written, there was much discussion of new block-grant funding. These program funds may no longer exist under the names that are used here, but the list helps you think about the categories of funds that may be available to assist in program funding. (See the Annotated Bibliography for an additional resource on block grants. Research current program funding from federal sources in the *Federal Register*, found at local and university libraries, in most public school grants management offices, and on the Internet.)

Category	Description
Alcohol and drug abuse block grant	These grants are based upon a state plan submitted annually pursuant to guidelines established by the Substance Abuse and Mental Health Services Administration, Center for Substance Abuse Services. They address planning, establishing, maintaining, coordinating, and evaluating projects for development of more efficient prevention, treatment, and rehabilitation programs and activities to deal with alcohol and other drug abuse. These are specific set-asides for target populations, including women and children.
Centers for Disease Control and Prevention	Within the Centers for Disease Control and Prevention (CDCP), the Division of Adolescent and School Health (DASH) addresses comprehensive health education, promotion, and services in schools. Funds are distributed to state education departments, several large cities, and twenty national health and education agencies for HIV education and training of health educators. Demonstration grants have been awarded for comprehensive school health programs in four states (Arkansas, Florida, West Virginia, and Wisconsin) and the District of Columbia. Another DASH initiative has been the Youth Risk Behavior Surveillance System. The survey monitors trends in substance use, sexual activity, violence, suicide, depression, and other risk behaviors among students in ninth through twelfth grade. Findings from this survey have been used to support the need for comprehensive school-based services.[1]

Category	Description
Chapter 1, financial assistance to meet special education needs of children; Part A, basic programs operated by local educational agencies	Chapter 1, Part A, provides funds to assist local school districts in meeting the educational needs of educationally deprived children in low-income areas. The population is defined by the local education agencies (LEA) and may include preschool through secondary programs. The funds may be used to fund equipment and instructional materials, books and school library resources, and employment of special instructional personnel. Funds must be used to supplement, not supplant, state and local funds, and the agency receiving the funds must maintain its fiscal effort. Grants are made to the LEAs based on the state's per pupil expenditure and number of children ages five to seventeen inclusive from low-income families, and the number of children ages five to seventeen inclusive living in institutions for neglected or delinquent children.
Part B, Even Start programs operated by local educational agencies	Even Starts are programs to improve educational opportunities of both children and adults by providing family-centered education programs involving parents and children in a cooperative effort to help parents become full partners in the education of their children and to assist children in reaching their full potential as learners. For those who are eligible for participation in an adult basic education program under the Adult Education Act and children (ages one to seven inclusive) of eligible parents.
	Services include identification and recruitment of eligible children and screening and preparation of parents and children for participation, including testing, referral to necessary counseling, and related services.
Part D, programs operated by state agencies, programs for migratory children	Part D provides grants to states to establish or improve, either directly or through local education agencies, programs designed to meet the special educational needs of migratory agricultural workers.
Part D, programs operated by state agencies Subpart 2, programs for handicapped children	Chapter 1 provides grants to sites to assist in delivering special education and related services to children with handicaps, from birth through age twenty, who are enrolled in state-operated facilities and programs. Programs and projects are designed to supplement the special educational needs of children with handicaps or the early intervention needs of infants and toddlers with handicaps. Funds are allocated based on the state's average per pupil expenditure and the number of children with handicaps, from birth through twenty-one, enrolled on December 1. Funds must be used to supplement, not supplant, state and local funds, and the agency receiving funds must maintain its fiscal effort.

Category	Description
Child and Adolescent Service System Program (CASSP)	These grants are based upon a state plan submitted annually, pursuant to guidelines established by the Substance Abuse and Mental Health Services Administration, Center for Mental Health Services. The grant provides for development of a full array of screening, assessment, treatment, and case management services for adults with mental illnesses and children with serious emotional disturbances.
Child care development block grant	The grant program began in 1991. It provides large-scale, direct federal support for child care. Interagency efforts may be able to use this funding for child care services for families at service delivery sites.
Community health centers, Public Health Services Act	Funding to community health centers is based upon annual awards by the Public Health Service. Covered services may include primary health services, supplemental health services necessary for adequate support of primary health services, referral to providers of supplemental health services, and payment for provision of such services. Some states have community health centers that include mental health services.
Comprehensive Child Development Act	This act supports projects that provide intensive, comprehensive, integrated, and continuous supportive services for infants and young children from low-income families.
Department of Agriculture	Among the programs administered by the Department of Agriculture are the Food Stamps Program; the Supplemental Food Program for Women, Infants, and Children (WIC); and the National School Lunch and School Breakfast programs. All assist low-income youth and are managed by USDA's Food and Nutrition Service.
Department of Justice	The Juvenile Justice and Delinquency Prevention Act, administered by the Department of Justice, was revised in 1992 to improve coordination and emphasize community-based programs and services, including family counseling. The department has a large grant program. The Justice Department also administers runaway and homeless grants, which support both street-based and family-based services. To qualify for these grants, providers must demonstrate coordination with health and other service agencies.[2]
Department of Labor	The Employment and Training Administration within the Department of Labor administers the Job Training Partnership Act (JTPA), which allocates funds to states to support job training and summer employment programs for young people. The department also administers a federal Job Corps program, which prepares young people to work in various trades while offering an educational component to program implementation.

Category	Description
Developmental Disabilities Assistance and Bill of Rights Act	Part B of this act provides grants to states for planning, coordinating, and delivery of specialized services to persons with developmental disabilities. The grant does not provide support for direct services. Part C provides grants to protection and advocacy systems. Part D provides grants to university-affiliated programs. The funding provides for interdisciplinary training for persons serving those with developmental disabilities.
Drug-free schools	The Drug-Free Schools and Community Act, enacted in 1986, targets reducing demand or preventing drug use. The program, administered by the Department of Education, allocates funds to states based on a formula that takes into account each state's school-age population and Chapter 1 funding. In each state, half of the grant goes to the state department of education and half to the office of the governor. The grants to state education departments are distributed to local education associations for drug education; substance abuse prevention strategies; and training and technical assistance to teachers, parents, administrators, and law enforcement officials. The governors' portion of the funds can be used to support other types of antidrug abuse efforts by parents' groups, community-based organizations, or other public or private groups.
Education of the Handicapped Act (Individuals with Disabilities Education Act), Part B, preschool grants	Funds are provided to states to encourage provision of special education and related services to all children ages three through five with handicaps. States are eligible only if they provide free appropriate public education to all children with handicaps, ages three to five inclusive. This includes the same services as in other Part B services.
Education of the Handicapped Act (Individuals with Disabilities Education Act), Part B	The purpose of this act is to assist states in providing free and appropriate public education to all children with thirteen specified disabilities, ages three to twenty-one. Funding is based upon the number of children with handicaps served by the site on December 1 of the fiscal year for which funds are appropriated. Services must be provided in the least restrictive environment by qualified personnel and may be provided through classroom instruction, home instruction, and instruction in hospitals and institutions, including private schools and facilities if eligible children are placed there by the state or local educational agency. Services include special education classes, speech pathology and audiology, and physical and occupational therapy. The state may retain up to 25 percent of the state's allocation, to be used for discretionary grants through the state for projects designed to benefit children with handicapping conditions.

Category	Description
Education of the Handicapped Act, Part H	Part H provides assistance to states to develop and implement a statewide, comprehensive, coordinated, multidisciplinary, interagency program to provide early intervention services for infants and toddlers with handicaps and their families. This is based upon a state application that describes the population and the service delivery system. Some states offer coordinated programs between departments of social services and education. The identified population often includes those children with established conditions and developmental delays. Emotional disturbance is considered within the categories. Services include comprehensive screening; development of an interagency family care coordination plan; and services detailed within the plan, including family training, counseling, home visits by professionals, speech-language pathology and audiology, occupation and physical therapy, and case management services.
Head Start program	The Head Start program provides comprehensive health, education, nutrition, social, and other services to economically disadvantaged preschool children and their families. The goals of the program are to assist children to cope with school and attain greater competence, and to enhance parent-child interaction. In addition to the standard model of a five-day-per-week program, home-based models may also be used. The health services component of the Head Start performance standards provides that "for each child enrolled in the Head Start program a complete medical, dental, and developmental history will be obtained and recorded, a thorough health screening will be given, and medical and dental examinations will be performed" (1304.3–1,2 Health Services).
Indian Health Service	The Indian Health Service (IHS) operates health clinics or provides funding to deliver health care to native Americans and Alaska natives.
Mental Health and Child Health (MCH) block grant	In addition to perinatal care, MCH program priorities include development of preventive and primary care systems for pregnant women and children, and creation and expansion of organized networks of comprehensive, coordinated, family-centered services for children with chronic and disabling conditions. The majority of the funds (about 85 percent) are sent directly to states. The remaining 15 percent is reserved for federal grants in research, training, and demonstration projects. Each state receives a predetermined amount, plus an amount dependent on the number of live births in the state and an adjustment for financial need. Funding priorities and eligibility criteria for services are decided by each state. The bureau's Division of Maternal, Infant, and Child Health recently created a separate office for adolescents.

Category	Description
Public Health Services Act, migrant health centers	Provides comprehensive primary health care to migrant and seasonal farmworkers and their families.
Stewart B. McKinney Homeless Assistance Act	Title VI-A is categorical grants for primary health services and substance abuse services for the homeless. Title VI-B provides funds for community mental health services to homeless individuals who are chronically mentally ill.
Substance Abuse and Mental Health Services Administration	The Substance Abuse and Mental Health Services Administration (SAMHSA) in the DHHS Public Health Service has five components: substance abuse treatment; substance abuse prevention; mental health services; and two institutes to examine causes, effects, and most promising treatments for substance abuse and mental health problems. The Center for Substance Abuse Prevention (CSAP) has established new goals: empowering communities, fostering competence, encouraging collaboration, and building comprehensive prevention programs. The CSAP has a large grant program that funds demonstration projects for high-risk youth, operates an information clearinghouse, provides technical assistance to states, and sponsors training for counselors and program administrators. Another grant program, initiated by the National Institute for Mental Health (NIMH) within the SAMHSA, is the Child and Adolescent Service System Program (CASSP). It was designed specifically to improve service delivery for emotionally disturbed children and adolescents.[3]
Title IV-A, Social Security Act, emergency assistance for families	The state submits a plan that defines criteria for determining emergency, income eligibility, population eligibility, and scope of services that can be authorized. The federal funding participation (FFP) is 50 percent of cost, which covers both services and administration costs. Some states define populations as families with children at risk of abuse or neglect and who do not have current resources to pay for needed treatment. Most states establish restrictions on the number of emergencies that may be covered in a twelve-month period and the types of service. The services may be restricted to those available on a statewide basis. The Title IV-A program is the only human services federal entitlement program except emergency Medicaid that does not require proof of citizenship.
Title IV-B, Social Security Act, child welfare services	Funding is based upon federal appropriation and is distributed to states based upon the state's per capita income and population under age twenty-one. The state submits a state plan that defines the population and services. Funds can be used for protective services, personnel, child care agency licensing, assistance in the home, prevention, reunification of families, and return of runaways. Some states cover mental health counseling for children and families under Title IV-B.

Category	Description
Title IV-E, Social Security Act	Title IV-E of the Social Security Act primarily reimburses states for foster care maintenance, but in 1980 it was expanded to include efforts to prevent placement and restore families. The FFP (federal funding participation) for out-of-home maintenance costs is reimbursed at the state's Medicaid matching rate. The FFP is 50 percent for administration and 75 percent for training. Maintenance costs may include food, clothing, shelter, supervision, and related costs for children in licensed family, group, or institutional care. Administrative costs include all "nontherapy" functions of the staff involved with these children. Some states support foster care, shelter care, and transitional independent living programs under Title IV-E. Title IV-E funds are also used to share costs in therapeutic foster and therapeutic group home programs by paying for the nontreatment costs. Depending on the state's plan, some states can fund summer camps, transportation, and day care for children in foster care homes. Title IV-E includes very complex paperwork and federal requirements and is best used for children already involved with the child protective services system. For children in the system, IV-E can be used for preschool, after-school, and summer school, as well as case management. Eligible services could be provided on school grounds.
Title IV-F, Social Security Act, jobs program	Title IV-F was created by the Family Support Act of 1988 (FSA) and provides federal matching funds for the Job Opportunity and Basic Skill Training Program (JOBS). JOBS funding includes the cost of program operation and support services such as child care transportation, tools, and books. Some states target AFDC clients for services. Local and state funds from other state agencies can draw down FFP to provide enhanced education, training, and employment-related services through a contract and memorandum of understanding. Federal regulations require the state to provide some mandatory, and allow for some optional, services. The state plan describes how services will be delivered. Salaries of staff assigned full-time to JOBS activities are matched at a 60 percent federal rate. Other administrative costs, including client transportation, are matched at 50 percent. AFDC-eligible teen parents could be covered for case management and other school-based supportive services.
Title V, Social Security Act, maternal and child health block grant	The grant was established in 1981 as a consolidation of seven programs operating since 1935 designed to serve children and pregnant women. Eligibility for MCH is set by individual states and federal appropriations. MCH block grant funds go to local health departments that could be linked to school-based services. Schools could also apply directly for MCH funds. The state plan describes how services will be delivered. Funds are distributed to states based on the state's proportion of low-income children, ages birth through twenty-one, at a matching rate of 75 percent federal money. Funds may be used to provide health services and related activities, including planning, administration, education, and evaluation activities. States must assure mothers and children access

Category	Description
	to quality maternal and child health services, reduce infant mortality and incidence of preventable disease and handicapping conditions, increase the number of children appropriately immunized, and increase the number of low-income children receiving health assessments and follow-up services. The program must be coordinated with EPSDT. Some states help support public health service clinic services using this funding. Collaboratives could use these funds to provide integration of services.
Title VI, Innovative Education Program Strategies	Title VI supports innovative programs in school improvement and professional development across the curriculum, and fosters instructional innovation.
Title XIX, Social Security Act, Medicaid	Medicaid was created in 1965 through Title XIX of the Social Security Act and is a state-administered program to provide health services to the poor. Each state submits a plan and amends the plan as necessary. The plan establishes income guidelines, definition of medical need and amount, and duration and scope of covered services. Each state sets the criteria for provider certification and enrolls providers. States have a good deal of leeway in putting together a plan. Beyond the core mandated services, states may choose up to thirty-one optional benefits. Case management is an optional benefit offered in many states that could be advantageous to collaborative efforts. States may choose to expand a category known as "rehabilitation services," which are defined as "any medical or remedial services recommended by a physician or other licensed practitioner of the healing arts for maximum reduction of physical or mental disability and restoration of any individual to his best function level" (sec. 4719 of the U.S. Omnibus Budget Reconciliation Act of 1990).
	All states participating in Medicaid must provide EPSDT comprehensive, well-child health care services and medically necessary treatment services to all Medicaid-eligible children birth through age twenty-one. The EPSDT is designed to detect, diagnose, and fully treat children's health needs. Basic benefits include health screening, vision, dental, hearing, and other necessary health care services. EPSDT could be used to finance special education-related services; case management services; and outreach, screening, and health prevention. EPSDT is very flexible and can reimburse for administrative costs as well as specific medical treatments.
Title XVI, Social Security Act, Social Security Disability Insurance (SSDI)	The Social Security Administration is required to give children an individual functional assessment (IFA) to determine whether a child's impairment so restricts his or her ability to engage in age-appropriate behaviors or activities that the impairments are comparable to those that would render an adult disabled. The basic eligibility requirements are a disability (conduct disorder diagnosis is defined as a disability), limited income and resources, and citizenship and residency.

Category	Description
Title XX, Social Security Act, social services block grant	States determine through a plan how services will be delivered. Services may include child care, protective services for children and adults, services for children and adults in foster care, transportation services, and services to special populations such as children with emotional disturbances, etc.
	Administration, personnel training and retraining, conferences or workshops, and purchase of technical assistance may also be provided under the plan. Some states use these funds as cost-sharing funds with children's mental health funds.
	This provides a definite funding opportunity for collaborative efforts. Most services that are offered in an interagency collaborative effort would be eligible for funding under Title XX.
Vocational-technical education programs	The focus of vocational-technical education is to improve the quality of life for youth and adults, individuals and family members, to prepare them to become self-sufficient. This is accomplished through concentrating resources on improving vocational education leading to academic and occupational skill competencies for paid and unpaid employment.

Part Two: State Funding Sources

Every state has a variety of programs available under different categories of service, depending on what the political climate is at the time. Here are some general categories of spending you might explore.

Category	Description
Alcohol, drug abuse, and mental health programs; children's mental health	Funds are usually available for hospitalizing children in need of crisis stabilization; residential treatment services; nonresidential services for an array of home, school, and community-based services; therapeutic services for children in state custody; and children's substance abuse services—residential, nonresidential, and school-based.
Children and families programs	Look for foster care funding, programs that address in-home services for family preservation, group and adoptive care, and subsidized child care. Subsidized child care resources may include state health and human services organizations, prekindergarten initiatives, teenage parenting programs, and federally sponsored programs implemented on a local level (such as the Job Training Partnership Act, handicapped programs, and subsidized before- and after-school programs).
Children's medical services	Diagnosis, evaluation, and intervention services funding is usually available, along with chronic health care funding.

Category	Description
Community-based training programs	There are a variety of programs designed to improve maternal and child outcomes, and to employ and train mothers and fathers from the community as peer support for pregnant women who are medically, socially, or economically at risk. Resource mothers and fathers monitor participants through their pregnancies; provide information on available social, educational, and medical services; and promote awareness of parents' roles as home educators.
Community development grants	Form a community coalition with a broad partnership base (policy advocacy networks; financial partners, such as banks, foundations, equity lenders, government programs); technical assistance agencies (such as housing associations); community organizations; neighborhood cultural centers; parks, museums, and theaters; social and child welfare agencies; health organizations, etc. The coalition can then apply for community development funds from state and federal funding agencies to meet specific program goals.
Department of education funding (e.g., prekindergarten and early intervention programs)	This initiative may or may not be found in the local education association. The programs are designed to assist free-lunch-eligible children, three to five years of age, and their families in a developmentally appropriate program. Other programs place emphasis on families of at-risk children, including families of children with disabilities, through home visitation and parent education models. Most of the prekindergarten and early intervention programs provide funding for parent resource centers that can be school-based.
Department of labor and employment	Programs in this category are aimed at relieving economic distress. In addition to mandatory education and job training services, participants can receive all or some of the following services: health care, child care, transportation assistance, life skills education, counseling, and other services necessary to break the cycle of poverty and welfare dependence. These are usually separate programs, such as Job Corps, that target economically disadvantaged youth. The rehabilitation division of state employment agencies addresses training and job services for individuals with disabilities.
Developmental services	The main area of emphasis is on children with recognized disabilities. Community residential services, funding for diagnosis and evaluation teams, and case management funds are available.
Division of social and human services	There are a variety of names for this agency in different states; generally, this is a large department that oversees social and human services such as drug and alcohol treatment, child abuse and neglect, mental health services, and other programs designed to address the needs of children and families.
Dropout prevention programs	Some states provide funding for at-risk student enrollment in targeted programs that provide alternative educational and social services. Teenage parent programs are often grouped in this category of service. They typically provide transportation, social services, health services, and child care.

Category	Description
Health	Community public health units, primary care funding, and special programs targeting infants and pregnant women are growing in number across the country. In some areas, special emphasis is being placed on collaborative efforts that involve children in public schools. Grants may be available to target high numbers of medically underserved and high-risk students.
Juvenile justice	Funding is rising in the area of residential programs and detention centers, as well as community services. Some states are providing grant opportunities to fund community projects based upon an interagency plan to address crime and delinquency.
Multiagency networks	Some states provide funding for facilitation of network planning and implementation for targeted populations, such as emotionally disturbed students.
Resource systems	Find out whether there are local resource centers that provide support and training opportunities for community service providers and school district personnel. These centers often assist local agencies with identifying, locating, and evaluating children who have disabilities.
Specific funding for collaborative efforts	Call the state department of education and ask whether your state has any specific money targeted for collaborative or interagency efforts. For instance, Kentucky is the site for family resource centers. Florida is the site of full-service schools. These grants provide incentives to schools, departments of social services, and other public agencies to provide integrated health, education, and social services for children and their families. Some states offer a statewide design with a core of mandatory services. Other states provide for locally designed programs. Some states also provide capital outlay money to construct or renovate physical facilities to prepare space for co-located services.
Vocational education	There is funding available in vocational education to provide educational and training services. Vocational education also qualifies for additional federal sources of funding. Vocational funding in your area may be tied to community-based programs stressing education and training for students and adults, guidance, counseling, assessment, juvenile justice and adult offenders, homemaking education, community employment centers, training for individuals with limited English proficiency, career assessment and counseling, child care and transportation, tutor training, and supplemental education services for immigrant children enrolled in elementary and secondary public and private schools.

Part Three: Elementary and Secondary Education Act Funding

[Title XI of the Elementary and Secondary Education Act (ESEA) offers local educational agencies (LEAs) on their own behalf or on behalf of one or more of their schools (or an individual school or group of schools if there is no governing LEA) an opportunity to use up to 5 percent of the ESEA funds they receive to develop, implement, or expand a coordinated services project.]

Office of State and Federal Education
Programs Funding
Division of Public Schools
522 FEC 488-6547
FUNDING OPPORTUNITIES
October 16, 1995

ELEMENTARY AND SECONDARY EDUCATION ACT FUNDING

Title

Coordinated Services Projects

Eligibility

Local education agencies, or in the case of no governing LEA, an individual school or group of schools.

Description

The education department is inviting applications for school districts to use a portion of their federal funds to provide health and social services through a coordinated site at or near a school. Coordinated services link public and private agencies with schools to improve access to health and social services for students and their families, including addressing inadequate or substandard nutrition, health care, and living conditions that adversely affect the ability of children to learn. ED will approve waivers for applicants to use up to 5 percent of all their Elementary and Secondary Education Act discretionary funds (both formula and competitive) in any fiscal year to provide coordinated services. Applicants may not use funds for direct provision of any health or health-related service. This application also applies to waiver of an annual reporting requirement that otherwise would apply to those projects.

Application Date/Deadline

None.

CFDA no.

N/A

Source

September 12 *Federal Register.*

Contact

Compensatory Education Programs, U.S. Department of Education, 600 Independence Ave. SW, Portals Bldg., Room 4400, Washington, DC 20202-6132, (202) 260-1854.

[A list of potential ESEA funding sources follows.]

Part Four: Opportunities for Coordinated Services Projects

1995 ESEA Funds Available to LEAs for Schools for Coordinated Services Projects[4]

Programs for Disadvantaged Children (Title I)

Basic LEA grants	Title I, Part A, Section 1124(a)	CFDA # 84.010
Concentration grants	Title I, Part A, Section 1124(a)	CFDA # 84.010
Set-aside for BIA/outlying areas	Title I, Part A, Section 1121	CFDA # 84.256
Capital expenses for private school children	Title I, Part A, Section 1120(e)	CFDA # 84.016
Even Start family literacy program	Title I, Part B	CFDA # 84.213, 84.214, 84.258
Migrant education	Title I, Part C	CFDA # 84.011
Prevention and intervention programs for children and youth who are neglected, delinquent, or at risk of dropping out	Title I, Part D	CFDA # 84.013
State school improvement	Title I, Part A, Sections 1116 and 1117	CFDA # 84.218

Impact Aid (Title VIII)

Basic support payments	Title VIII, Section 8003(b)	CFDA # 84.041
Payments for children with disabilities	Title VIII, Section 8003(f)	CFDA # 84.041
Payments for heavily impacted districts	Title VIII, Section 8003(f)	CFDA # 84.041
Payments for federal property	Title VIII, Section 8002	CFDA # 84.041

School Improvement Programs

Eisenhower professional development program	Title II, Part B	CFDA # 84.281
Innovative education program strategies	Title VI, Part A	CFDA # 84.298
Arts in education	Title X, Part D	not applicable
Public charter schools	Title X, Part C	CFDA # 84.282
Instruction in civics, government, and the law	Title X, Section 10602	CFDA # 84.123
Magnet school assistance	Title V, Part A	CFDA # 84.165
Women's educational equity	Title V, Part B	CFDA # 84.083
School dropout prevention demonstration program	Title V, Part C	CFDA # 84.201
Foreign language assistance program	Title VII, Part B	CFDA # 84.249, 84.293, 84.294
Safe and drug-free schools and communities: state grants	Title IV, Part A, Subpart 1	CFDA # 84.186
Safe and drug-free schools and communities: national programs	Title IV, Part A, Subpart 2	CFDA # 84.184

Education for native Hawaiians	Title IX, Part B	CFDA # 84.208, 84.209, 84.210, 84.221, 84.296, 84.297
Education infrastructure	Title XII	CFDA # 84.284

Indian Education

LEA grants	Title IX, Part A, Subpart 1	CFDA # 84.060
Special programs for Indian children	Title IX, Part A, Subpart 2	CFDA # 84.061
Special programs for adult Indians	Title IX, Part A, Subpart 3	CFDA # 84.062
National activities	Title IX, Part A, Subpart 4	CFDA # 84.299

Bilingual and Immigrant Education

Bilingual instructional services	Title VII, Part A, Subpart 1	CFDA # 84.003, 84.288, 84.289, 84.290, 84.291
Bilingual support services	Title VII, Part A, Subpart 2	CFDA # 84.194, 84.292
Bilingual professional development	Title VII, Part A, Subpart 3	CFDA # 84.195
Immigrant education	Title VII, Part C	CFDA # 84.162

Education Research, Statistics, and Improvement

Eisenhower professional development: national activities	Title II, Parts A and C	CFDA # 84.168
Technology for education: K–12 technology learning challenge	Title III, Part A, Section 3136	CFDA # 84.302, 84.303
Star schools	Title III, Part B	CFDA # 84.203
Fund for the improvement of education	Title X, Part A	CFDA # 84.215
Javits gifted and talented education	Title X, Part B	CFDA # 84.206
21st-century community learning centers	Title X, Part I	CFDA # 84.287
Civic education	Title X, Part F, Section 10601	CFDA # 84.215

Endnotes

1. Dryfoos, J. G. *Full-Service Schools. A Revolution in Health and Social Services for Children, Youth, and Families.* San Francisco: Jossey-Bass, 1994.

2. Dryfoos (1994).

3. *Integrated Approaches to Youths' Health Problems: Federal, State, and Community Roles.* (Background briefing report). Family Impact Seminars, July 7, 1989, Washington, D.C.

4. Funds may not be available under some of these programs for FY 1995, as some of the programs have been proposed by the U.S. House of Representatives or the U.S. Senate for rescission.

Resource H

Program Evaluation

💾 Part One: Example Goals, Basis for Measurable Objectives, and Suggested Measurements[1]

Goal	Basis for Measurable Objectives	Suggested Measurements
Improve advocacy for children and families	Rates of volunteerism Amount of funding for children's programs	Logs of volunteer hours per program site, documentation of funding received from school, county, and agency budgets
Decrease child abuse or neglect	Rates for program participants (reports to child protective agencies; court decisions; removal of child from biological family) Rates of prevention cases that do not go on to receive intensive intervention from another agency	Logs of caseworker and investigator activities or reports generated by agencies providing services, courthouse records, arrest records, agency logs
Reduce communitywide rates	Teen pregnancy reduction Child abuse and neglect reduction Unemployment Recidivism within the juvenile justice system	Check for existing reports completed on a communitywide system already in place. If none are in existence, set up means for collecting data from census, agency records, vital statistics, and county records.
Improve costs and cost efficiencies	Sources of funding Amount of funding Direct cost of services and personnel Indirect costs of services and personnel Use-of-time studies for individual personnel Rates of use for physical facilities	Document each source of funding with amount. Use cost reports generated at each program site. Standard calculations for all sites for indirect costs of services and personnel. Use time sheets to conduct time-on-task analysis.
Reduce drug, alcohol, and tobacco use	Rates of use decrease Student attitudes toward use Student knowledge of drug effects	Self-report through student survey, rate-of-arrest records, agency logs of referrals, student attitude survey, pretest and posttest design of knowledge gained from instruction.

Goal	Basis for Measurable Objectives	Suggested Measurements
Enhance home environment	Ability to promote child development Safety Enrollment in in-home counseling programs Child-family interaction	Self-report observation by home visitor, medical records, and agency logs.
Enhance community connection	Parental attitudes toward schools and partners Parental knowledge of community services available Rates of community partnership and participation	Self-report agency logs of referrals to other interagency partners, and rates of use of community resources based on agency logs.
Enhance parent-child interaction	Increase in parent participation for at-home and at-school events Improvement in parent-child interaction	Activity logs of at-home and school events, observation, self-report, and family support plan progress goals met.
Improve family education and participation	Parent participation in student-teacher conferences Family satisfaction with services	Logs of conferences, self-reports, and observation.
Improve service utilization	Services offered by partner agencies Services used by participants Referrals to other agencies Services delivered by other agencies Patterns of utilization across different groups of students and parents Comprehensive multiservice delivery plan Utilization rates of automated service directory (hotlines or rates of using computerized access to directory of services)	Record agency reports, program logs, parent interviews, copies of interagency referral forms, evidence of plan and collaborating partners, and computer reports on rate of using computerized access to directory of services.
Improve service availability	Service delivery policy Directory of available services and programs Directory of businesses that support available services and programs Computerized automation of information Installation of directory of services telephone hotline Installation of directory of services computerized access	Record evidence of directories and system for keeping information current, documented progress toward automated information referral system, and logs of referral system.

Goal	Basis for Measurable Objectives	Suggested Measurements
Increase community awareness	Number of media stories on initiative Number of stories on issues addressed by the initiative	Record number of stories covered by each type of media (TV, radio, newspaper, other).
Enhance interagency collaboration	Existence of memoranda of understanding Frequency of meetings among partner agencies Existence of steering committee with representation from partner agencies Partner satisfaction with partner arrangements Existence of waivers to document changes in funding streams Existence of interagency parental consent forms	Archive copies of memoranda, agreements, and consent forms; logs of meeting dates; surveys; documentation of process to obtain waivers.
Increase job placement	Job rates while enrolled in school Job rates after exit (graduation, dropout) Job rates after employability training component Postsecondary job readiness	Record agency records, self-reports, and standardized tests.
Improve mental health	Suicide rates Scores on depression scales Scores on self-esteem scales Satisfaction with services Enrollment in mental health counseling	Record self-reports, medical records, police reports, standardized tests, and agency records.
Improve parental mental and physical health	Suicide rates Scores on depression scales Scores on self-esteem scales Satisfaction with services Enrollment in mental health counseling Blood pressure Cholesterol level Pulse rate Body weight Exercise levels Health education classes	Record self-reports, medical records, police reports, standardized tests, physical examinations, and pretesting and posttesting for educational component.

Goal	Basis for Measurable Objectives	Suggested Measurements
Improve physical health	Diet and nutrition test scores Cholesterol level Blood pressure level Percent overweight Exercise levels Health education class enrollment Health education class grade point averages Health professional available: hours of services, percentage of time in direct contact services Wellness fair with screenings Clinic referrals for sickness and accidents	Record pretesting and posttesting, blood test, physical examination, self-report, agency logs, time and task analysis, and attendance rates.
Increase school achievement	Grade point average Homework completion rates Classwork completion rates Acquisition of computer skills Standardized test scores Absenteeism and attendance rates Promotion rates Dropout rates School reentry rates for dropouts Student attitudes toward school Teacher ratings of student performance Observation of in-class behavior GED completions Vocational education completions Scholarships awarded	Record school records, teacher observation, self-report, pretesting and posttesting, standardized test scores, communitywide indicator reports from vital statistics and census data, teacher ratings, teacher observation, and agency records.
Enhance social skills	Ability to withstand peer pressure (e.g., in role-playing, observations of class behavior, on the playground) Rates of juvenile delinquency Rates of disciplinary referral Rates of corporal punishment Rates of suspension or expulsion	Record observations, communitywide indicators from agency records, vital statistics or census data, school records, arrest records, and court records.

Goal	Basis for Measurable Objectives	Suggested Measurements
Enhance social skills *(continued)*	Rates of suspension or expulsion (violence- or drug-related) Rates of repeat offense	
Streamline procedures	Existence of new, simpler forms Number of family contacts with multiple agencies Time spent waiting for services	Record agency files, program logs, number of contacts families have with multiple agencies, observation, family interviews, time and task analysis.
Improve systems	Safe, orderly environment Program appropriateness Use of volunteers Dissemination of services available Augmentation of paraprofessional personnel (e.g., media specialist, career counselor, nutritionist, etc.) Staff attendance at sensitivity workshops	Record observation with checklist, program logs, self-report, logs of dissemination activities, evidence of new job descriptions, and agency logs.
Prevent teenage pregnancy	Student attitudes toward sex and contraception Student knowledge about sex and contraception Rates of contraceptive use Rates of pregnancy (self-report, clinic report) Rates of repeat pregnancies Live birthrates Weights of newborn	Record self-reports, pretesting and posttesting, vital statistics, medical records, physical examinations, and agency records.
Increase use of extracurricular activities	Use of extended day programs Enrollment in tutorial programs Enrollment in vocational and career counseling programs Enrollment in weekend and vacation programs Enrollment in summer programs Use of adult education opportunities Number of extracurricular activities offered per site	Keep agency logs.

Endnote

1. Adapted from *Survey of Full-Service School Sites in Florida.* Tallahassee: Florida Department of Education, University of South Florida Institute for At-Risk Children and Their Families, 1993.

⊞ Part Two: Teacher Perception Survey

Learning and Social Behaviors Related to School Success

This survey is designed to measure the effectiveness of our full-service school program, based on your evaluation of a student before AND after the full-service school staff has worked with him or her.

For each indicator listed below, place a check mark in the space that most closely matches this student's behavior (5 = always, 4 = often, 3 = sometimes, 2 = seldom, 1 = almost never). If an indicator does not apply to this student, write "N/A"; if you don't know about a particular indicator for this student, write "D/K".

Date: _____

Student's name: _____ Student's I.D. # _____

Your name: _____ Room # _____

1. Pays attention in class				
5	4	3	2	1
2. Practices good listening habits				
5	4	3	2	1
3. Follows directions				
5	4	3	2	1
4. Works well independently				
5	4	3	2	1
5. Completes assignments on time				
5	4	3	2	1
6. Follows school rules				
5	4	3	2	1
7. Gets along well with others				
5	4	3	2	1
8. Works well in a group				
5	4	3	2	1
9. Respects others' rights and feelings				
5	4	3	2	1
10. Claims appropriate share of attention				
5	4	3	2	1
11. Shows self-confidence				
5	4	3	2	1
12. Shows respect for authority				
5	4	3	2	1

13. Is respected and liked by others

5	4	3	2	1

Please add any comments that may help the full-service school staff serve this child:

_____

_____

_____

Resource I

💾 Characteristics of an Effective Evaluation Plan

Assess your evaluation plan with this checklist, to be sure that:

☐ Your plan is outcome-oriented. The questions your evaluation plan answers must be keyed to the program's outcomes for families, individuals, collaborating agencies, and the community.

☐ It is collaborative. It should involve individuals and community agencies at all levels of data collection, analysis, and interpretation. The evaluation plan should be relatively nonintrusive to service providers and families; this is accomplished by using existing data-collection methods and initiating little or no additional paperwork.

☐ It requires multiple-level data collection. The data come from families; component organizations; site information; and states, districts, and counties.

☐ It tracks outcomes. The plan should consider and appropriately include developmental, evolutionary, or longitudinal tracking (over more than a one-year period) of anticipated outcomes in order to assess program effectiveness over time.

☐ It provides for distribution of information. The information to be disseminated must be useful, timely, and relevant to stakeholders at all levels, including program managers.

☐ It establishes measurement. Measures are needed for multiple aspects of the program, including inputs, processes, and outcomes.

☐ It specifies measurement of barriers being overcome. It is important to know the extent to which the program succeeds in service integration, delivery, and collaboration.

☐ It documents how the program is implemented. The plan reveals whether the needs assessment has adequately identified available resources, and how administrative or funding problems are overcome.

☐ It assesses change. The plan requires assessment of change by using baseline data with multiple and repeated standardized measures over reasonable intervals.

☐ It is flexible. The plan has to accommodate likely changes in community resources and personnel.

☐ It focuses on standards. It establishes expectations of multiservice collaborative programs, while valuing the uniqueness of each individual program's contributions.

☐ It contracts for outside evaluation as needed. With a large project, there is likely to be a need for professional, impartial evaluation. The cost of an outside evaluation may average 5–10 percent of the entire budget, unless otherwise specified in the RFP or guidelines.

☐ It displays data effectively. The plan uses figures and tables to display evaluation data as it relates them to program mission, goals, and objectives. Redundant information is sometimes helpful to proposal reviewers.

☐ It stipulates provision of information. It makes explicit what information will be provided and when the information will be available.

Resource J
Sharing Information

⊞ Part One: Consent to Share Information

I authorize the following organizations providing specialized services and cooperating agencies to exchange information related to _____ [student name]. This information will be kept confidential by the receiving organization or cooperating agency. This agreement will expire on _____ [date].

Educational service organizations
Social service agencies
Law enforcement agencies
Mental health service providers
Health care providers

The information exchanged will be used to provide medical, education, and welfare management services in the best interests of the student.

I understand that personal records are protected by various federal and state laws and cannot be disclosed without this, my written consent, unless otherwise authorized. I have received and understand the informational flyer on confidentiality and information sharing.

Consent:

_____	_____	_____
Signature	Relationship	Date
_____		
Name (PRINTED)		
_____		_____
Student signature (optional)		Date
_____		_____
Witness		Date

This form has been sent to:

_____	_____
Agency name	Date
_____	_____
Agency name	Date
_____	_____
Agency name	Date

🖫 Part Two: Informational Flyer on Confidentiality

[Suggested title: *Confidentiality in a Full-Service School*]

Increasingly, public school students are victims of complex social, emotional, health, and educational problems that were unheard of thirty or forty years ago. Children often bring problems to the school setting that make educational success difficult. As these problems increase, schools are becoming increasingly more involved in meeting the needs of children and families.

The full-service school program at your child's school brings health and human services from the community together with educational services in support of children and families.

In order to meet the needs of students and families, it is necessary to share information between these agencies in an attempt to provide the following benefits to you:

1. Ensure that you are getting the help that you need.
2. Ensure that your services are not interrupted.
3. Avoid duplication of services.
4. Reduce the number of times you have to fill out forms.
5. Provide services that are focused on your family's needs.
6. Protect your legal rights.
7. Provide more effective services and programs for you.

It is always important to ensure that the individual's confidentiality rights are protected. Information can be shared within the departments of one agency. Whenever personal information is to be shared between agencies so that you can benefit from additional services, your written consent is required. Only the information that is necessary to provide the services that you need will be released to another agency. Without written consent, your services may be delayed or limited.

We look forward to working with you to meet your needs and those of your family.

Resource K
Interagency Agreements

💾 Part One: School-Based Interagency Agreement

Parts of a School-Based Interagency Agreement

1. *Period of agreement.* The period of the agreement also includes a list of the partners, initiation date, duration, and renewal dates. This section sets the parameters for renewal of the agreement.

2. *Witness section.* The witness section gives the writers an opportunity to document the program's mission and goals using "whereas" statements. Each collaborating agency may want to state its purpose for participating in the partnership.

3. *Services, reimbursement rates, and requirements, if applicable.* If money is exchanged, state the amount; if special personnel qualifications are required, so note. If there is no exchange of money involved, this section may instead ensure a reporting schedule for data collection and evaluation of program outcomes. The type of service is described, along with the hours, locations, any additional revenue sources, reporting requirements, pay schedules, breakdown of expenses, addresses of the provider and the funding agency, and discussion of benefits and travel expenses.

4. *Hiring, supervision, and conflict resolution.* Document how an employee or volunteer will be hired and supervised. What will you do if personnel problems arise, such as poor attendance, inappropriate behavior, or tardiness? Agree to a negotiation process before problems begin. The negotiation process may include an established personnel advisory board, a review and evaluation process, and

a method for recommending removal of personnel who do not work out.

5. *Evaluation.* Document the importance of data collection as part of your full-service school program's ongoing evaluation effort. You may want to specify what types of data must be collected and include a copy of any data collection forms in an attachment to the agreement.

6. *In-kind services.* The funding philosophy for a full-service school promotes use of existing resources. Document the resources that you are not paying for; supervision, screening and referral services, space, and data collection activities are examples of in-kind services that can be documented. Documenting these services in an interagency agreement has the advantage of verifying in-kind services for grant or other funding proposals.

7. *Information sharing and confidentiality.* Collaborating agencies can reemphasize their philosophy or position in recognizing and safeguarding the confidential nature of case records and student information in conformance with all applicable federal and state laws, rules, and regulations. If guidelines have been developed for addressing confidentiality within the full-service school setting, refer to those guidelines in this section. If existing state laws reinforce the notion of sharing information in special circumstances, cite the law.

8. *Insurance.* Specify what liability coverage the collaborating agencies have; include written verification of liability protection if necessary.

9. *Retention of records.* Financial records, supporting documents, statistical records, and any other documents pertinent to the agreement should be preserved for a minimum of three years; some states require a five-year retention period.

10. *Publicity.* All notices, informational pamphlets, press releases, research reports, and other public notices that refer to the full-service school should have the prior approval of one person, one agency, or a representative team from collaborating agencies before release. This process also helps ensure family confidentiality.

11. *Renegotiation and notification.* Document a process for changing any part of the agreement by submitting requests for changes in writing.

12. *Assignment and subcontracting.* Can any portion or services of the program be assigned or subcontracted by either party? If so, establish a process of written notification for major changes.

13. *Civil rights and statement of assurance of nondiscrimination.* Many agreements reinforce equal employment opportunities by referring to Titles VI and VII of the Civil Rights Act of 1964. Depending on which agency has primary fiscal responsibility, this section may be a requirement for the contract.

14. *Indemnification clause.* An indemnification clause is a step toward minimizing liability. This clause is often referred to as the "hold harmless clause."

15. *Termination.* How can the agreement be terminated? We suggest that you provide for termination with or without cause, with a thirty-day written notice to the other party.

16. *Attorney fees.* Standard contracts usually state that a provider of services understands and acknowledges that if PURCHASING AGENCY incurs any expenses in enforcing the terms of this agreement, whether or not a suit is brought, the provider agrees to pay all such costs and expenses, including but not limited to court costs, interest, and reasonable attorney's fees.

17. *Provisions for service.* Use this section to document what will be provided. Office space, utilities, equipment, furniture, clerical supplies, maintenance, telephone installation, and coordination activities are examples of services that may be provided by the agency that is housing the program.

18. *Language and form.* The document is written so that the feeling is very neutral.

19. *Copies of the agreement.* List the recipients of all copies of the agreement to avoid any confusion about who received signed copies.

20. *Signature page.* Include signatures, titles, addresses, and dates. You may want to include the signature of an attorney, all of the highest-ranking administrative officials, and the signature of the full-service school program manager.

Note: Sections may be added to cover such topics as training and staff development, definition of terms, movement of students to and from programs during the school day, or joint administrative functions and procedures.

[SAMPLE] INTERAGENCY AGREEMENT

between

_____

and

_____

1. Partners, initiation date, duration, and renewal: This AGREEMENT made and entered in this _____ day of _____ , _____ by and between _____ , hereinafter called PURCHASING AGENCY, and _____ , hereinafter called the PROVIDER, shall end on _____ , _____. This AGREEMENT may be renewed each year upon mutual agreement by both parties.

    WITNESSETH:

2. WHEREAS, the Full-Service Schools Program exists to stimulate the creation of collaborative partnerships among education, health, and human services providing agencies to more effectively and efficiently meet the needs of children, youth, and their families in support of children's success in school; and

    WHEREAS, the PROVIDER desires to provide appropriate educational and early-intervention opportunities at selected schools (list names) through provision of a prevention specialist to students who may be experiencing family problems related to substance abuse or indications of personal substance abuse;

    Now, therefore, in consideration of the foregoing, the parties agree as follows:

3. Services:

    Note: If there is not exchange of money involved, this section may be included to ensure a reporting schedule for data collection and evaluation of program outcomes.

The maximum amount reimbursable to the PROVIDER by PURCHASING AGENCY under this AGREEMENT shall be _____ dollars ($00,000.00).

   A. Level of expertise: PROVIDER agrees to provide a counselor with qualifications as follows: master's-level education, experienced licensed preferred, but an individual with a bachelor's-level education with appropriate training and experience may fill the position. A particular criterion will be thorough knowledge of community resources.

   B. Types of service: Any one of the following mental health and related services may be provided: individual, group and family counseling, classroom presentations, case management.

   C. Hours, locations: Services will be provided twelve months per year at _____ School on school grounds, in family homes, in community centers, or at appropriate "summer camp" settings. Individual will provide forty hours per week of service with at least five hours scheduled during evening hours convenient for parents. Attendance at Full-Service Schools scheduled meetings may be billed toward weekly hours.

D. It is agreed that Full-Service Schools grant funds shall not be utilized for any service covered by any other funding source. In addition, the PROVIDER shall assess Full-Service Schools clients for fees on the sliding scale as per agency policy. Provider shall keep accurate and complete records of any fee, reimbursement, or compensation of any kind, assessed against or collected from any client or other third party, for any service covered by this AGREEMENT, and shall make all such records available upon demand. PROVIDER shall report such fee, reimbursement, compensation, and funding to PURCHASING AGENCY for such payments received for each unit from all sources to the extent such payments exceed the actual cost per service. This reimbursement may be deducted from PROVIDER's invoices.

E. The PROVIDER shall provide PURCHASING AGENCY with monthly statements reporting hours worked and units of service delivery with signatures from school site employees certifying attendance. PROVIDER may choose to document units delivered in excess of contracted levels and not paid by any other source. The PURCHASING AGENCY shall pay the PROVIDER monthly at an hourly rate of $_____ . [If a rate schedule is used, delineate the service and rate per hour of each service.] The PROVIDER will invoice on a monthly basis by the fifteenth of the month following provision of services. The contract amount per month is for 200 hours; however, units of service so documented may be used to augment subsequent months' billings when service levels are lower than contracted amounts. Written justification for failing to deliver contracted service levels must be submitted with billing whenever this deficit occurs. Adjustments enabling PROVIDER to collect maximum monthly payment(s) for the month(s) showing unit shortages (or hourly shortages) will be made so long as written justification for uneven service delivery is submitted and justification is not in violation of the requirements for delivery of services. Allowable expenditures will include:

A. Salaries and benefits . . . . $_____

B. Materials and supplies . . . . $_____

C. Travel expenses for staff directly involved in this program . . . . $_____

D. Postage . . . . $_____

NOTICES, AUTHORIZATIONS, BILLINGS, AND REPORTS or any other documentation required by this agreement to be provided by one party to the other shall be sent as follows:

Full-Service Schools Program Office

[address]

F. The PROVIDER shall bear responsibility for all financial, clerical, and administrative duties in hiring the professional staff, and PURCHASING AGENCY shall not be billed if a position is vacant and equivalent coverage is not provided.

G. The PROVIDER will provide all personnel with salary and benefits, and pay the employer's match of FICA. If travel expenses are reimbursable via this agreement, documentation must comply with state statute.

4. Hiring and Supervision. To assist in ongoing interagency coordination, an administrative representative from the Full-Service Schools department of the school board will be available to co-interview potential employees for the position. All final applicants in the interview process will participate in an interview with the school site administrator before formal employment. The job performance of the worker will be evaluated each semester by the PROVIDER supervisor with the input of the principal at

the school site assigned. The PROVIDER supervisor and the coordinator of the Full-Service Schools project agree to meet as often as needed to solve mutual problems and plan for future operations.

5. Evaluation. Accurate and timely documentation and other requested information as required by the Full-Service Schools Program shall be considered a factor in evaluating future funding requests. Invoices and/or documentation returned to PROVIDER for corrections shall be cause for delay in receipt of reimbursement.

6. In-kind services documented. Consistent with the mission of the Full-Service Schools Program, the PROVIDER has agreed to IN-KIND services, including but not limited to the following:

    (a) Clinical supervision, training, and administrative management of professional staff (valued at $_____ per contract period).

    (b) Screening and referral of Full-Service Schools clients for any of the range of services offered by the Full-Service Schools network, such as counseling for truancy and runaway students, twenty-four-hour crisis line counseling, case management, economic services, etc. (valued at $ _____ per contract period).

    (c) Attendance and participation in the Full-Service Schools oversight council meetings.

    (d) Ongoing collaboration with PURCHASING AGENCY in endeavors to improve and expand the Full-Service Schools concept.

    (e) Ongoing collaboration with PURCHASING AGENCY to collect data, evaluate, and report on services provided. Information will include goals listed in treatment plan documents, number of services offered by category, and the percentage of students seen in prevention services who are not subsequently referred for significant at-risk behaviors.

7. Information sharing. The Parties shall recognize and safeguard the confidential nature of case records and student information in conformance with all applicable federal and state laws, rules, and regulations and both Parties' policies pertaining to the right of privacy of parents, guardians, and students. PROVIDER and PURCHASING AGENCY agree to abide by the "Guidelines for Confidentiality" document developed by the Full-Service Schools oversight council. [See Confidentiality Guidelines in Resource J for additional details.]

8. Insurance. The PROVIDER shall furnish PURCHASING AGENCY with written verification of liability protection prior to final execution of said AGREEMENT.

9. Retention of records. The PROVIDER shall preserve and make available all financial records, supporting documents, statistical records, and any other documents pertinent to this AGREEMENT for a period of three (3) years after termination of the term of service specified; if any audit has been initiated and audit findings have not been resolved at the end of those three (3) years, the records shall be retained until resolution of the audit findings.

10. Publicity. All notices, informational pamphlets, press releases, research reports, and other similar public notices that refer to the collaboration must have prior approval, by [time] prior to publication and release. Family confidentiality will be provided for at all times in any publications.

11. Renegotiation. This AGREEMENT contains the entire understanding between the parties regarding the matters contained herein, and no amendment or modification to this AGREEMENT shall be valid unless in writing and signed by all parties.

12. Assignment and subcontracting. No portion of this AGREEMENT may be assigned or subcontracted by either party without the affected party's prior written authorization.

13. Titles VI and VII, Civil Rights Act of 1964. Both Parties shall comply with the provision of Title VI and VII of the Civil Rights Act of 1964 and all other federal laws applicable to equal employment opportunity.

14. Indemnification clause. Any PROVIDER agrees to be fully responsible for its acts of negligence, or its agents' acts of negligence when acting within the scope of their employment or agency, and agrees to be liable for any damages resulting from said negligence. Nothing herein is intended to serve as a waiver of sovereign immunity by any PROVIDER to which sovereign immunity may be applicable. Nothing herein shall be construed as consent by a state agency or political subdivision of the state of _____ to be sued by third parties in any matter arising out of any contract.

15. Termination. This AGREEMENT may be terminated by either party at any time, with or without cause, upon thirty (30) days' written notice to the other party. In the event of termination, PROVIDER shall be paid for services rendered under this contract prior to termination. PURCHASING AGENCY shall be the final authority as to availability of funds and allocation of available funds among providers. PURCHASING AGENCY reserves the right to terminate the services covered by this AGREEMENT with a two-week notice in the event funds are unavailable or if a minimum enrollment of twenty-five students is not maintained in the program.

    If the PROVIDER fails to provide services called for by this AGREEMENT within the time specified herein or any extension thereof, or if the PROVIDER fails to perform any of the other provisions of this AGREEMENT, PURCHASING AGENCY may, by written notice of breach to the PROVIDER, terminate this AGREEMENT. Termination shall be upon no less than twenty-four (24) hours' notice, in writing, delivered by registered mail with return receipt requested, or in person, with proof of delivery to the address specified in the agreement.

16. Attorney fees. The PROVIDER understands and acknowledges that if PURCHASING AGENCY incurs any expenses in enforcing the terms of this AGREEMENT, whether the suit be brought or not, PROVIDER agrees to pay all such costs and expenses including, but not limited to, court costs, interest, and reasonable attorney's fees.

17. PURCHASING AGENCY agrees to:
    (a) Provide office space within the Full-Service School building to accommodate staff for the program's services.
    (b) Provide utilities, equipment, furniture and clerical supplies, interior and exterior building maintenance, and telephone installation costs for the program site.
    (c) Provide administrative staff who will assist in direction and coordination of the program's operation.

18. Language and Form. The form or any of the language contained in this AGREEMENT shall not be interpreted or construed in favor of or against either party hereto as the drafter thereof.

19. Copies of the AGREEMENT. Copies shall be placed on file and be available in the office of:
    1. The Full-Service Schools Program
    2. Director of finance
    3. The PROVIDER agency

20. Signatures (with titles) and addresses. (Include an attorney, signatures of highest-ranking administrative officials, signature of chairperson of interagency group.)

IN WITNESS WHEREOF, the Parties hereto, by the undersigned, do bind said Parties, set their hands and seal on this _____ day of _____ , _____.

NAME OF ORGANIZATION

By _____

Title _____

Address _____

Witness _____

NAME OF ORGANIZATION

By _____

Title _____

Address _____

Witness _____

💾 Part Two: Community-Based Interagency Agreement

Parts of the Community-Based Interagency Agreement

This alternative form of an interagency agreement is used to document the ways in which the agencies collaborate to provide services. The form begins with the same documentation as the School-Based Interagency Agreement: give the document a title, state the purpose (or mission statement) of the full-service school effort, list the partners involved, and date the agreement.

The next part of this agreement concentrates solely on the collaborative effort. The writers choose four or five objectives around which collaboration will take place. Examples of these specific objectives are administrative, policy, or technological changes. Some other examples include policy changes that could modify eligibility rules, setup of a central referral process, or application for state and federal waivers to expedite service delivery. Administrative changes could include applying flexible wraparound funding to services for a target population or establishing a trust fund to ensure flexibility in expenditure. The group may want to develop ways to better use existing resources, such as establishing a toll-free hotline for information, setting up joint eligibility and screening tools, and using more effective case management strategies through multidisciplinary team staffing and family support plan meetings. Collaborators may want to include a major technological project such as tracking families who are receiving services from the program through a computerized comprehensive service delivery system.

The interagency agreement is the mechanism to document each collaborating agency's participation in the full-service school's specific objectives. For example, if your full-service school decides to improve the screening process for families, part of the document may read:

Together we will:
Collaborate to determine developmentally appropriate screening tools and procedures, train our individual staff members in administering the screening, decide on mutually agreeable dates and procedures for screenings, conduct the screenings as appropriate, obtain parental consent with the use of the interagency Consent to Share Information form, and share screening results among agencies.

(See Resource J for a sample of the Consent to Share Information form.) After deciding on the specific objective for the interagency agreement (in this case, improving the screening process), the collaborators begin to collect specific information. What types of screening are being done? When are screenings conducted? What is the purpose for each screening? What types of screening tools are being used? The more specific the information, the more opportunity collaborators will have to identify common ground.

The next section of the interagency agreement documents what each individual agency will do toward the specific task of improving the screening process. For example, a public health unit may document its participation with the following statements:

The Public Health Unit will:
Conduct early and periodic screening, diagnosis, and treatment (EPSDT) screenings on Medicaid-eligible children to include a health and developmental history; physical examination; nutritional and developmental assessment; routine immunizations; laboratory tests; health education; and vision, dental, and hearing screenings. If a problem is identified, Medicaid providers can arrange for treatment. With parental permission, screening results will be reported to other appropriate collaborating agencies.

The last part of the agreement could include general statements about the collaborative effort. This is an opportunity for collaborating partners to document their beliefs (see Chapter Four). Examples of these beliefs may include the value of the family unit to the community, expanding the communication process among collaborating agencies, developing joint funding opportunities that target prevention and early intervention, and protecting confidentiality of information. As each member of the full-service school program signs and dates the agreement, the document becomes a powerful symbol of how individuals working together can make the world a better place for families. The family support plan is central to the idea of a full-service school, developing a family-centered prevention and early intervention system. The following principles form the foundation of the family support plan and reinforce the full-service school's central theme of strengthening the family unit.

1. Family-driven collaboration makes the family an active participant with community agencies in planning and making decisions about participation in the full-service school program.

2. Respect for and acceptance of each family's unique structure, roles, values, beliefs, and coping style are cornerstones of an effective program.

3. Intervention strategies must respect the racial, ethnic, and cultural diversity of families.

4. Family autonomy, independence, and decision making must be respected; family members must be able to choose the level and nature of the community's involvement or intervention in their life.

5. Services should be flexible, accessible, and responsive to family needs.

6. Services must be provided in as normal, humane, and empowering a fashion and environment as possible, promoting the family's integration into the community.

7. Because no one agency or discipline can meet the diverse and complex needs of children and their families, a team approach to planning and implementing the family support plan is necessary, requiring equal involvement by the family and community agencies.

8. Services are based on a holistic approach to answering families' needs, integrating educational, medical, and social services; ensuring continuity and appropriate intensity; and eliminating duplication of effort.

9. Whenever possible, families should receive the support necessary to maintain their children at home (in a family unit). Family supports should build on existing informal networks and natural sources of support.

10. A team of community agency professionals and family members will collect information in accordance with established confidentiality guidelines in order to make decisions regarding eligibility and intervention strategies.

[SAMPLE] COMMUNITY-BASED INTERAGENCY AGREEMENT

FULL-SERVICE SCHOOLS PROGRAM

Collaborating Partners:

Children's Medical Services	Children's Learning Place
_____ School District	Retired Senior Volunteer Program
Head Start	Family Network
Public Health Unit	

PURPOSE

The Full-Service Schools Program exists to stimulate creation of collaborative partnerships among education, health, and human services providing agencies to more effectively and efficiently meet the needs of children, youth, and their families in support of children's success in school. The intent of this agreement is to document an interagency planning process to identify target groups of children, youth, and families to be served based on need; identify significant health, social, and economic problems facing families; identify services that families need and want; identify areas of duplication of effort and gaps between services among agencies; and identify barriers to receiving services within the families and within the agencies providing services.

The intent of this agreement is to clarify agency roles and responsibilities in the process of streamlining access to services in the areas of screening, referral, assessment, family support planning, service delivery, and transition planning for children from birth through age seven and their families.

SCREENING AND REFERRAL

Together we will:

- Develop and update an interagency Consent to Share Information form with accompanying parental informational pamphlet for the purpose of obtaining consent from parents or guardians to exchange information between service agencies.

- Collaborate to determine developmentally appropriate screening tools and procedures, train our individual staff members in administering the screening, decide on mutually agreeable dates and procedures for screenings, conduct the screenings as appropriate, obtain parental consent with the use of the interagency Consent to Share Information form and share screening results among agencies. (See Resource J for a sample of the Consent to Share Information form.)

The Public Health Unit will:

Conduct early and periodic screening, diagnosis, and treatment (EPSDT) screenings on Medicaid-eligible children to include a health and developmental history; physical examination; nutritional and developmental assessment; routine immunizations; laboratory tests; health education; and vision, dental, and hearing screenings. If a problem is identified, Medicaid providers can arrange for treatment. With parental permission, screening results will be reported to other appropriate collaborating agencies. (For example, if the child is 2½ to 5 years of age, results will be reported to Children's Medical Services.)

Children's Medical Services will:

Conduct developmental screenings for children age 2½ to 5 years of age using the Dial-R or other instruments as appropriate. These will include vision and audiometric screenings and will be documented year-round with the exception of July, dependent on continued funding. Screenings will be conducted in the agency's office, on school campuses, and/or in homes. With parental permission, results will be reported to other appropriate collaborating agencies.

ASSESSMENT

Together we will:

- Cooperate to ensure that parents are involved in the evaluation and assessment process of each child.
- Cooperate to develop a joint eligibility form between programs to ensure that duplication of efforts will be eliminated or minimized to the fullest extent possible in conducting evaluations and assessments on children and families for the purpose of determining eligibility and need for services.

Children's Medical Services will:

Apply for a state waiver in order to accept one or more of the school system's assessment instruments, including but not limited to the Arizona Articulation Profile, Preschool Language 3, REEL, or Nonspeech Assessment as accepted assessment tools to determine eligibility for the Children's Medical Services program.

Children's Learning Place will:

- Conduct multidisciplinary evaluations on children referred to determine eligibility for early intervention services.

MULTIDISCIPLINARY TEAM STAFFING AND FAMILY SUPPORT PLANS

Together we will:

- Participate in family support plan meetings for families of children referred to or receiving services among collaborating agencies.

TRANSITION PLANNING

Together we will:

- As part of the family support plan process, develop individualized transition plans for children receiving services and transitioning to other services among collaborating partners.

The School District will:

- Review referrals from collaborating partners who are serving children age two years, six months, to determine eligibility for services for the school system's preschool program at age three.
- Meet with the families of transitioning students.
- Facilitate a meeting between parent, child, sending teacher, and receiving teacher for children age two years, eleven and a half months, who are entering the prekindergarten program.
- Work collaboratively with partners to provide services for children who do not meet eligibility criteria.

Children's Learning Place will:

- Forward Children's Learning Place referral forms and transition packets to the school.
- Meet with the families of transitioning students.
- Facilitate a meeting between parent, child, sending teacher, and receiving teacher for children age two years, eleven and a half months, who are entering the prekindergarten program.
- Work collaboratively with partners to provide services for children who do not meet eligibility criteria for the school system prekindergarten program for their children age two years, six months, who will be transitioning.

GENERAL AGREEMENTS

[See Chapters Three, Four, and Six]

- Members of the Full-Service School Program value the family unit in our community and agree that families are the primary resource for children.

- There will be ongoing and expanded communication among collaborating partners to ensure collaborative efforts. Whenever possible, joint funding opportunities that target prevention and early intervention services for families will be pursued.
- Collaborating partners agree to abide by state and federal laws and procedures to ensure confidentiality of information.

Note: Collaborating partners may wish to add clarifying language for interagency sharing of information and confidentiality guidelines.

_____

Resource L

Family Services Program Tools

🖫 Part One: Family Needs Assessment[1]

Name of person completing form: _____

Relationship to child: _____ Date: _____

Parents and guardians of children have many different needs. Not all parents need the same kinds of help. For each of the needs listed below, please check (✓) the space that best describes your need or desire for help in that area. Although we may not be able to help you with all your needs, your answers will help us connect you to community resources.

	I really need some help in this area.	I'd like some help, but my need is not that great.	I don't need any help in this area.
1. Someone who can help me feel better about myself			
2. Help with child care or after-school and summer supervised activities			
3. More money or financial help			
4. Someone who can baby-sit for a day or evening so I can get away			
5. Better medical care for my child or another member of the family			
6. More information about child development			
7. More information about behavior problems			
8. More information about programs that can help my child (educational, health, social)			
9. Counseling to help me cope with my situation better			
10. Day care so I can get a job			
11. Information about adult education opportunities			
12. Information about job training and employment opportunities			
13. A bigger or better house or apartment			
14. More information about how I can help my child with a specific problem			
15. More information about nutrition or feeding			
16. Learning how to handle my other children's jealousy of their brother or sister			
17. Help with how to deal with problems with in-laws or other relatives			
18. Help with how to deal with problems with friends or neighbors			

	I really need some help in this area.	I'd like some help, but my need is not that great.	I don't need any help in this area.
19. Special equipment to meet my child's needs			
20. More friends who have a child like mine			
21. Someone to talk to about my problems			
22. Problems with my spouse			
23. A car or other form of transportation			
24. More time for myself			
25. More time to be with my child			

Please list any needs we have forgotten:

26.

27.

28.

29.

💾 Part Two: Family Support Scale[2]

Name: _____ Date: _____

Listed below are people and groups that often are helpful to members of a family raising a child. This questionnaire asks you to indicate how helpful each person or group of people is to *your family*. Please *circle* the response that best describes how helpful the sources have been to your family during the past *three to six months*. If a source of help *has not been available* to your family during this period of time, circle the NA (not available) response.

How helpful has each of the following been?	NA Not Available	1 Seldom Helpful	2 Sometimes Helpful	3 Generally Helpful	4 Very Helpful	5 Extremely Helpful
1. My parents	NA	1	2	3	4	5
2. My spouse's or partner's parents	NA	1	2	3	4	5
3. My relatives	NA	1	2	3	4	5
4. My spouse's or partner's relatives	NA	1	2	3	4	5
5. Spouse or partner	NA	1	2	3	4	5
6. My friends	NA	1	2	3	4	5
7. My spouse's or partner's friends	NA	1	2	3	4	5
8. My own children	NA	1	2	3	4	5
9. Other parents	NA	1	2	3	4	5
10. Neighbors	NA	1	2	3	4	5
11. Coworkers	NA	1	2	3	4	5
12. Parent groups	NA	1	2	3	4	5
13. Social groups or clubs	NA	1	2	3	4	5
14. Church members or minister	NA	1	2	3	4	5
15. My family's or child's physician	NA	1	2	3	4	5
16. Intervention program for special needs	NA	1	2	3	4	5
17. School or day care center	NA	1	2	3	4	5
18. Professional helpers (social workers, therapists, case managers, teachers, etc.)	NA	1	2	3	4	5
19. Finding someone to talk to about my child	NA	1	2	3	4	5
20. _____	NA	1	2	3	4	5
21. _____	NA	1	2	3	4	5

💾 Part Three: Family Needs Scale[3]

Name: _____ Date: _____

This scale asks you to indicate if you have a need for any type of help or assistance in a variety of different areas. Please circle the response that best describes how you feel about needing help in those areas. At the end of the exercise, you will be asked to put a star next to those areas you feel most strongly about.

To what extent do you feel the need for any of the following types of help or assistance?	NA Not Applicable	1 Almost Never	2 Seldom	3 Sometimes	4 Often	5 Always
1. Having money to buy necessities and pay bills	NA	1	2	3	4	5
2. Budgeting money	NA	1	2	3	4	5
3. Paying for special needs of my children	NA	1	2	3	4	5
4. Saving money for the future	NA	1	2	3	4	5
5. Having clean water to drink	NA	1	2	3	4	5
6. Having food for three meals a day for my family	NA	1	2	3	4	5
7. Having time to cook healthy meals for my family	NA	1	2	3	4	5
8. Feeding my child	NA	1	2	3	4	5
9. Getting a place to live	NA	1	2	3	4	5
10. Having plumbing, lighting, and heat	NA	1	2	3	4	5
11. Getting furniture, clothes, and toys	NA	1	2	3	4	5
12. Completing chores, repairs, and home improvements	NA	1	2	3	4	5
13. Getting a job	NA	1	2	3	4	5
14. Having a satisfying job	NA	1	2	3	4	5
15. Planning for a future job for my child	NA	1	2	3	4	5
16. Getting where I need to go	NA	1	2	3	4	5
17. Getting in touch with people I need to talk to	NA	1	2	3	4	5
18. Transporting my child	NA	1	2	3	4	5
19. Finding someone to talk to about my child	NA	1	2	3	4	5
20. Having someone to talk to	NA	1	2	3	4	5
21. Having medical and dental care for my family	NA	1	2	3	4	5
22. Having time to take care of myself	NA	1	2	3	4	5
23. Having emergency health care	NA	1	2	3	4	5

To what extent do you feel the need for any of the following types of help or assistance?	NA Not Available	1 Almost Never	2 Seldom	3 Sometimes	4 Often	5 Always
24. Finding special dental and medical care for my child	NA	1	2	3	4	5
25. Planning for future health needs	NA	1	2	3	4	5
26. Managing the daily needs of my child at home	NA	1	2	3	4	5
27. Caring for my child during work hours	NA	1	2	3	4	5
28. Getting respite care for my child	NA	1	2	3	4	5
29. Getting therapy or special services for my child	NA	1	2	3	4	5
30. Having time to take my child to appointments	NA	1	2	3	4	5
31. Exploring future educational options for my child	NA	1	2	3	4	5
32. Expanding my education, skills, and interests	NA	1	2	3	4	5
33. Doing things that I enjoy	NA	1	2	3	4	5
34. Doing things with my family	NA	1	2	3	4	5
35. Participation in parent groups or clubs	NA	1	2	3	4	5
36. Traveling or vacationing with my child	NA	1	2	3	4	5
37. Having emergency child care	NA	1	2	3	4	5

Now put a star next to the needs that you feel most strongly about.

Endnotes

1. Adapted from Dunst, C. J., Trivette, C. M., and Deal, A. G. *Enabling and Empowering Families: Principles and Guidelines for Practice.* Cambridge, Mass.: Brookline, 1988.

2. Dunst, Trivette, and Deal (1988).

3. Dunst, Trivette, and Deal (1988).

💾 Part Four: Family Care Coordination Plan

(The plan may be modified each time the family care coordination team meets with the family, *if* the family chooses to make changes.)

1. Background Information

   A. Initial information

   Primary referral on (child or person initially referred): _____

   Nickname: _____ or other names known by: _____

   Date of birth: _____ Age: _____

   Ethnic background: _____ Type of interpreter services needed: _____

   Primary language in home: _____

   Social Security no.: _____

   Address: _____

   _____

   Health insurance company: _____ Policy no.: _____

   Medicare no.: _____

   Student no.: _____

   Disabilities: _____

   Phone number: _____

   Address and directions to home: _____

   _____

   Transportation: ☐ self ☐ bus ☐ taxi ☐ walk ☐ none ☐ volunteer ☐ other

   Parent's name: _____ Mother's maiden name: _____

   Parent's name: _____ Guardian's name: _____

   Caregiver (if other than parent or guardian): _____

   Family status: ☐ migrant farmworker ☐ temporary resident ☐ permanent resident

   Caregiver's place of employment: _____

   Programs or agencies currently involved with child, family, or individual (include educational, medical, social, and human services agencies):

   _____

   _____

   B. Referral information

   Referral date: _____ Referral source: _____

   Family care coordination plan date: _____

   Review dates: _____ _____ _____

Names of family members	Relationship	Age	Date of birth
_____	_____	_____	_____
_____	_____	_____	_____

2. Family Care Coordination Team Members

Role	Name, Program, and Address	Phone No.
1. _____	_____	_____
2. _____	_____	_____
3. _____	_____	_____
4. _____	_____	_____
5. _____	_____	_____
6. _____	_____	_____
7. _____	_____	_____
8. _____	_____	_____
9. _____	_____	_____
10. _____	_____	_____

3. Reason for Referral

In your family's own words:

4. Family Strengths

Based on the family support scale, the social support scale, and the child needs scale, what are the strengths of your family unit?

5. Family Needs

Based on the family support scale and the family needs assessment, what are your main concerns and priorities for your family?

Concern	Summary of Present Status
e.g., son's grades	Failing 3 subjects
_____	_____
_____	_____

6. Goal Setting

What do you want for yourself? for your child? for your family? What are your short-term goals for your family? What are your long-term goals for your family?

7. Steps to Reach Goals

How can your family reach those goals?

Action and Resources: What needs to happen to reach this outcome? Who is responsible?	Description of Resource or Service In what ways will this happen?	Evaluation How will we know if the goal is reached?
_____	_____	_____
_____	_____	_____
_____	_____	_____
_____	_____	_____
_____	_____	_____

8. Signature of Agreement

The members of my family care coordination team have supported me in developing this plan, and I agree to the provisions of the plan.

Signed: _____

Date: _____

Witness: _____

Family Care Coordination Plan Meeting Attendees

Meeting Date	Signature	Agency	Phone No.
_____	_____	_____	_____
_____	_____	_____	_____
_____	_____	_____	_____
_____	_____	_____	_____
_____	_____	_____	_____

The family care coordination team members will review my plan on:

date: _____ time: _____ place: _____

Resource M
Examples of Training Topics

1. Building trust and commitment over time

2. How to respond if the public misunderstands your agenda:

   a. "Yes, you may be right."

   b. Identify some common ground to begin the conversation.

   c. Remain calm, cool, and collected!

   d. Take the advice offered.

   e. Use the media to respond.

3. Selecting your battles

4. How to include malcontents as stakeholders and "turf guarders"

5. The art of accepting some pieces as negotiable

6. Don't assume your own folks aren't part of the problem!

7. Know your information sources. Recognize informal and formal mechanisms for communication. For example, bus drivers, secretaries, and janitors are major sources of information about school for parents.

8. How to design your program with consensus, gradually build stakeholder involvement, create continuity, and constantly *revise*

9. How to redesign your program to accommodate changes

10. Choosing an independent evaluation and evaluator

11. Using a third party as a negotiator

12. Invite them in and invite them to be honest: how to conduct focus group discussions

13. Knowing and dealing with the malcontents: offering the choice of nonparticipation

14. Educating the public: telling the truth, good or bad, and building trust on facts and handouts

15. Sticking to parliamentary procedure during meetings to allow a controlled forum of discussion

16. Dealing with questionable practices (examples: individuals tying up fax machines with emotional messages, stormy meetings, undemocratic proceedings)

17. Assessing the purpose of your group: deciding how much quality time will be dedicated to how many meetings

18. Keeping up a proactive campaign with individuals of influence

19. Staying involved in related issues to expand your influence

20. Being a "dreamer and doer"

21. Writing interagency agreements: reducing verbal commitments to contracts between agencies and with parents

22. Communication techniques for parents only

23. Business and industry partnerships: what they are and how to build them

24. The art of the home visit to maintain personal contact

25. Asking the top brass to visit local sites

26. Understanding systems for strategic planning

27. Change management

28. Expanding and institutionalizing

29. Service projects for students, parents, and community members

30. Sharing the resources of schools

31. Including students and teachers on planning teams: standing committees, recognition programs, seeing teachers and students as innovators, etc.

32. Including teachers in support programs (examples: blood pressure checks, wellness programs, support groups and services, AIDS education, counseling services)

33. Writing goals and objectives—and tying them to real outcomes (also, how to tie outcomes to social issues)

34. How to collect data without driving everyone crazy (or, how to design reporting requirements)

35. How to report outcomes in terms of dollars

36. How to develop surrogate measures (examples: Are children of parenting teens immunized by age two? How many children of parenting teens are abused and neglected?)

37. Leadership abilities and traits

38. Technological advances that may benefit families

39. Understanding funding [plan for about a year for this one]

40. Grant writing

41. How does an idea become law?

42. The legal rights of parents

43. Confidentiality

44. What is a block grant, and what does it mean to me?

45. How does the public know about schools and what they do?

46. Research on at-risk students and families

47. Research on successful parent education programs

48. Stress management

🖫 Companion Diskette for *Building a Full-Service School*

As indicated by icons, much of the preceding material is available in electronic format on a separately purchased companion diskette. For ordering information you may call Jossey-Bass Publishers directly at (888) 378-2537, fax to (800) 605-2665, or visit the website at www.jossey-bass.com. Following are details about the electronic files and the system requirements for using them:

System Requirements

Windows PC

- 3.5 floppy disk drive capable of reading high-density disks
- Microsoft Word 6.0 for Win 95 or later or software capable of reading Microsoft Word 6.0/95
- Memory sufficient to open file sizes of 50+K

Macintosh

- 3.5 floppy disk drive capable of reading high-density IBM disks
- Microsoft Word 6.0 for Mac or later or software capable of reading Microsoft Word 6.0 for Win 95
- Memory sufficient to open file sizes of 50+K

Using the Files on Disk

Each page in your workbook that is marked with a disk icon has been saved onto the disk as a Microsoft Word 6.0 for Win 95 .DOC file. These .DOC files can be opened with many Windows- and Macintosh-based word processors or desktop publishing programs for viewing or editing as you see fit. Not all software will read the files exactly the same, but the .DOC file attempts to preserve the formatting as accurately as possible.

To use the Word files, do the following:

1. Copy all the .DOC files to a directory or folder on your hard drive.
2. **For Windows 95 and Windows NT:** *If you have Microsoft Word 6.0 or greater,* double-click on the file that you would like to use, or select the file and choose File, Open. Microsoft Word will launch and the file will open within Word.

   *If you do **not** have MS Word 6.0 or greater,* double-click on the file that you would like to use. You will then see a box with a list of the alternate programs that you can use to open the file. Select the program that you want to use and open it. In some cases, the program may give you the message that it has to translate the file, and it may bring up a translation program such as Conversions Plus. In that event, follow the directions on the screen to translate the file, and the program that you selected will be automatically launched at the end of the translation so that you can use the file.

   For Macintosh: *If you have Microsoft Word for Mac 6.0 or greater,* open Word and then use File, Open from within Word to find and open the file that you want on the disk.

   *If you do **not** have MS Word 6.0 or greater,* double-click on the icon for the disk and then double-click on the Word_6 folder. Double-click on the file that you would like to use. You will then see a box with a list of the alternate programs that you can use to open the file. Select the program that you want to use and open it. In some cases, the program may give you the message that it has to translate the file, and it may bring up a translation program such as MacLink Plus. In that event, follow the directions on the screen to translate the file, and the program that you selected will be automatically launched at the end of the translation so that you can use the file.

Note: Each file is coded to the corresponding resource section in the text to make it easy for you to find the one you want. For example, part two of Resource J has been named RES-J2.DOC.

Glossary

Action research

a systematic reflection on practice, including (1) identifying a problem, (2) studying the problem by gathering data as a program continues, and (3) reflecting on the data in order to make decisions grounded in evidence

Assessment services

diagnostic and evaluative services usually involving professional diagnosis of child or family problems, a consideration of strengths and weaknesses of a child, and the family environment. Assessment may determine eligibility for program services or develop a plan of service provision, whether in a single program or multiprogram environment.[†]

At risk

the concept that any person at any time may be exposed to the chance of injury or loss, or that a person may not be able to achieve her or his full potential because of inhibiting factors

Barriers

policies, conditions, problems, insufficiencies, or attitudes that obstruct the achievement of outcomes[†]

Billing unit financing

designing service delivery around the concept of services that can be billed (to Medicaid, health insurance providers, etc.), thus paying for themselves as they go

Blended financing

melding of federal and state funding to cut across historically separate service domains. To maximize federal funding, categorical agencies (as with education, mental health, and child welfare) work cooperatively to fund noncategorical service packages for individual children and youth.

Blueprint 2000

Florida's plan for education accountability and school improvement in instruction and assessment

Capital outlay

long-term expenditure for physical assets such as buildings or major pieces of equipment; funds specifically used for fixed assets or additions of fixed assets such as land or existing buildings, improvement of grounds, construction of buildings, additions to buildings, remodeling, initial equipment, and additional equipment

Capitation rate

any preset or fixed fee for which persons receive as much service as appropriate. The provider or a group of providers accept a periodic fee, generally on a per-person, per-month basis. For example, health professionals receive a capitation rate of X dollars per client assigned to their office for primary care services.

Care coordination

activities that link families to service providers through screening, referral, delivery, and follow-up

Carve-out

a program separate from the primary plan of service delivery designed to provide a specialized type of care. For example, a mental health service may be a carve-out of a group health plan.

Case management

a broad range of functions where eligible persons with specific needs are identified, and a plan is written to optimize client outcome in the most effective manner; process that identifies, assesses, plans, implements, and evaluates client needs and service delivery; sometimes used interchangeably with "care coordination"

Case manager

a person or a team that works with families, providers, and insurers to coordinate all services deemed necessary in a case management plan

Caseloads

general term used by social service agencies to describe the number of cases per month that a worker is responsible for. Some agencies limit the number of caseloads. The number of caseloads usually dictates how many workers are assigned to a geographic region.

Categorical funding

funding designated for specific services only. For example, funds for volunteer programs cannot be used to purchase student supplies.

Child welfare services

supportive services provided to help students and support a family unit, including financial assistance and protective supervision assisting children within the home (if a family cannot remain intact, then substitute services).

Respite care may be a child welfare or a mental health service, depending on the service provided.[†]

Collaboration

process of working jointly with others, including those with whom one is not normally or immediately connected, to develop and achieve common goals. Characteristics: partners establish common goals; partners agree to pool resources and jointly plan, implement, monitor, and evaluate new services and procedures; co-located services are designed to further mutually agreed-upon goals; collaboratives use input from each partner to make necessary changes to develop a comprehensive service delivery system; collaboratives directly negotiate policies leading to more comprehensive service delivery system.[‡]

Co-locate

the act of relocating community agencies or their representatives to the campus of a full-service school[‡]

Community agency

an organization of any type, public or private, for profit or not for profit, including those that offer assessment, prevention, and intervention services (mental health, child welfare, juvenile justice, educational, medical, vocational, recreational, operational, etc.)

Community-based governance

organizational structure involving broad representation from community agencies; designed to guide or influence initiation, development, evaluation, and sustainability of a full-service school; based on the premise that long-term viability requires community involvement and participation at all levels of the program

Confidentiality guidelines

written or verbal practices designed to keep spoken and written information about individuals private

Consortium

group of agencies that join forces to contribute to funding a program that cannot be funded by one agency alone

Cooperation

process of associating and acting together for mutual benefit. Characteristics: partners help each other meet their respective programmatic goals; goals and objectives of each program are designed, staffed, funded, and evaluated autonomously; partners may agree to share space, information, and referrals, or establish co-located services while pursuing their respective goals.[‡]

Coordination

process of linking the functions of autonomous entities in an effort to achieve the most effective results and to avoid duplication. Characteristics: caseworker in a particular agency is assigned to communicate with other agencies about their respective services to determine appropriateness for individual clients or customers and to avoid duplication of effort; basic agency functions and services are defined by the individual agency; agencies share only as much information as is necessary to avoid duplication of services and to direct customers to other services that may be helpful or to which they are entitled; the primary goal is to identify and connect clients with the variety of services that they desire or to which they may be entitled; cafeteria-style service delivery system is maintained.[‡]

Cost-effective

relationship between the price paid for a service or program and how well the program served its purpose (produced the intended or expected results), measured in dollars or percentage of purpose achieved, or expressed as a ratio

Cost reimbursement

sometimes termed cost-based reimbursement, provides global reimbursement for all services provided. For example, an institution such as a nursing home has a cost-reimbursement rate based on all services provided in the home. Reimbursement is no greater than the actual cost.

Cost sharing

occurs when agencies agree to share the cost of a particular program or position, frequently used as a technique to generate matching funds. Cost sharing makes the most of existing funding, as when staff are "repositioned" or co-located to the site or to another community agency or school.

Crossover funding

ability to use funds from one source of categorical funding for families that may meet slightly different criteria. For example, if families or a program design meet eligibility criteria for more than one funding source or program, a full-service school may be able to apply funds from different sources to meet the families' needs. May require requesting waivers of a funding source's requirements.

Cross-training

process by which interagency partners in a full-service school program share experience, expertise, and information in an effort to build the collaborative skills necessary to meet the complex and diverse needs of students and families

Database

a computer program designed to collect and store large numbers of facts, quantities, or conditions for further research or analysis

Decategorization

flexibility sometimes offered to local programs to use funds for purposes other than those the funds were originally earmarked for

Demographics

information such as age, sex, marital status, occupation, income, education, or zip code; often used as "predictor variables" in data analysis to establish whether subjects with similar demographics will respond to survey questions similarly

Discretionary funds

sums of money whose spending is left to the organization's own judgment; funds not specifically targeted for a particular purpose

Draw-down

use of state or local funds to qualify a program for additional money from another source. For instance, if a state can generate the match dollars required by a federal funding source for a particular program, the state can qualify for those federal funds.

Educational services

offering knowledge and socialization-skills development for students; by law, free and appropriate to all students. Students with emotional and behavioral problems may require special services to obtain an education.[†]

Eligibility

status of an individual or family that qualifies them for certain funds or services, based on rules and regulations that govern how money is distributed to clients

Entitlement

right of an individual or family to claim funds for a specific program based on need (food stamps, for example), regardless of how many other families are in need of the service. A nonentitled program has a set limitation on the number of participants, regardless of eligibility.

Evaluation

securing data on an ongoing basis (formative evaluation) and in conclusion (summative evaluation) in order to support the effectiveness of the full-service school program

Expert systems

computer systems designed to facilitate the decision-making process through use of extended database applications

Family support plan

written document resulting from a family-centered process that identifies the family's strengths, concerns, and goals, and that coordinates community resources and services in support of those goals

Federal funding

federal program dollars. For full-service schools, there are five major programs: Medicaid, Early Periodic Screening and Diagnosis and Training

Service (EPSDT), Title IV-F JOBS Program, Title IV-E Child Welfare Assistance, and the Family Support Act of 1988.

Fee for service

a flat rate charged per family for a specified service regardless of the complexity of service delivery, time involved in the service, or actual cost

Flexible dollars

a general term referring to funding regulations that allow spending to be adapted or modified to meet family and program needs

Formative evaluation

measures progress of objective achievement while the project is ongoing; therefore, an assessment of both progress toward completion and effectiveness of the process (cf. summative evaluation)

Foundation

a nonprofit organization established through donations or endowment for the support of an institution (such as a hospital or research organization), or in honor of an individual or idea and in support of a particular population

Front-end priorities

results of ranking funding needs in such a way as to support intervention and prevention strategies, which are more effective when offered sooner rather than later in response to a family's or child's needs

Full-service school

a school intended to integrate educational, medical, social, and human services that are beneficial to meeting the needs of children, youth, and their families on school grounds or in locations that are easily accessible

Funding consortium

contractual arrangement documenting collaboration of funding sources to meet particular needs in a community program. If one agency does not have adequate funding to meet its clients' needs, multiple agencies may form a consortium to function as the funding unit.

Funding stream

how money travels from the source to the family; another term for categorical funding, targeted to a specific population and often with strict eligibility criteria

Glue money

sums of money used to join or hold together different parts of programs. For example, funds from one organization can be used as a match to bring dollars into a second program, or two or three organizations can share the cost of a program administrator that none of the parties could afford on their own.

Goals

general statements of overall intent with a long-term perspective, sometimes referred to as outcome measures

Governance structure

an organizational arrangement designed to guide or influence a program's initiation, development, evaluation, and sustainability

Grant

transfer of money, privilege, property, or power from one source to another, by deed or in writing. Funding grants usually require a detailed proposal submitted in a particular format and are awarded on the basis of competition.

Grant cycle

time frame that includes receipt of the request for proposal, writing of the proposal, funding source review of the proposal, and notification of award or denial

Grant proposal

written plan of action that forms the basis for a contract between the grantee and the funding source

Guidelines

instructions or forms that define a funding source's requirements for grant proposals, including format, content, and length

Health services

activities that include detection and treatment of physical impairments or bodily damage, such as routine physical examinations, follow-up care, prenatal or postnatal care of pregnant teens, and treatment of sexually transmitted diseases[†]

Hooks

sums of money used in a program design to catch, hold, or pull other funding sources together. For example, funds for child care from one program may be "hooked" to parent education or job training and employability classes funded through a second program. In order to receive child care funds, the family must participate in the second activity.

In-kind resources

products or services, offered either within or in association with an organization, that have cash value. For example, a sponsoring agency may provide ten hours of training valued at $15 per hour, or a school board may provide office space that has a value of $75 per month. In-kind resources are used to demonstrate stability and self-sufficiency to the funding source by showing how the community supports a program with in-kind contributions.

In-service training

workshops or training sessions for collaborating agencies, concentrating on the design principles of the full-service school initiative

Intake

point at which a student or family first enters a program. The intake activity includes collecting basic demographic information in order to determine a family's eligibility for services.

Integration

process by which a community determines ways to combine appropriate community-based programs along a continuum of care for maximized efficiency and program effectiveness[‡]

Interagency agreement

a mutually agreed-upon, written contract designed to structure partnerships among collaborating community agencies in a full-service school program; specifies contributions to be made by each partner to the program

Juvenile justice services

services in response to offenses committed by juveniles, with services ranging from county agency supervision to detention and other residential programs. Some services may be provided at staff members' discretion. Most are court-ordered.[†]

Leveraged funding

reallocating funds previously spent on specific services (and general funds spent in state on an unmatched basis) to make the cost of these services matched dollars. The objective of leveraged funding is to draw down additional federal dollars.

Line workers

workers directly involved with families: teachers, social workers, law enforcement personnel, parent educators, health professionals, and others

Linkages

firm commitments of collaboration and cooperation, including memoranda of understanding, interagency agreements, or other binding agreements supported by documented actions pursuant to these agreements[‡]

Managed care

term commonly used in the health care industry. One provider (a physician) is designated as a primary care provider. All referrals for additional medical services must come from the primary care provider. Options available under managed care include health maintenance organizations (HMOs), freedom-of-choice waivers, and home-based and community-based services waivers.

Mapping

graphic representation of needs assessment information about a whole community or a portion thereof. For example, zip codes of teen parents may be graphically displayed over a map of the community to identify high areas of need for teen parenting programs.

Match rate

a percentage rate established by a local, state, or federal funding source that must be reached by a potential service provider before drawing down additional dollars. For example, a state may have a match rate of 25 percent in cash to draw down an additional 75 percent of federal funds, or a local grant program may have a match rate of 20 percent in cash to draw down 80 percent in matching dollars from the funding source.

Matching funds

funding dollars that can be used to match or draw down additional dollars. For example, state and local funds can be used to match federal funds.

Maximization

how agencies offer services to optimize efficiency, effectiveness, and accessibility for families; requires a philosophy that advocates offering long-term, client-appropriate, adequate services to eligible individuals when and where the service is most beneficial

Mental health services

residential and nonresidential programs and services directed to treatment and resolution of emotional problems of students, families, and community members[†]

Need-to-know policy

A need-to-know policy answers three questions:

1. What information is needed?
2. Under what circumstances may this information be released, and to whom?
3. What is the intended use of the information?

Network

a connection of computers allowing the computers to operate separately but communicate with each other

Objectives

statements that identify specific, concrete, and measurable ways in which goals will be fulfilled

Operational services

the service infrastructure of a full-service school; spans domain boundaries and encompasses case management, advocacy, self-help and support, transportation, legal services, and volunteer services[†]

Parents

within a family, adults who serve as primary caregivers to one or more children[†]

Partnership

variety of relationships involving cooperation, coordination, and collaboration; ongoing processes of identifying common goals and planning; implementing; and evaluating joint efforts. Partners may thus be agencies or individual agents, such as volunteers, and the term may include a school district, full-service schools project, or full-service site.[†]

Planning

careful and deliberate process of using decision making to build collaboration; the basis for sound implementation of a full-service school program

Prevention services

actions to prevent problems in mental health, health, or education, such as promoting physical and mental health, reducing incidence of disease, and identifying problems and intervening early (secondary)[†]

Random sample

sample selected so as to guarantee equal probability of selection to all possible samples of this size that could be formed from all the members of the population involved

Recreational services

activities including age-appropriate formal and informal interactions or amusements for students with peers and adults, providing youth with social skills and interpersonal activities[†]

Redirected funding

altering the delivery pattern of existing funding sources to shift funding from existing, separate programs to more comprehensive programs that offer a related but broader range of services. The goal is to reduce duplication and categorization. For example, existing child care funds may be redirected to a wraparound program for families that includes parenting classes, credit counseling, and adult education to ensure a comprehensive delivery approach.

Reinvestment

process of maximizing an existing program's services and dollars, and then taking the money or resources gained and returning them to the program in the form of expanded services. For example, if you are able to draw down additional funds or receive matching funds for a specific program, the money saved is reinvested in the program to serve families.

Representative sample

cross-section of a population, often used to provide a convenient estimate of some characteristic of the entire population

RFP

Request for proposal; contains the funding source's guidelines for format, content, length, and purpose of a solicited grant proposal

School-based services

basic social, economic, and health services that are integrated, available, and delivered to clients by being located on or near a school site

School-linked services

services offered by schools that are linked to at least two or more other children-and-family-service agencies in an ongoing, collaborative relationship

Screening

determining the nature of the family's or individual's risk and eligibility for needed services

Site-based governance

organizational plan based on the premise that those individuals working directly with students and families at the "site" of a full-service school should have the most influence on initiation, development, evaluation, and sustainability of the program

Sliding scale

a system that bases fees for service on the participant's income level

Soft money

money that is accessible for only a limited time or for separate, discrete projects

Staffing

meeting of family members, social and human service agency representatives, and education system representatives to arrive at a common understanding of the strengths and issues facing a family, and to develop a unified family care coordination plan outlining action to be taken

Stakeholder

any potential participant in the full-service school: children, parents, extended family, neighbors, school personnel at all levels, community agencies (mental health, child welfare, juvenile justice, health, vocational, recreational, economic), businesses, and college faculty and staff

Streamline

process of improving the cost-effectiveness and efficiency of community services and their delivery. For example, streamlining may include simplifying processes by using joint eligibility forms, building collaborative relationships, eliminating unnecessary tasks, cutting repetitive work, reducing time required for certain tasks, and relocating services nearer to families.

Streamlining access

improving cost-effectiveness and efficiency of service delivery by effecting change in policy, administration, and technology, and maximizing existing resources

Students

children of ages ranging from birth to conclusion of full-time school enrollment. Thus, infants and toddlers, whether attending a prekindergarten or not, are considered students; so are school-enrolled teenage parents. Adults are people sixteen to eighteen years old who are not enrolled in high school, or anyone eighteen or older.[†]

Subsidized cost

partial funding of the cost of a particular service or program by using a second funding source. For example, the cost of health insurance premiums may be subsidized for low-income families. Subsidized fees can also be set up on sliding scales.

Summative evaluation

evaluation building on the information of ongoing formative evaluation (see that entry) to produce a final analysis of program progress

Tasks

steps, activities, or procedures to accomplish objectives

Taxing authority

authority given to local boards (such as welfare or children's services boards) to generate funding by taxing a community's general population. Taxing authority regulations vary from state to state.

Transition study

a systematic examination of the individuals or groups of individuals that pass or change from one place or situation to another. For example, detailed information may be kept about students as they move from an elementary school to a middle school.

Triage

system that ensures the greatest benefit from limited facilities or resources by giving priority treatment to those who must have it and little or no treatment to those who can survive without it or who are certain not to survive even with treatment

Tuition

funding option where individual families pay a fee per service; usually refers to payment for enrollment in an instructional course over a specified period of time

Vocational services

services designed to help youth (with or without disabilities) move from education to employment, including development of skills in career selection, job finding and retention, and specific technical skills for doing a job[†]

Waiver

process by which a funding authority, such as the federal Health and Human Services Department, grants exceptions to established requirements

Welfare board

an executive board charged with administration of funds generated through a taxing authority. The advantage of establishing a local welfare board is that there are no federal mandates on its spending. Boards can create their own restrictions on service provision according to what local funding sources want. The funds received from taxes can be used as match to draw down revenue from other sources. Boards can also target specific funding streams or change funding to accommodate the community's special needs. A welfare board may be dedicated to one particular issue, such as juvenile justice, or it may be more general, such as welfare of children and families. Boards may be established independently or as part of county or city government.

Wraparound funding

a funding mechanism to provide all-inclusive services to a child, from a variety of sources, staying consistent over time

Endnotes

[†]   As defined through the evaluation efforts of the University of South Florida for the Florida Full-Service School Program.

[‡]   From Office of Juvenile Justice and Delinquency Prevention, State of Florida, FY 1995 Competitive Discretionary Program Announcements and Application Kit.

Annotated Bibliography

All efforts have been made to provide as complete and accurate a listing as possible for each entry. Entries are formatted in the following manner:

Title (in alphabetical order).

Author, year of publication, relevant page numbers.

Name and address of publisher; if periodical, volume, issue, and inclusive page numbers.

Brief description of content; ERIC or other identifying number.

1.   *Adolescent Health Technical Assistance and Training Resource Guide.*
        Maternal and Child Health Bureau (1994), pp. 1–76.
        Adolescent Health Project, National Center for Education in Maternal and Child Health, 2000 15th St. North, Suite 701, Arlington, VA 22201-2617.
    Provides information on thirty-four projects designed to improve adolescent health care. Each entry contains the program's name, address, phone number, project director, contact person, mission statement, goals and objectives, areas of technical expertise, audience or clientele, training, fees, and materials available.

2.   "Altered Destinies: Making Life Better for Schoolchildren in Need."
        Maeroff, G. I. (1998).
        Phi Delta Kappan, 79(6), 425–432.
    Discusses a "sense of connectedness as a means of gaining a feeling of belonging so that students regard themselves as part of an academic enterprise. . . . The sense of connectedness is strengthened by bonds that the school establishes with home, neighborhood and community." Advocates that schools in impoverished neighborhoods should strengthen ties to students by building links to the community and its activists. Argues that a range of services (including medical and dental services, mental health therapy, drug prevention sessions, tutoring, mentoring, after-school

recreation, Saturday workshops, summer programs) increases well-being for disadvantaged youth.

3. "Assessing the Coordination of Children's Services: Dilemmas Facing Program Administrators, Evaluators, and Policy Analysis."
   Kahne, J., and Kelley, C. (1993).
   Education and Urban Society, 25(2), 187–200.

   In-depth discussion of ways to "improve the efficiency and effectiveness of children's service programs by coordinating the efforts of service providers," and by addressing the needs of the whole child. Also discusses strengthening the relationship between parents, children, and service providers; accessibility of appropriate services; duplication of services; organizational structure and goals; and present accountability systems and appropriate alternatives. UMI EJ 460628

4. *Basics of Program Evaluation for School-Linked Service Initiatives.*
   Gombay, D. S. (1993), pp. 1–24.
   David and Lucile Packard Foundation, Center for the Future of Children, 300 Second St., Suite 102, Los Altos, CA 94022.

   Addresses the evaluation component for school-linked services: what services were provided, who received the services, and whether the services have an impact. Depending on a program's evaluation design and purpose, it may be sufficient to answer only one or two of the questions. Provides numerous examples of general outcome measures and corresponding specific outcome measures as well as the techniques that may be employed to measure them. Also addresses the issues of evaluation design, random assignment, generalizability, and statistical significance. Working paper no. 1932

5. *A Blueprint for Success: Community Mobilization for Dropout Prevention.*
   National Foundation for the Improvement of Education (1987), pp. 1–32.
   NFIE, 1201 Sixteenth St. NW, Washington, DC 20036.

   Addresses the problem of school dropouts and maintains that dropout rates "must be solved at the local level, where the problems originate." Calls upon the community as a whole to mobilize to address the issue. Focuses on the how-to's of mobilizing individuals, coalitions, agencies, and the public. Nine possible routes are presented.

6. *A Blueprint for Success. Lessons Learned: NFIE's Dropout Initiative.*
   National Foundation for the Improvement of Education (1990), pp. 1–38.
   NFIE, 1201 Sixteenth St. NW, Washington, DC 20036.

   Discusses lessons learned through the Drop-Out Prevention Initiative: empowered teachers, programs tailored to student needs, realistic expectations, community collaboration, early intervention, school district support, and encouragement of parents. Lists forty-seven NFIE projects, project directors, and a one-sentence description of each project.

7. *A Blueprint for Success: Operation Rescue.*

> National Foundation for the Improvement of Education (1986),
> pp. 1–44.
> NFIE, 1201 Sixteenth St. NW, Washington, DC 20036.

Outlines seven principles and essential elements for success of a dropout prevention program. Resulted from information exchanges in Denver, Los Angeles, Louisville, and Bridgeport (Connecticut) that explored various programs and what made each successful. Contains a sample scenario of a restructured school, a listing of national organizations, as well as the programs analyzed for the blueprint. Each program listing contains an address, phone number, contact person, and brief description of the program.

8. *Blueprint 2000: A System of School Improvement and Accountability for 1994–95 School Improvement Plans.*

> Florida Commission on Education Reform and Accountability (1994).
> Florida Department of Education.

Purpose is to "guide and oversee the implementation of a system of school improvement and accountability which will result in educational excellence and the highest level of student learning, and thereby, the opportunity for every Florida student to be successful in a global economy and a changing social structure, and a contributing citizen in our democracy." Provides specific information regarding background; developing the system; funding; recommendations for repeal or revision of laws; and goal standards, assumption, and outcomes.

9. *Building a Community Agenda: Developing Local Governing Entities.*

> Center for the Study of Social Policy, pp. 1–23.
> Center for the Study of Social Policy, 1250 Eye St. NW, Suite 503, Washington, DC 20005-3922.

Poses ten specific questions and describes each in depth:

1. What do we mean by collaboration?
2. What problems is collaboration designed to solve?
3. At what organizational level should collaboration occur?
4. How do we know if collaboration is happening and if it is working?
5. How effective can state-level interagency groups be in reducing system fragmentation and improving services to children and families?
6. What strategies can state policy makers initiate to further collaboration at the local level?
7. What strategies can states employ to promote collaboration across jurisdictions, including those where obstacles are greatest?
8. What is the role of the private sector in collaboration initiatives?
9. What are the risks of collaboration?
10. What problems won't collaboration solve?

Gives seven keys to successful collaboration.

10. *Building a Community School: A Revolutionary Design in Public Education.*
    Children's Aid Society (1993), pp. 1–56.
    Children's Aid Society, 105 East 22nd St., New York, NY 10010.
    Addresses the issue and need for a community school. Shares "steps we had to take to reach our goals, some of the obstacles we encountered along the way, and the overall philosophy that inspired our every move" in Washington County (New York). Also discusses services that can be incorporated into a community school, funding strategies, and practical steps for starting a community schools program. Appendixes contain suggested readings and resources.

11. *Building Bridges: A Review of the School-College Partnership Literature.*
    Wallace, J. (1993), pp. 1–18.
    Education Commission of the States, 707 17th St., Suite 2700, Denver, CO 80202-3427.
    Addresses school-college partnerships, beginning with a look at how such partnerships began and progressing to a discussion of types of partnerships (programs and services for students, those for educators, research and resources, and restructuring of the education system). Also talks about lessons learned from these partnerships and where future research studies should be directed. Annotated bibliography.

12. *Building Bridges: Supporting Families Across Service Systems.*
    Family Resource Coalition (1994).
    Family Resource Coalition, (312) 341-0900.
    Spring/summer, vol. 13 (I, II), 52 pages.
    Seven essays and profiles of programs addressing education, child welfare, health care, youth development, people with disabilities, the welfare system, and child mental health. Family Resource Coalition publishes the *FRC Report*; operates the National Resource Center for Family Support Programs and its school-linked services division; provides technical assistance, training, and consulting services; communicates family support issues and information to policy makers; tracks federal, state, and local policy initiatives; disseminates current knowledge on program design, administration, staffing, financing, and outcomes; sponsors national conferences; and encourages networking and collaboration among local programs.

13. *Building Bridges: Using State Policy to Foster and Sustain Collaboration.*
    Gomez, M. N., and de los Santos Jr., A. G. (1993), pp. 1–14.
    Education Commission of the States, 707 17th St., Suite 2700, Denver, CO 80202-3427.
    Addresses the topic of collaboration through state policy. The authors' goal "is to help policy makers create strategies to establish and sustain partnerships—particularly partnerships between schools and colleges." Discusses higher education (successful collaboration and lessons learned) and state policy (areas, levels, and questions that need to be addressed). Stresses importance

of state policy taking the lead in creating collaborative delivery systems to improve education and social programs for children and their families. S-93-1

14.   *Building Coalitions.*
          Ohio State University.
          Tapping Private Sector Resources (June 1992), pp. 1–58.
From OSU's Cooperative Extension Service, contains sixteen fact sheets regarding coalition development: introduction; coalition facilitator guide; coalition functioning; coalition goal setting; developing members; communication in coalitions; evaluating the collaboration process; extra resources for a coalition; making a difference; mobilizing the community; structure; turf issues; understanding the process; working with diverse cultures; networking; and how to tap private sector resources. 6/92-1M-97832

15.   *Building Communities from the Inside Out: A Path Toward Finding and Mobilizing a Community's Assets.*
          Kretzmann, J. P., and McKnight, J. L. (1997), 375 pages.
          Center for Urban Affairs and Policy Research Neighborhood Innovations Network, Northwestern University, 2040 Sheridan Rd., Evanston, IL 60208.
Discusses the issue of devastated communities and paths to rebuilding, specifically: releasing individual capacities, releasing the power of local associations and organizations, capturing local institutions for community building; rebuilding the community economy, asset-based community development, and providing support for asset-based development.

16.   "Building Parent Partnerships."
          Gutloff, K., ed. (1996), pp. 1–96.
          NEA Professional Library, P.O. Box 509, West Haven, CT 06516-9904.
Features stories by teachers who have tackled the challenge of expanding parent partnerships with schools. Describes six different programs as well as giving tips and ideas on how to build strong partnerships. Also includes selected resources and worksheets.

17.   "California's Healthy Start School-Linked Services Initiative: Summary of Evaluation Findings."
          Wagner, M., and Golan, S., prepared for the Foundation Consortium for School-Linked Services, the Interagency Children and Youth Services Division, California Department of Education (1996), pp. 1–21.
          SRI International, 333 Ravenswood Ave., Menlo Park, CA 94025-3493.
Reports the answers to six questions: (1) To what extent did the Healthy Start local initiatives reflect principles of effective service delivery? (2) What contributes to effective service delivery (and what does not)? (3) What improvements were noted among core clients? (4) What schoolwide improvements in student performance and behavior and in school climate were experienced by schools affiliated with school-linked services initiatives? (5) Did

improvements among children, families, or schools occur more often when services reflected principles of effective service delivery? Were other factors associated with improvements in results? (6) What attributes of local initiatives contributed to sustaining school-linked services and service reforms?

18. "Capitalizing on Community Resources: Three Cosponsorship Programs."
     Harris, J. (1988).
     Community Services Catalyst, 18(1), 13–15.
     Focuses on three cosponsorship programs, the key to which "is to discover what each participant really wants and to organize the operation to produce a win-win situation." Discussion topics include achieving the win-win situation, advantages and disadvantages, financial arrangements, and ten guidelines for cosponsorship. EJ 365136

19. "The Changing Local Community School Board: America's Best Hope for the Future of Our Public Schools."
     Shannon, T. A. (1994).
     Phi Delta Kappan, Jan., pp. 387–390.
     Discusses the vision, philosophy, approaches, and structure of the new and changing school board. Stresses that the "comprehensive needs" of children must be met through collaboration of services. The National School Boards Association endorses that the "schools are a natural place in which to deliver the services."

20. *Child Care Recipients Face Service Gaps and Supply Shortages. (Testimony Before the Committee on Labor and Human Resources, U.S. Senate.).*
     Ross, J. L. (1995), pp. 1–12.
     U.S. General Accounting Office, P.O. Box 6015, Gaithersburg, MD 20884-6015.
     Testimony before the U.S. Senate Committee on Labor and Human Resources addresses subsidized child care and the welfare system; historical and descriptive background; child care programs and their service delivery problems, current child care supply, and implications of welfare reform on child care services for low-income mothers. GAO/T-HEHS-95–96

21. "Children and Divorce."
     Behrman, E. E., ed. (1994).
     The Future of Children, 4(1), 1–255.
     Explores the relationship of divorce to children's well-being; contains articles from fourteen authors. Topics include an analysis of policy and program changes, statistical analysis of trends, financial impact, child support orders, child custody, high-conflict divorce, and the role of the father.

22. *Collaboration: The Prerequisite for School Readiness and Success.*
     Kunesh, L. G., and Farley, J. (1993), pp. 2–3.
     ERIC Clearinghouse on Elementary and Early Childhood Education, University of Illinois, 805 West Pennsylvania Ave., Urbana, IL 61801.

Discusses problems with current service delivery systems, and offers collaboration and a profamily system as a solution. Lists characteristics that are essential to any profamily system: comprehensive; preventive; family-centered; family-driven; integrated; developmental; flexible; sensitive to cultural, gender, and racial concerns; and outcomes-oriented. Offers these guidelines for successful collaboration: "(1) involving all key players; (2) ensuring visionary leadership; (3) establishing the expected outcomes for families and children; (4) ensuring commitment to change from all levels of member organizations and among community members; (5) establishing communication and decision-making processes; and (6) encouraging member agencies to include collaborative goals in their institutional mandates." ERIC ED 356 906

23.   *Collaboration to Build Competence: The Urban Superintendent's Perspective.*
      Clark, T. A. (1991), pp. 1–65. U.S. Department of Education.
      U.S. Government Printing Office, Superintendent of Documents, Mail Stop: SSOP, Washington, DC 20402-9328.

Discusses comprehensive community collaboratives, specifically: building partnerships, key collaborative players, characteristics of successful collaboratives, measuring success, and shaping collaboratives for the future. Appendixes list selected school-community partnerships and include a program description, key partners, participant descriptors, and contact address and phone number for each. ISBN 0-1603-6037-4

24.   "Combating Violence and Delinquency: The National Juvenile Justice Action Plan."
      Coordinating Council on Juvenile Justice and Delinquency Prevention (1996), pp. 1–167 plus appendixes.
      U.S. Department of Justice, Office of Justice Programs, Office of Juvenile Justice and Delinquency Prevention, Washington, DC 20531.

Reports a statistical analysis of juvenile offenses and factors influencing delinquency prevention. Suggests an eight-step plan for intervention and prevention. Provides a comprehensive list of resources and an annotated bibliography related to juvenile justice programs.

25.   *Concept Paper.*
      Interagency Workgroup on Full-Service Schools (1992).
      Florida Department of Education, Tallahassee.

Provides a brief overview of the full-service school program, including purpose, description of the problem, target population, which schools should become full-service schools, current status, guidelines for development, desired outcomes, funding, barriers, and interagency resources and contacts. Appendixes include information regarding legislation, criteria for dropout prevention programs, and key events for full-service schools.

26.   "Conceptualizing the Costs of Comprehensive, Community-Based Support Systems for Children."
      Rice, J. K. (1995).
      The Finance Project, 1341 G Street, NW, Washington, DC 20005, pp. 1–36.

Presents the rationale for developing new approaches to conceptualizing the costs associated with implementation and operation of models supporting comprehensive, community-based reform. Contains a template for community partners to use in computing total and marginal costs of resources required to operate community-based initiatives.

27.   "Concerns About School-Linked Services: Institution-Based Versus Community-Based Models."
>   Chaskin, R. J., and Richman, H. A. (1993).
>   David and Lucile Packard Foundation, Center for the Future of Children, 300 Second St., Suite 102, Los Altos, CA 94022.
>   *Education and Urban Society,* 25(2), 201–211.

Addresses concerns regarding school-linked services and the controversy of selecting a single institution, such as a school, versus a community-based institution as a delivery-system site. The authors prefer the community-based models and provide a strong basis for their rationale.

28.   *Confidentiality: A Guide to the Federal Laws and Regulations.*
>   Legal Action Center (1991).
>   Legal Action Center, 153 Waverly Place, New York, NY 10014.

Provides an extensive review of federal statutes and regulations regarding prevention and treatment programs for drug abuse.

29.   *Confidentiality and Collaboration: Information Sharing in Interagency Efforts.*
>   Breenberg, M., and Levy, J. (1992), pp. 1–54.
>   Education Commission of the States Distribution Center, 707 17th St., Suite 2700, Denver, CO 80202-3427.

From the Center for Law and Social Policy, Joining Forces, American Public Welfare Association, Council of Chief State School Officers, and the Education Commission of the States. Discusses information sharing and interagency collaboration in the belief that "confidentiality is neither an impenetrable barrier nor something which can be casually disregarded." Topics include confidentiality restrictions, developing information sharing, informed consent, automated systems, strategies for safeguarding confidentiality, and legislature. Appendixes contain sample release forms, checklists for obtaining consent, and staff oaths. Federal statutes and regulations regarding confidentiality are also included.

30.   "Controlling Crime Before It Happens: Risk-Focused Prevention."
>   Hawkins, J. D. (1995).
>   *National Institute of Justice Journal,* Aug., pp. 10–17.

Argues for juvenile justice prevention programs based on the public health model. The new model would identify risk factors in community, family, school, and individuals, and build in protective factors that "buffer exposure to risk." Ends with community guidelines for preventive intervention and implications for criminal justice.

31.   "Coordinated Services for Children: Designing Arks for Storms and Seas
        Unknown."
                Crowson, R. L., and Boyd, W. L. (Feb. 1993), University of Chicago.
                American Journal of Education, 101, 140–179.
        Deals with school-community relations, focusing on "increased parental
        involvement in governance, instructional partnerships, school-to-
        community outreach, and children's service coordination." Also deals
        with the issue that "the full potential is unlikely to be realized without a
        better theoretical and practical understanding of the organizational,
        administrative, and implementation issues associated with such ven-
        tures." Recommends increased understanding of these issues if service
        integration initiatives are to be successful.

32.   "Creating Effective Interagency Collaboratives."
                Dunkle, M., and Nash, M. (1989).
                Education Week, Mar. 15, pp. 44–45.
        Focuses on interagency collaboration as a necessity to successful prevention
        and service programs. Espouses the goal that agencies must work together
        to treat the whole child. Explores barriers to collaboration and how to over-
        come them; provides strategies and examples for positive interagency col-
        laboration.

33.   *Dade County Public Schools Adolescent Outreach Program: Jointly Funded
        Contract with Project Independence 1994–95.*
                Full-Service Schools (1995), pp. 13–35.
                Dade County Public Schools, Miami, Fla.
        Issues discussed are statement of need, services provided, staff and general
        program information, project implementation, measurable objectives, eval-
        uation, coordination, and payment/funding. Contains detailed charts of
        budget and expenditure report and budget summary worksheet.

34.   *Developing a Family-Centered Prevention and Early Intervention System: A
        Training Series. Module 1: The Family Support Plan Process.*
                Center for Prevention and Early Intervention Policy (1992), pp. 1–115.
                Florida Department of Education, Office of Early Intervention and
                School Readiness, Florida Education Center, 325 West Gaines St.,
                Tallahassee, FL 32399-0400.
        Participants' training manual for the family support plan process, the pur-
        pose of which "is to provide families and professionals with a philosophi-
        cal and process framework in which to develop individualized Family
        Support Plans for infants and toddlers and their families." Discusses
        requirements for family support plans, family-centered philosophy, family-
        centered service coordination, and phases of the family support plan
        process. Appendixes contain information on assisting families in identify-
        ing their concerns, priorities, and resources; the family support plan meet-
        ing; and family case studies and sample family support plans.

35.   "Editor's Introduction."
            Koppich, J. E., and Kirst, M. W. (1993).
            Education and Urban Society, 25(2), 123–128.
       Discusses integrated children's services and how the journal's articles
       address this topic. Briefly describes three problems associated with integra-
       tion: underservice, lack of prevention, and service fragmentation. Other
       issues are funding, space availability, confidentiality, staff training, and
       governance.

36.   *Education and Health: Partners in School Reform.*
            Chervin, D. D., and Northrop, D. (1994), pp. 1–42.
            BellSouth Foundation, 1155 Peachtree St. NE, Atlanta, GA 30367-6000.
       BellSouth Foundation and Education Development Center offer this guide
       for schools and communities to meet the health, human service, and educa-
       tional needs of children. Identifies numerous school districts and respective
       programs that are successfully meeting these needs and reforming the
       school environment. Discusses lessons learned from these programs and
       the opportunities they provide for the future. Includes a listing of the
       school districts and program contact persons.

37.   *Education Data Confidentiality: Two Studies.*
            Pechman, E. M., O'Brien, E., Hightower, A., and Williams, A. (1994),
            pp. 1–75. U.S. Department of Education.
            Policy Studies Associates, Inc., 1718 Connecticut Avenue NW, Suite
            400, Washington, DC 20009.
       From the National Forum on Education Statistics, contains two studies
       relating to the issue of confidentiality. The first "contains a survey, abstract,
       and analysis of federal and state restrictions and stipulations regarding
       data confidentiality issues." The second "covers major court challenges,
       data collection issues germane to education, and trends anticipated to affect
       data confidentiality policy." NCES 94-635.

38.   *Education Development Center, Inc., Annual Report 1992.*
            Education Development Center, Inc. (1992), pp. 1–48.
            Education Development Center, 1250 24th St. NW, Suite 300,
            Washington, DC 20037.
       Collection of information about active 1992 projects, divided into three
       categories: innovation in education, health and human development, and
       equity and cultural diversity. Contains 122 project descriptions and a report
       by Independent Certified Public Accountants regarding the financial posi-
       tion of Education Development Center.

39.   *The Effectiveness of Comprehensive Case Management Interventions: Findings
       from the National Evaluation of the Comprehensive Child Development Program.*
            St. Pierre, R. G., Layzer, J. I., Goodson, B. D., and Bernstein, L. S.
            (Sept. 1997) pp. 1–30.
            Abt Associates, Inc., 55 Wheeler St., Cambridge, MA 02138; (617)
            349-2794.

Reports the results of an evaluation study of the Comprehensive Child Development Program (CCDP), an innovative attempt to ensure the delivery of early and comprehensive services with the aim of enhancing child development and helping low-income families to achieve economic self-sufficiency. Findings show that a case management approach does not lead to improved outcomes for parents or children.

40. *Enabling and Empowering Families: Principles and Guidelines for Practice.*
        Dunst, C. J., Trivette, C. M., and Deal, A. G. (1988).
        Cambridge, Mass.: Brookline Books.
    Funded through the Center for Prevention and Early Intervention Policy, Institute for Science and Public Affairs, Florida State University. Copies available from the Florida Department of Education, Office of Early Intervention and School Readiness, Florida Education Center, 325 W. Gaines St., Tallahassee, FL 32399-0400; (904) 488-6830. Source of family needs scale and family support scale.

41. *Ensuring Student Success Through Collaboration: Summer Institute Papers and Recommendations of the Council of Chief State School Officers.*
        Council of Chief State School Officers (1992), pp. 1–132.
        Council of Chief State School Officers, One Massachusetts Ave. NW, Suite 700, Washington, DC 20001-1431.
    Contains eleven papers covering community support in education, implementing school-linked services, youth development approach in schools, human service reforms, family-centered approaches, financing school-linked services, collaboration in education, and comprehensive school health services. Appendix contains the council's policy statement regarding student success through community collaboration, including four guiding principles and seven strategies for change to ensure the success of community collaboration and to promote a common vision for the well-being of the nation's children.

42. *Executive Guide: Improving Mission Performance Through Strategic Information Management and Technology.*
        Browsher, C. (1994), pp. 1–48.
        U.S. General Accounting Office, Washington, DC 20548-0001.
    Addresses "what agencies can do now to improve performance by using new approaches to managing information and their related technologies." Focuses on eleven practice principles learned from senior management staff in leading organizations in three areas: deciding to change, directing change, and supporting change with respect to information management. Each principle is described fully and contains information on specific characteristics, how to get started, and a case study incorporating the practice principle. GAO/AIMD-94-115.

43. *Expanding School Health Services to Serve Families in the 21st Century.*
        Igoe, J. B., and Giordano, B. P. (1992), pp. 1–36.

Office of School Health Programs, University of Colorado Health Sciences Center, Denver, Colo.

Discusses family health centers as a means of addressing the needs of families, enabling the community to take responsibility for their children and families. Provides numerous examples of programs throughout the country that have successfully implemented family service centers.

44. "Family Involvement in Children's Education: Successful Local Approaches."

U.S. Department of Education, Superintendent of Documents, P.O. Box 371954, Pittsburgh, PA 15250-7954; stock number: 065-000-01085-2; (1997), pp. 1–150.

A 150-page idea book describing successful programs across the nation that involve parents in school planning and governance activities and as volunteers. Some programs described also provide coordinated noneducational services for families to support academic achievement. Organized around strategies for overcoming barriers to family involvement in schools.

45. *Family Matters Newsletter.*

Robert Wood Johnson Foundation (summer 1993), pp. 1–19.
Mental Health Services Program for Youth, Washington Business Group on Health, 777 North Capitol St. NE, Suite 800, Washington, DC 20002.

Addresses concerns of serving children through collaboration, advocacy, system reform, etc. Discusses programs from California, Kentucky, North Carolina, Ohio, Oregon, Pennsylvania, Vermont, and Wisconsin that provide services to children. Each program discussion addresses program dynamics and financing strategies. Also outlined and briefly discussed are individualization of care, management of care, financing of care, and normalization of care as the "four essential values for building systems of care." Glossary of terms.

46. *Family Support Programs and School-Linked Services: Overview of Family Support Programs.*

Administration for Children, Youth, and Families (1991), pp. 1–5.
Family Resource Coalition, 200 S. Michigan Ave., Suite 1520, Chicago, IL 60604

Discusses family support programs and school-linked services. Describes the premises of family support programs, program components, and four family support program initiatives. A brief description of resource organizations is provided to enable the reader to request additional information. ERIC ED 352145

47. "Fighting Fragmentation: Coordination of Services for Children and Families."

Soler, M., and Shauffer, C. (1993).
Education and Urban Society, 25(2), 129–140.

Provides an overview of the CASSP (Child and Adolescent Service System Program), the Willie M. Program, and the Ventura County Model, all of which utilize integrated services to address mental health issues with children. Also outlines characteristics of effective "coordinated service programs: clear value statement, family-centered orientation, broad community involvement, involvement of the educational system, accessible intake location, evaluation of all needs, case management, service plan, dispute resolution, high-quality services, flexibility in funding, information system, measurement of effectiveness, planning of additional services, and communication capability."

48. "Financing School-Linked, Integrated Services."
   Farrow, F., and Joe, T. (1992).
   The Future of Children, 2(1), 56–67.
   Addresses the issue of financing school-linked services, including potential funding sources for education, social services, and health care. Outlines three barriers to financing: categorical funding, crisis orientation, and the absence of a universal entitlement approach. Discusses strategies that may counteract the negative effects of the barriers. Also contains information regarding development and implementation of a fiscal strategy for school-linked services.

49. "Financing School-Linked Services."
   Kirst, M. W. (1993).
   Education and Urban Society, 25(2), 166–174.
   Addresses the issue of financing school-linked services. Suggests a new technique of utilizing existing money from the state and local governments and community as matching funds to supplement federal funding. Provides three examples from school-linked services in California, New Jersey, and Kentucky as to how the techniques may be successfully implemented.

50. "Financing School-Linked Services."
   Kirst, M. W. (1992).
   University of Southern California, Center for Research in Education Finance, School of Education, Waite Phillips Hall 901, Los Angeles, CA 90089-0031.
   University of Southern California Policy Brief (7), 1–7.
   Discusses funding school-linked services, specifically collaboration, the need for a new children's service strategy, funding principles, and federal funding sources such as Medicaid, Maternal and Child Health Block Grant, Title IV-E of the Social Security Act, and AFDC. Also describes three school-linked service programs (New Beginnings, San Diego; New Jersey's High School Program; and Family Resource and Youth Service Centers in Kentucky) and their funding issues.

51. *Florida Full-Service Schools Training Conference. Summary of the Proceedings.*
   Florida Department of Education (1992), pp. 1–163.
   Institute for At-Risk Infants, Children and Youth, and Their Families, College of Education, University of South Florida, Tampa, FL 33620.

Topics addressed are collaboration, information sharing, networking, after-school programs, co-locating services, mental health services, family service center model, Full-Service Schools Act, and the challenges facing full-service schools. Appendixes contain full-service school concept paper; newspaper articles; conference agenda; and a directory of conference presenters, addresses, and phone numbers.

52.   *The Florida Legislature, Commission on Juvenile Justice. 1993 Annual Report.*
      Florida Commission on Juvenile Justice (1993), pp. 1–142.
      320 Holland Building, Tallahassee, FL 32399-1300.
Outlines the commission's activities, recommendations, history of juvenile justice in Florida, and general juvenile justice facts. Contains numerous tables, charts, and maps. Focuses on the issues of public safety, deterrence, and prevention of crime and rehabilitation of youth. Includes glossary of juvenile justice terms.

53.   *Florida's Full-Service Schools: A Case Study of Three Oversight Committees.*
      Reynolds, J. E. (1994), pp. 1–37.
      Florida Department of Education, 325 West Gaines St., Tallahassee, FL 32399
Provides three case studies in interorganizational collaboration. Methodology, research design, and results are discussed in detail. Also discusses implications of findings with regard to system-oriented change, leadership, collaboration coordination, and cooperation. Concludes with recommendations for policy makers and practitioners, as well as recommendations for further research on the topic of interorganizational collaboration.

54.   *Focus on Parents: Strategies for Increasing the Involvement of Underrepresented Families in Education.*
      Office of Community Education (1989), pp. 1–43.
      Massachusetts Department of Education, 1385 Hancock St., Quincy, MA 02169.
Discusses strategies and approaches for increasing parent and family involvement in education. Three parts address principles of effective parent involvement, seven steps for effective outreach to families, and twenty-six sample strategies. Sample strategies are divided into categories of outreach, education, and empowerment. Appendix summarizes key research on parent involvement. 16098-5000-82, 11/89.

55.   *Formative Evaluation of the Kentucky Family Resources and Youth Service Centers: A Descriptive Analysis of Program Trends.*
      Illback, R. J. (1993), pp. 1–74.
      R.E.A.C.H. of Louisville, Inc., 101 East Kentucky St., Louisville, KY 40203.
Summarizes the Kentucky Family Resource and Youth Service Center Program, which was designed "to reduce barriers to learning through school-based family support and parent involvement initiatives." Topics:

program history and development, literature and research summary, evaluation component, program results, summary, and recommendations. Emphasis on program's results and outcomes. Appendixes contain child and family demographics, risk factors, needs checklist, educational status checklist, service delivery matrix, support helpfulness scale, and program participant survey.

56. "Fragile Families, Fragmented Services: A Strategy for Reform."
     Rude, J. C. (1992–93).
     AACC Journal, Dec.–Jan., 27–30.

Addresses collaboration in the Beacon College Grant Project, which involved six Oregon community colleges. Project's vision is for community colleges to act as "leading architects in building new communities in America" through collaborative partnerships with employers and public and private community agencies. Outlines guidelines for collaborative projects: focus on needs of individual client, share information, decrease client dependency on agency, cultivate internal teamwork, and strive for tangible and measurable outcomes.

57. *Fulfilling Reform's Promise: A Need to Expand the Vision of Education in the South.*
     BellSouth Foundation (1991), pp. 1–52.
     BellSouth Foundation, 1155 Peachtree St. NE, Atlanta, GA 30367-6000.

Highlights findings and suggestions of a twenty-two-member group organized to investigate education reform. Focuses on how philanthropy in education can improve learning, teaching, higher education technology in education, and the overall process of education. Appendixes contain an evaluation questionnaire as well as a listing of task force, management panel, and advisory committee members.

58. *Full-Service Schools: A Revolution in Health and Social Services for Children, Youth, and Families.*
     Dryfoos, J. G. (1994), 310 pages.
     Jossey-Bass, 350 Sansome St., San Francisco, CA 94104.

Describes full-service schools as "the movement to create an array of integrated support services in schools that responds to the declining welfare of many American families and the rising new morbidities of sex, drugs, violence, and stress among youth." Builds a compelling case for broad public commitment to full-service schools based on a historical and current overview of national efforts and an exploration of cost-effectiveness. Brief descriptions are given on how programs are organized, staffed, and funded, with emphasis on school-based clinics. Contains glossary, bibliographical notes, and index.

59. "Getting Our Acts Together."
     Kirst, M., McLaughlin, M., and Massell, D. (1991).
     Thrust for Educational Leadership (Florida Policy Review), 5(1), pp. 22–24.

Discusses schools providing integrative services, specifically addressing the new role of the principal, various service and program options for integration, case management, and the need for a children's service coordinator. Using these concepts, schools "move from the role of deliverer of educational services to the role of broker of the multiple resources that can be applied to achieve successful, productive, and happy lives for children."

60. "Getting Ready to Provide School-Linked Services: What Schools Must Do."
Jehl, J., and Kirst, M. W. (1993).
Education and Urban Society, 25(2), 153–165.
Addresses successful school-linked services that result from a restructuring of traditional school operations. Successful restructuring or change in school personnel, levels of district leadership, middle management, principals, and teachers are discussed in length. Also considers restructuring parent-school interactions and goal accountability. EJ 460625

61. *Getting Schools Ready for Children: The Other Side of the Readiness Goal.*
Southern Regional Education Board (1994), pp. 1–40.
Southern Regional Education Board, 592 Tenth St. NW, Atlanta, GA 30318-5790.
Focuses on Goals for Education: Challenge 2000, Goal One (readiness for school), and how it is essential that schools be prepared to meet the needs of students. Outlines eight changes that schools can institute to successfully achieve Goal One. Selected reading list.

62. *Glass Walls: Confidentiality Provisions and Interagency Collaborations.*
Soler, M. I., Shotton, A. C., and Bell, J. R. (1993), pp. 1–85.
Youth Law Center, 114 Sansome St., Suite 950, San Francisco, CA 94104.
Focuses on confidentiality and interagency collaboration, analyzing statutes and regulations and identifying successful mechanisms and strategies of confidentiality models. In addition to analysis of federal statutes, also looks at California, Iowa, New York, and Washington state statutes and regulations. Topics include privacy interests of children, families, and agencies; confidentiality restrictions; protecting privacy; consent forms; release forms; interagency agreements; and aggregate information systems.

63. *Handbook: Legal Issues for School-Based Programs.*
Legal Action Center (1991).
Legal Action Center, 153 Waverly Place, New York, NY 10014.
Explores the issue of confidentiality in school-based programs. Contains discussion of federal regulations governing confidentiality and of student information disclosures to parents under the Federal Educational Rights and Privacy Act.

64. *Handbook of School-Based Interventions: Resolving Student Problems and Promoting Health Educational Environments.*
Cohen, J. J., and Fish, M. D. (1993).
Jossey-Bass, 350 Sansome St., San Francisco, CA 94104.

Describes interventions for major problem behaviors that students may exhibit from kindergarten through grade twelve. Interventions are research-based and drawn from the literature.

65.   *Head Start Program Performance Standards (45-CFR 1304).*
        U.S. Department of Health and Human Services (1991), pp. 15–37.
        U.S. Department of Health and Human Services; Head Start, Mary E.
        Switzer Building, 330 C St., Room 2050, Washington, DC 20201;
        http://www.dhhs.gov/programs/hsb/goals.htm

Gives Head Start program's health services objectives, performance standards, and guidance statements.

66.   "Health and Social Services in Public Schools: Historical Perspectives."
        Tyack, D. (1992).
        The Future of Children, 20(1), 19–31.

Addresses historical perspectives of health and social service programs in the public school system. As far back as 1890, "reformers" saw the need for school lunches, health services, and social services. Looks at why these programs were proposed, how they affected the school, and who received the services. Current reform proposals, how they relate to history, and lessons learned from the historical perspective are also addressed.

67.   *Healthy Caring: A Process Evaluation of the Robert Wood Johnson Foundation's School-Based Adolescent Health Care Program.*
        Marks, E. L., and Marzke, C. H. (1993), pp. 1–93.
        Mathtech Inc., Suite 200, 210 Carnegie Center, Princeton, NJ 08540.

Describes the program, established to meet the health needs of adolescents by utilizing the school environment. Data regarding the school-based adolescent health centers was collected from twenty-four centers. Covers starting up, services, personnel, organizational management and environment, relationships with school staff and students, costs and revenues, and lessons for the future.

68.   *Healthy Youth 2000: National Health Promotion and Disease Prevention Objectives for Adolescents.*
        American Medical Association (1990), pp. 1–50.
        American Medical Association, Department of Adolescent Health, 515
        North State St., Chicago, IL 60610.

Objectives are divided into primary adolescent health objectives (physical activity and fitness; nutrition; tobacco, alcohol, and other drugs; family planning; mental health and mental disorders; violent and abusive behavior; educational and community-based programs; unintentional injuries; environmental health; oral health; maternal and infant health; HIV infection; sexually transmitted diseases; and clinical preventive services) and additional objectives regarding roles (health care professionals, schools, communities, and governments). Also provides a listing of Healthy People 2000 resources, which may be ordered from the ODPHP National Health Information Center.

69.   "Home Visiting."
       Behrman, R. E., ed. (1993).
       David and Lucile Packard Foundation, Center for the Future of
       Children, 300 Second St., Suite 102, Los Altos, CA 94022.
       The Future of Children, 3(3), 1–214.

Devoted to multidisciplinary discussion of home visiting programs.
Contains eleven articles in these categories: description, research, economic
analysis, recommendations for improvement, implications, providing services to diverse families while respecting cultural contexts, and universal
home visiting as a means of preventing child abuse and neglect.
Appendixes describe home visiting programs nationwide. Also included
are program contact persons, addresses, and phone numbers

70.   "How Shall We Study Comprehensive, Collaborative Services for Children
      and Families?"
       Knapp, M. S. (1995).
       Educational Researcher, 24(4), 5–16.

Reviews current efforts in a variety of studies of comprehensive, collaborative services, with discussion of assumptions, issues confronting research
and evaluation, engaging divergent perspectives, measuring independent
variables, and attributing results to influence. Suggests ways to address
issues including desirable attributes, locating and measuring the bottom
line, and samples of some promising kinds of studies.

71.   "Identifying Potential Dropouts Through School Health Records."
       Swanson, N., and Leonard, B. J. (1994).
       Journal of School Nursing, 10(2), 22–26, 46.

Study focused on identifying potential dropouts by analyzing school
records of 225 ninth graders in a midwestern inner-city school. Found these
variables significant in predicting student dropout: vision and scoliosis
screening, health room visits, age, and absences. Results state that it is not
the health problems themselves for which students drop out, but the high
correlation between the identified variables. Implications for school nursing practice are also outlined; school nurses are perceived as key personnel
in assessing at-risk students.

72.   *Improving Public Policy Through Collaboration: States, Communities, and
      Grantmakers Working Together. A Policy Forum on Full-Service Schools in
      Florida.*
       Hercik, J. M. (1994), pp. 1–51.
       Council of Governors Policy Advisors, 400 North Capitol St., Suite
       390, Washington, DC 20001.

Written "to provide the Florida Policy Forum participants with a record of
the proceedings of the two days, and to give them an historical perspective
and a framework for thinking through an implementation strategy for their
counties. In addition, this report will provide other states wrestling with
some of the same issues and concerns as the state of Florida with an outline

for strategic planning and development for going to scale with their version of full-service schools or school-linked services."

73. *Information Systems to Support Comprehensive Service Delivery.*

> National Center for Service Integration (1994).
>
> Symposium, Sept. 22–23, Washington, D.C.

Provides results of a nationwide study of community and state information system initiatives that support delivery of comprehensive and integrated services to children and their families. Addresses human services delivery reform, framework for initiatives, system development, functional focus, challenges, lessons learned, and case studies. Appendixes contain samples of planning documents and memoranda of understanding and consent forms.

74. *Ingredients for Success: Comprehensive School-Based Health Centers. A Special Report on the 1993 National Work Group Meetings.*

> Brellochs, C., and Fothergill, K. (1995), pp. 1–48.
>
> Janin/Cliff Design, Inc., School Health Policy Initiative, Montefiore Medical Center, Albert Einstein College of Medicine, Department of Pediatrics, Division of Adolescent Medicine, 111 East 210th St., Bronx, NY 10467-2490.

Addresses school-based health centers, staff requirements, integration of school personnel and resources, service capacity and delivery, funding, and the implications of these centers on children's health and education needs. Also discussed are the eleven principles the initiative outlined as essential to school-based health centers. Appendixes contain a directory of the 1993 National Work Group Meeting members.

75. *Integrated Approaches to Youths' Health Problems: Federal, State, and Community Roles.*

> Family Impact Seminars (July 7, 1989).
>
> Background briefing report, Washington, D.C.

Secondary source: found on page 255 of *Full-Service Schools* by J. G. Dryfoos.

76. *Integrated Services: A Summary for Rural Educators.*

> Nawal, L. M. (1993), Information Analysis-ERIC Clearinghouse Products.
>
> ERIC/CRESS, Appalachia Educational Laboratory, P.O. Box 1348, Charleston, WV 25325.

Discusses the issue of integrated services and two models: school-linked and community-based. Promotes the idea that case management is essential to both models. Discusses integrated services in the scope of rural communities. ERIC Digest EDO-RC-92-9

77. *Integrating Community Services for Young Children and Their Families.*

> North Central Regional Educational Laboratory (1993), pp. 1–23.
>
> North Central Regional Educational Laboratory, 1900 Spring Road, Suite 300, Oak Brook, IL 60521-1480.

Discusses the issue of integrating services, specifically addressing the current delivery system, early childhood education, school readiness, caring communities, profamily system, effective service integration initiatives, and guidelines for effective collaboration. Also discusses regional actions and agendas regarding collaboration from Illinois, Indiana, Iowa, Michigan, Minnesota, Ohio, and Wisconsin. Each state action agenda is explained by statewide directives, legislation, funding sources, implications, constraints, and future outlook. Report 3, 1993SR

78.   *Integrating Education, Health, and Social Services in Rural Communities: Service Integration Through the Rural Prism.*

> Bhaerman, R. D. (Dec. 1994), 137 pages.
>
> Research for Better Schools, 444 N. Third St., Philadelphia, PA 19123-4107.

Conveys the importance of financial, human, technical, and knowledge resources to successful service integration in rural schools and communities. Contains four parts: overview of service integration, rural context, planning, and summary. Appendixes contain information on major funding sources, sample surveys, national and regional organizations, state resources, local resources, university resources, and the National Center for Service Integration's Resource Briefs. OERI contract No. RP91002004

79.   *Integrating Human Services: Linking At-Risk Families with Services More Successful Than System Reform Efforts.*

> McDonald, G. J. (1992), pp. 1–45.
>
> U.S. General Accounting Office, Washington, DC 20548.

Report to the chairman, Subcommittee on Children, Family, Drugs and Alcoholism, Committee on Labor and Human Resources, U.S. Senate. Addresses the issue and the importance of integrating human services. Addresses initiatives (system-oriented and service-oriented) and benefits and obstacles that each faces. Concludes with a discussion of policy considerations. Appendixes contain past federal efforts to integrate services and a description of service integration programs GAO visited. GAO/HRD-92-108

80.   *Interagency Collaboration: Improving the Delivery Services to Children and Families.*

> Kadel, S. W. (1992), pp. 1–104. Office of Educational Research and Improvement, U.S. Department of Education.
>
> South Eastern Region Vision for Education (SERVE), 345 S. Magnolia Drive, Suite D-23, Tallahassee, FL 32301-2950.

Addresses interagency collaboration and family service centers. A family service center "is a form of collaborative action which brings together staff and programs from various agencies into one location to serve a community." Covers the benefits of family service centers, steps for development and implementation, and potential obstacles and how to overcome them. Provides brief examples of successful programs and techniques, and includes contact person, address, and phone number. Also lists state and national initiatives dealing with collaborative services. Appendixes provide examples of needs assessment forms, staff oath of confidentiality forms, and release forms.

81. *Interagency Collaboration in the Heartland: Challenges and Opportunities. Proceedings of the NCREL Early Childhood Connection.*
> Raack, L., Kunesh, L. G., and Shulman, D., with contributions from Kirst, M., Walter, S., and Wolff, P. (1991), pp. 1–51.
> North Central Regional Educational Laboratory, 1900 Spring Road, Suite 300, Oak Brook, IL 60521.

Discusses issues in interagency collaboration: barriers to collaboration, implementation recommendations, handicapped children as clients, family-based and community-based services, a model for linking social services, concerns regarding collaboration within a state, and the future of collaborative services. Also contains a list of advisory council and staff members, addresses, and phone numbers.

82. "Interagency Data Systems for Accountability."
> Sullivan, C., and Sugarman, J. (1995).
> Council of Chief State School Officers, Center on Effective Services for Children, P.O. Box 27412, Washington, DC 20038-7412.
> *Issue Brief,* Spring, pp. 1–32.

Discusses the purposes of interagency data systems, their inputs and examples of data elements, and eight issues to consider when designing a cross-program, cross-agency system. Also describes six data systems from around the country. Appendixes contain recent federal legislation and examples of data systems.

83. *Interagency Task Force State Implementation Plan.*
> Interagency Task Force on Family Resource and Youth Services (1991), pp. 1–107.
> Secretary for Human Resources, Commonwealth of Kentucky, Frankfort, KY, 40621.

Describes establishing family resource and youth service centers in Kentucky, "designed to promote the flow of resources and support to families in ways to strengthen the functioning and enhance the growth and development of the individual members and the family unit." Provides guiding principles and a plan of action. Appendixes contain information on statutes, budget, a state resource directory, program component options, and program tours.

84. *Joining Forces: Linking the Education and Social Welfare Systems to Help At-Risk Children and Youth.*
> National Association of State Boards of Education (1989), pp. 1–7.
> National Association of State Boards of Education, 1012 Cameron St., Alexandria, VA 22314.

Addresses the issue of education and social welfare systems working together for the good of the children. Describes the Joining Forces effort, goals, responsibility, approach, and participants. Encourages change in early intervention to prevent future problems; strengthening family involvement in schools and academic achievement; responding early to children experiencing problems; and changing policies to support children and school success. ED 302 917.

85.   "Joining Hands."
    Cohen, B. (1995).
    Education Week, May 3, pp. 35–38.
Supports the idea that "only by working together can schools and communities hope to salvage young lives and fulfill education's promise of literacy and opportunity." Argues for changes in families, societal structure, and welfare reform.

86.   *The Journal of At-Risk Issues.*
    Reitzammer, A. F. (ed.) (1995), pp. 1–48.
    Department of Education, Huntington College, 1500 East Fairview Ave., Montgomery, AL 36101-2148.
Provides articles on the topics of the at-risk student, full-service schools, intervention martial arts programs, effective teacher strategies, lessons learned after high school, and violence in schools.

87.   *Kentucky Family Resource and Youth Services Centers Guide for Planning and Implementation.*
    Kentucky Family Resource and Youth Services Centers (1992), pp. 1–29.
    Family Resource Coalition, 200 South Michigan Ave., Suite 1520, Chicago, IL 60604.
Intended to "walk through the proposal planning process with potential applicants." Outlines the philosophy of family resource and youth service centers, the distinguishing characteristics of a center, planning a center, establishing an advisory council, completing a community needs assessment, funding issues, and evaluation strategies. Also lists elements essential to a successful proposal: understanding and applying basic principles; responding to community needs; planning collectively with community and participants; developing a realistic evaluation component; and planning to encounter program changes.

88.   "Key Issues in Developing School-Linked, Integrated Services."
    Gardner, S. L. (1993).
    Education and Urban Society, 25(2), 141–152.
Addresses key points to consider when planning and implementing school-linked services: planning, targeting, governance, information systems, staffing, and community controversy. Discusses these topics in depth and provides useful strategies for success.

89. *Kids Count Data Book: State Profiles of Child Well-being.*
       Annie E. Casey Foundation (1997), pp. 1–174.
       Annie E. Casey Foundation, 701 St. Paul St., Baltimore, MD 21202;
       (410) 547-6600; www.aecf.org

Provides a national profile, published annually, of state-specific data regarding percent of low-birthweight babies, infant mortality rate, child death rate, percentage of all births that are to single teens, juvenile violent crime arrest rate, percentage graduating from high school on time, percentage of teens not in school and not in the labor force, violent death rate among teens, percentage of children in poverty, and percentage of children in single-parent families.

90. *Know Your Community.*
       Samuels, B., Ahsan, N., and Garcia, J. (1996), pp. 1–109.
       Family Resource Coalition, 200 S. Michigan Ave., 16th Floor, Chicago,
       IL 60604.

A step-by-step guide to community need and resource assessment. Includes information on establishing a community planning team, defining boundaries, developing a statistical profile, assessing needs from residents' perspectives, identifying assets and resources, and setting community priorities.

91. *Leadership for Collaboration: A Training Program.*
       South Eastern Regional Vision for Education (SERVE), pp. 3ff.
       SERVE, 41 Marietta St. NW, Suite 1000, Atlanta, GA 30303.

Promotes skills necessary to ensure positive collaboration: strategies for teamwork, skills that enable positive working relationships, information and benefits of collaboration, samples of collaborative models, and knowledge regarding the collaboration process. Provides an in-depth guide to setting up the training program.

92. "A Look at Current School-Linked Service Efforts."
       Levy, J. E., and Shepardson, W. (1992).
       The Future of Children, 2(1), 44–55.

Describes six school-linked service programs: School-Based Youth Services Program, New Jersey; Project Pride, Illinois; Probtsfield Elementary School, Minnesota; Youth At Risk Program, New York; Wallbridge Caring Communities, Missouri; and New Beginnings, California. Describes in detail the "goals of the effort, who is served, what services are offered, where services are located, and who is responsible for providing services." Also addresses the process of designing a school-linked service strategy and systemic change to improve long-term goals. EJ 448071

93. *Mainstream Assistance Teams: A Handbook on Prereferral Intervention.*
       Fuchs, D., Fuchs, L. S., Reeder, P., Gilman, S., Fernstrom, P., Bahr, M.,
       and Moore, P. (1989).
       MAT Project, John F. Kennedy Center, Box 40, George Peabody
       College, Vanderbilt University, Nashville, TN 37203.

Describes a well-researched effort to implement a behavioral consultation model of intervention assistance.

94.   *Making It Simpler: Streamlining Intake and Eligibility Systems.*
      Kraus, A., and Pillsbury, J. B. (1993), pp. 1–27.
      National Center for Service Integration Information Clearinghouse,
      National Center for Children in Poverty, Columbia University, 154
      Haven Avenue, New York, NY 10032.

Looks at streamlining federal, state, and local government programs in an effort to simplify intake and eligibility systems. Streamlining simplifies processes, removes unnecessary tasks, reduces repetitive work, reduces manual transfers of information, and builds partnerships among agencies. Suggests changes in policy, administration, and technology. Barriers such as turf issues, confidentiality, restrictive rules, technology limitations, and cost-benefit factors are discussed, along with lessons learned and implementation strategies. Resource Brief 6

95.   *Making the Case: Evidence of Program Effectiveness in Schools and Classrooms.*
      Ralph, J., and Dwyer, M. C. (1988), pp. 1–54.
      U.S. Department of Education, Program Effectiveness Panel,
      Recognition Division, 555 New Jersey Ave. NW, Room 510,
      Washington, DC 20208-5645.

Outlines guidelines for the Education Department's Program Effectiveness Panel, whose mission is to evaluate a program's effectiveness. Programs that are submitted for evaluation and approved "become a member of the National Diffusion Network and eligible to apply for federal dissemination funds." Describes the submission process and proper format, claims, case study methodology, types of evidence and educational impact, evaluation design, meaningful results, and realistic expectations of data. Describes four claim types: "academic achievement—changes in knowledge and skills, improvements in teachers' attitudes and behaviors, improvements in students' attitudes and behaviors, and improvements in instructional practices and procedures."

96.   *Measuring Program Outcomes: A Practical Approach.*
      United Way of America (1996), pp. 1–170.
      Publication supported by grants from Ewing Marion Kauffman
      Foundation and W. K. Kellogg Foundation. Developed by United
      Way of America Task Force on Impact. Effective Practices and
      Measuring Impact, 701 North Fairfax St., Alexandria, VA 22314-2045;
      (703) 836-7100. To order, call sales service/America, (800) 772-0008;
      item number 0989.

Presents a "Summary of Program Outcome Model" to clarify the use of outcomes in program evaluation. The step-by-step guide provides exhibits, worksheets, and examples of how to use evaluation as an essential part of program development, improvement, and continuation. Contains an extensive bibliography on performance measurement, data collection, and performance indicators.

97.   *Medicaid Financing for Mental Health and Substance Abuse Services for Children and Adolescents.*

    Fox, H. B., Wicks, L. N., McManus, M. A., and Kelley, R. W. (1991), pp. 1–69.

    U.S. Department of Health and Human Services, Public Health Service, Substance Abuse and Mental Health Services Administration, Center for Substance Abuse Treatment, Rockwall II, 5600 Fishers Lane, Rockville, MD 20857.

Provides "an explanation of the basic structure of the federal Medicaid program and current information on the availability of Medicaid coverage for mental health and substance abuse prevention and treatment services across states." Data resulted from telephone interviews of state Medicaid personnel from all fifty states and the District of Columbia in 1989. Major parts of the report are: basic information, requirements, and operations in the Medicaid system; analysis of benefits and mandatory and optional benefit categories; and survey results and recommendations. Appendixes contain the results of the "Fifty-States Survey of State Medicaid Coverage Policies and Practices" and a list of terms and abbreviations. (SMA) 93-1743

98.   *National Conference of Lieutenant Governors Education Task Force Subcommittee on At-Risk Students.*

    National Conference of Lieutenant Governors (1992), pp. 1–20.

    National Conference of Lieutenant Governors, Lexington, Ky.

Addresses the issue of at-risk students and their families, defining *at-risk* and providing indicators of students who are potentially at risk: family-related, social-economic, and student/self. "By developing a comprehensive and collaborative model involving the family, the schools, community-based service agencies, other community leaders, state human service agencies, and state leaders, a more efficient and effective service delivery mechanism can result" to aid at-risk students in learning. Discusses program models with respect to overall structure, program characteristics, budget, implementation, and evaluation and accountability. Appendixes contain a program outline of twenty state collaborative initiatives. Contact names and phone numbers are provided. ED 352 133

99.   *National Health Education Standards: Achieving Health Literacy.*

    Joint Committee on National Health Education Standards, American Cancer Society (1995), pp. 1–81.

    Health for Success, Excellence in School Health Education; (800) ACS-2345.

Discusses each national health education standard. Includes standard and corresponding rationale statements and performance indicators. Also addresses the supports required at the federal, state, and local levels to achieve the national health standards. Attachments contain a listing of the joint committee members, a listing of key events, an article titled "Making Time in the School Day for Health Instruction," a statement from the joint secretaries of education and health, and a reference list of key documents.

100.   *National Organizations Working for Healthy Youth: 1997 Project Summaries.*
    Centers for Disease Control and Prevention (1997), pp. 1–174.
    Atlanta: U.S. Department of Health and Human Services, Centers for Disease Control and Prevention.
  Lists and describes thirty-one national organizations, with a mission statement, project overview, project activities and products, and contact information for each.

101.   *The New Futures Initiative: A Midpoint Review.*
    Center for the Study of Social Policy (1991), pp. 1–12.
    Center for the Study of Social Policy, 1250 Eye St. NW, Suite 503, Washington, DC 20005-3922.
  Reviews the progress of the initiative in Dayton, Ohio; Little Rock, Arkansas; Pittsburgh, Pennsylvania; and Savannah, Georgia, whose goal is "to test new ways in which existing systems could better meet the needs of a growing proportion of youth." This midpoint review merely discusses certain key issues that have arisen in the cities and is not an evaluation of the initiative. Key issues include problems, goals, collaboration, oversight committee, case management, management information systems, educational interventions, teen health, and youth employment.

102.   *The Olympia School Project: A Summary and Recommendations for a Program Evaluation.*
    Mason, C. (1993), pp. 1–13.
    Olympia School District, 113 Legion Way SE, Olympia, WA 98501.
  First part describes community and interagency involvement. Second portion discusses a possible evaluation component. Project does not have a systematic evaluation component in place to substantiate its successes; however, this paper suggests several evaluation proposals: track services currently being offered; posttest consumer satisfaction; pretest and posttest participants in a selected number of programs; pretest and posttest families of new students; track referrals; monitor CPS referrals; and compare with a similar school.

103.   "One District's Strategies for Collaboration."
    Donofrio, R. I. (1992). Murphy Elementary School District, Phoenix, Ariz.
    The Executive Educator, Apr., p. 20.
  Briefly discusses the need for collaboration and outlines four guidelines as strategies for collaboration: "know the scope and mission of your own institution—including how far you are willing to go to provide noninstructional services"; "assess how well the social service needs of your students

and families are being met outside the schools"; "before embarking on collaboration with other agencies, assess what your school district is already doing to meet the broader needs of children"; and "set up ground rules that will govern attitudes and expectations." Provides other practical do's and don'ts regarding collaborative relationships. UMI EJ 441189

104.   *Parent Involvement Resource Manual.*
>   Cain, H. (1995).
>   Webster's International, Inc., 5729 Cloverland Place, Brentwood, TN
>   37027; (800) 727-6833.

Covers types of parental involvement, organizational strategies, what's working in the field, and federal requirements for the Title I educator. Also provides complete workshops on:

- Communicating with your child
- Use of computer
- Parent-student-teacher conferences
- Library
- Make and take sessions
- Using the newspaper
- Taking charge
- Discipline without tears
- Homework
- Self-esteem
- Television
- Using everyday strategies to help your child with reading and math

105.   *The Path of Most Resistance.*
>   The Annie E. Casey Foundation, 701 St. Paul St., Baltimore, MD
>   21202; pp. 1–29.

Reports eight lessons learned from a comprehensive, five-year reform initiative entitled "New Futures," aimed at preparing disadvantaged urban youth for successful lives as adults. Lessons learned include: (1) comprehensive reforms are very difficult; (2) it takes time; (3) it's not for every community; (4) building local ownership is no simple matter; (5) refine and modify plans; (6) communicate; (7) real change often depends on increases in economic opportunity and social capital; (8) stay at it.

106.   "The Politics of Evaluating Collaborative Efforts: Political Pressures and Methodological Responses." Presented at the 1994 American Education Finance Association Conference.
>   Herrington, C. D., and Lazar, I. (1994), pp. 1–14.

Begins with a discussion regarding the importance and necessity of collaborative children's services at the school site and then focuses on macropolitics and micropolitics of linking education and other human services; designing a politically and substantively responsive evaluation; program implementation; and outcome evaluation. Presents four concerns as essential in balancing the needs of the client versus the "political pressures converging on collaborative attempts." Also poses numerous questions regarding collaboration to help the reader think through the evaluation process.

107.   *Portraits of Interagency Collaboration.*
         Guthrie, L. F., Scott, B., Guthrie, G. P., and Aronson, J. Z. (1993), pp. 1–60.
         Office of Educational Research and Improvement, Washington, DC
         Far West Laboratory for Educational Research and Development, 730 Harrison St., San Francisco, CA 94107-1241.

Uses five case studies to address the issue of interagency collaboration. Covered in each case study are program overview, services provided, strategies, keys to success, and barriers and challenges. Vignettes illustrate selected topics. ERIC ED 356 573

108.   *The Power of Integrating Education and Human Services: Achieving the Potential of the Northwest.*
         Nissani, H., and Hagans, R. (1992), pp. 1–30.
         Northwest Regional Educational Laboratory, 101 S.W. Main St., Suite 500, Portland, OR 97204.

Addresses the issue of integrative services. Specifically discusses regional activities that support integration; historical, social, and political contexts; new roles and relationships; six key elements; new approaches; and results of a study of four service integration partners. Appendixes contain a description of partners: Portland Leaders Roundtables, Lincoln County Student/Community Assistance Program, Puget Sound Early Childhood Assistance Program, and Youth Information Management Task Force. ERIC ED 351 762

109.   "Preparing Leaders for Change-Oriented Schools."
         Thurston, P., Clift, R., and Schacht, M. (1993).
         Phi Delta Kappan, Nov., pp. 259–265.

Discusses administrative training for school administrative personnel, outlining "four postulates as essential elements of change-oriented leadership that benefits students: (1) leaders for change are transformational and engage in relationships with school personnel that inspire all participants . . . (2) leaders for change create collaboration . . . (3) leaders for change are oriented toward continuous learning . . . (4) leaders for change use a variety of student outcomes to evaluate the effects of improvement efforts." Four case studies (two elementary schools, one middle school, and one high school) explore the postulates, and four attributes of a successful administrative leader are identified: he or she is child-centered and a communicator, collaborator, and information processor.

110.   *Prevention Abstracts: Current Research on Prevention Issues.*
         Aboud, M. J., ed. (1994), pp. 1–24.

Southeast Regional Center for Drug-Free Schools and Communities, Spencerian Office Plaza, University of Louisville, Louisville, KY 40292.

Contains a collection of thirteen prevention abstracts that deal with adolescent substance use and abuse, coping skills and resilience, juvenile delinquency, adolescents' major concerns and perceived resources, and aggression.

111. *Principles to Link By. Integrating Education, Health and Human Services for Children, Youth, and Families: Systems That Are Community-Based and School-Linked.*

Elders, J. (1994), pp. 1–12. Centers for Disease Control and Prevention, Ewing Marion Kauffman Foundation, Maternal and Child Health Bureau, and Stuart Foundations.

U.S. Department of Health and Human Services, 601 Thirteenth Street NW, Suite 400 North, Washington, DC 20005.

An overview of the National Consensus Building Conference, where more than fifty private and public agencies assembled to share their views regarding integrating services. Focuses on "assuring effective services, building capacities for communities to conduct needs assessments and evaluations, initiating more collaborative funding practices, and expanding or developing structures for integrated services." As a result of the focus, thirty-one principles were established, addressing all levels of government and described in detail as a guide to integrating services for children and their families.

112. *Problem Solving and Barrier Removal in an Interagency Collaborative Program.*

Florida Department of Education (1993), pp. 1–42.

Diana Lincoln, HRS education coordinator, Department of Health and Rehabilitative Services, 1317 Winewood Blvd., Building 1, Room 218, Tallahassee, FL 32399-0700.

Results of a survey by the Interagency Work Group on Full-Service Schools. Focuses on problem areas that have hindered the full-service school program, including lack of understanding; lack of resources; funding procedures; management, coordination, collaboration; information system and sharing; involvement and participation; and mobility. Corresponding problem statements, causes, proposed solutions, and workgroup suggestions are offered. Contains a copy of the full-service school problem-solving survey, along with a list of respondents.

113. *Proceedings of a Joint Conference on School Health and Full-Service Schools, June 27–29, 1994.*

Hetrick, M., ed. (1994), pp. 1–437.

Institute for At-Risk Infants, Children and Youth, and Their Families, College of Education, University of South Florida, Tampa, FL 33620.

Collection of the conference proceedings, with workshop topics including integration of school health services; full-service schools; health reform effects on school health; using Medicaid reimbursement in schools; facing controversy in health education, teen sexuality, and HIV/AIDS; sexual abuse and teenage pregnancy; health education, school improvement, and service integration; comprehensive health services: knowledge, skills, and techniques. Directory of conference presenters.

114.   *Project Abstracts, Educational Partnerships Program.*
>> Danzberger, J. P., and Gruskin, S. J. (1993), pp. 1–88.
>> D. Williams, U.S. Department of Education, 555 New Jersey Ave. NW, Washington, DC 20208-5644.

Collection of project abstracts from across the country about this program, created "to encourage the creation of alliances between public schools or institutions of higher learning and the private sector," as well as to disseminate information regarding the program's projects and activities. Each abstract contains descriptive title, funding, project partnership, target student population and focus, objectives, description, program activities, evaluation plan, contact person, and U.S. Department of Education Office of Educational Research and Improvement project officer. Also includes the Educational Partnerships Program Evaluation and Documentation Project by Southwest Regional Laboratory.

115.   *Promoting Nebraska's Future. National Education Goal One: by the Year 2000 All Children in America Will Start School Ready to Learn. A Primer for Community-Level Planning Groups.*
>> Office of Child Development (1992), pp. 1–12.
>> Nebraska Department of Education, 301 Centennial Mall South, Lincoln, NE 68509-4987.

Discusses national education Goal One with regard to children in Nebraska. Also speaks about how the state board of education, citizens, and communities have responded to Goal One. Briefly describes ten collaborative programs in Nebraska, along with contact person and phone number. A Goal One community report card is provided as a means to rate your community with respect to twenty-four education and health indicators. ERIC ED 352 190

116.   *Putting Children First: State-Level Collaboration Between Education and Health.* (pamphlet)
>> Foley, C.
>> National Health and Education Consortium, Institute for Educational Leadership, 1001 Connecticut Ave. NW, Suite 310, Washington, DC 20036.

Discusses the need for each of us to become a child advocate, promoting collaboration between education and health services at the state level. Provides a framework for developing a state-level education and health consortium that focuses on children's issues and needs. Framework contains ten action steps. Full report available from the consortium for a $10 fee.

117. "Putting Services in One Basket."
   Rist, M. C. (1992).
   The Executive Educator, Apr., pp. 18–24.
   Discusses the issue of collaboration: schools, communities, and human service agencies working together to meet the needs of children and their families. Compares and contrasts community-based and school-based delivery systems. Advises how to get started and offers four important guidelines: (1) study local as well as nationwide demographics; (2) work to develop a sense of interagency teamwork; (3) commit the resources necessary for success; and (4) do not overlook the importance of training. Stresses the importance of commitment to successful partnerships for interagency collaboration. UMI EJ 441188

118. *Putting the Pieces Together: Comprehensive School-Linked Strategies for Children and Families.*
   Regional Educational Laboratory Network, U.S. Department of Education, Office of Educational Research and Improvement (OERI) (1996), pp. 1–98.
   Southeastern Regional Vision for Education, P.O. Box 5367, Greensboro, NC 27435.
   Illustrates a guidebook approach for school leaders who want to expand their efforts to help children and families succeed. Includes examples of building collaborative partnerships, conducting a community assessment, finding and developing resources, evaluating school-linked strategies, moving from vision to action, and maintaining the momentum in collaboration.

119. *Reaching All Families: Creating Family-Friendly Schools.*
   Moles, O. C., ed. (1996), pp. 1–53.
   U.S. Department of Education, Partnership for Family Involvement in Education, 600 Independence Ave. SW, Washington, DC 20202-8173.
   Suggests practical strategies for school outreach to promote family involvement in children's education. Includes introducing school policies and programs, personal contacts, ongoing communications, special practices and programs, special groups, and a description of services from the Department of Education in support of family involvement.

120. *Readiness for School: The Early Childhood Challenge.*
   Southern Regional Education Board (1992), pp. 1–36.
   Southern Regional Education Board, 592 Tenth St., NW, Atlanta, GA 30318-5790.
   Focuses on Goals for Education: Challenge 2000, Goal One (readiness for school). Essential to this goal is the realization that readiness for school begins even before a child is born and that a child's physical and mental well-being are crucial for successful learning. Outlines strategies for change at the state level; addresses obstacles that can hinder change and discusses the issue of financing.

121. *Recommendations for a Coordinated, Need-Responsive System of Assessment and Program Eligibility.*

> Shared Service Network. Client Assessment/Program Eligibility Ad Hoc Work Group (1991), pp. 1–40.
>
> Shared Service Network, 1950 W. Tennessee St. #10, Tallahassee, FL 32304.

Investigates the need "for system improvements in local practices of multi-agency client assessment and eligibility determination that would improve the quality of intake process for consumers and service coordinators and reduce potential inefficiencies in the use of public funds." Outlines key recommendations for system improvement and discusses system issues identified from eight current illustrative cases. Appendixes contain notes from the workgroup meetings.

122. "The Relationship Between School Boards and General-Purpose Government."

> Usdan, M. D. (1994).
>
> *Phi Delta Kappan,* Jan., pp. 374–377.

Addresses the notion that school board leadership is essential to the success of collaborative efforts for children and families. Contains research from the Institute for Educational Leadership regarding school board efforts and general-purpose government, showing that these two organizations must work together for collaborative leadership.

123. *Report of the Ad Hoc Committee on Full-Service Schools.*

> Dade County Ad Hoc Committee on Full-Service Schools (1994), pp. 1–58.
>
> Office of Instructional Leadership, Dade County Public Schools, 1500 Biscayne Blvd., Miami, FL 33132.

Summarizes the committee's conclusions, given their charge to establish the framework for implementing full-service schools across the district. Offers recommendations with respect to site selection, funding, staffing, facility design, implementation, needs assessment, interagency agreement, confidentiality, and Medicaid. Concludes that Blueprint 2000 Goals One, Two, Five, and Seven will be addressed through implementation of full-service schools.

124. "Restructuring Education Support Services and Integrating Community Resources: Beyond the Full Service School Model."

> Adelman, H. S. (1996).
>
> *School Psychology Review,* 25(4), 431–445.

Highlights major gaps in initiatives to restructure education, community health, and social services. Introduces the enabling component as a unifying, policy-oriented concept to address gaps and accelerate reform beyond the full-service school model. Outlines current efforts to operationalize the concept. Stresses implications for changing roles and functions of school psychologists.

125. *Rethinking Block Grants: Toward Improved Intergovernmental Financing for Education and Other Children's Services.*

> Hayes, C. D., with Daneggar, A. E. (1995), pp. 1–33.
>
> Finance Project, 1341 G St. NW, Washington, DC 20005.

Focuses on financing for education and other children's services. Uses research from the 1980s regarding the impact of the Reagan block grants. Topics addressed are program flexibility, streamlining, replacement of lost federal funding, accountability, and target populations. Also discusses block grants and how the nation's past experience with them can assist in this debate.

126. *Rethinking Children's Policy: Implications for Educational Administration.*

> Kirst, M., and McLaughlin, M., pp. 1–29. Unpublished paper.

Addresses the increasing number of children who are exposed to negative experiences. Uses information from Policy Analysis for California Education (PACE) to present statistics and trends regarding poverty, family structure, work, and health measures. Also discussed are problems associated with children's service implementation such as overservice and service fragmentation. Provides goals and suggestions, and concludes that the "school moves from the role of deliverer of educational services to the role of broker of the multiple resources that can be applied to achieve successful, productive, and happy lives for children."

127. "Rethinking Family-School Interactions: A Prologue to Linking Schools and Social Services."

> Smrekar, C. E. (1993).
>
> *Education and Urban Society, 25*(2), 175–186.

Deals with the issue of school-linked social service programs, focusing particularly on the "organizational conditions and social processes related to family-school interactions." Contains a case study of two schools with regard to the elements that foster and hinder connections between family and school. Stresses the importance of trust, familiarity, and understanding to successful school-linked social service delivery. Suggests and briefly describes the following strategies: collectively develop a vision statement, establish communication channels, conduct home visits, and use team teaching for continuity of care.

128. *Safeguarding Our Future, Children, and Families First. The Report of the Texas Commission on Children and Youth.*

> Texas Commission on Children and Youth (1994), pp. 1–262.
>
> Texas Commission on Children and Youth, Price Daniel Sr. Building, Room G-04, 209 West 14th St., P.O. Box 13106, Austin, TX 78711.

Addresses the need to improve and coordinate public programs to focus more on prevention and early intervention regarding the juvenile and criminal justice systems, stressing that the only way to combat increased juvenile crime is to focus on what places juveniles at risk in the first place. Identifies goals: fostering stable, nurturing families; promoting healthy children; ensuring school readiness; guaranteeing school success; deterring youth from crime; and ensuring serious consequences for violent and habitual juvenile offenders. Elaborates with findings, recommendations, and fiscal impact, and recommends partnership between local communities and the state. Appendixes contain mission statement, indicators, goal strategies, and descriptions of thirty model programs across the state.

129.   *School-Based Integrated Services: Replication Guide.*
       Funded by a grant from the U.S. Department of Health and Human Services and the Danforth Foundation.
       Department of Social Work, Institute on Children and Families at Risk, Florida International University, 3000 N.E. 145 St., North Miami, FL 33131-3600; (305) 950-5746.

Provides general guidance on the topics of families as action systems: parent partners, professional staff, consortia, mission, rights and goals, facilitation, service tailoring, nurturing change, and training.

130.   "School/Community Collaboration: Comparing Three Initiatives."
       Stone, C. R. (1995). Alternative School Programs for the Madison Metropolitan School District, Madison, Wisconsin.
       Phi Delta Kappan, June, pp. 794–800.

Explores school and community collaboration through three program approaches (executive collaboration, professional collaboration, and parental collaboration) and examines relative strengths and weaknesses. Concludes that to accentuate strengths and counterbalance limitations, integration of all three program approaches would be beneficial.

131.   *The School-Community Cookbook: Recipes for Successful Projects in the Schools. A "How-to" Manual for Teachers, Parents, and Community.*
       Hyman, C. S., ed. (1992), pp. 1–235.
       Cookbook, Fund for Educational Excellence, 605 N. Eutaw St., Baltimore, MD 21201.

"Cookbook" for successful school-community projects contains forty-three articles from writers experienced in such collaboration. Articles are divided into three categories: role of participants, "step-by-step instructions," and a potpourri of issues (evaluation, advocacy, goals and philosophy). A practical and resourceful manual for those who wish to improve schools and services to children and their families. Appendixes contain community resources from Baltimore and Maryland. ERIC ED 348 723

132.   *School/Community Networks for Successful Families: Project Success. Final report from Lt. Gov. Bob Kustra and the Coordination of Social Services Action Group.*
       Kustra, B. (1991), pp. 1–22.
       Office of the Lieutenant Governor, State of Illinois, 214 State Capitol Building, Springfield, IL 62706.

Makes recommendations with respect to service delivery systems, given the group's goal of ensuring that "all Illinois children come to school prepared to learn." Describes the service delivery system model that the action group created, along with six core service components essential to the model's success. State-level responsibilities as well as local community responsibilities with respect to collaboration are also outlined. Collaboration is seen as the key component to successful service delivery systems. ERIC ED 353 050

133. "School-Community Relations: A Process Paradigm."
    Wanat, C. L., and Bowles, B. D. (1993).
    Community Education Journal, Winter, pp. 3–7.

    Addresses the need for collaboration between school and community services and personnel, using research conducted at the University of Wisconsin-Madison Research and Development Center during the 1970s and the resulting model, Home-School-Community Relations. Explains model's impact and implications.

134. *School-Linked Comprehensive Services for Children and Families. What We Know and What We Need to Know.*
    U.S. Department of Education, Office of Educational Research and Improvement (OERI), (1995).
    New Orders, Superintendent of Documents, P.O. Box 361954.
    Pittsburgh, PA 15250-7954.

    Presents findings of an agenda-setting conference convened by Sharon P. Robinson, assistant secretary of OERI, and Jane Stallings, president of the American Educational Research Association (AERA). Six ideas were prevalent among participants: committed leadership, cultural sensitivity and congruence, participant-driven services, interprofessional development, new research approaches, and flexibility in policies. Stock no. 065-000-00754-1

135. *School-Linked Human Services: A Comprehensive Strategy for Aiding Students at Risk of School Failure. (Testimony).*
    Report to the chairman, Committee on Labor and Human Resources, U.S. Senate (1993), pp. 1–66.
    U.S. General Accounting Office, P.O. Box 6015, Gaithersburg, MD 20884-6015.

    Presents school-linked approaches with "at least three of four primary services: health, education, social services, and employment training," at a school site. Analyzes ten comprehensive school-linked services and discusses strengths, weaknesses, problems, and obstacles of each. Appendixes contain statements from the Department of Health and Human Services and the Department of Education, as well as evaluation data. GAO/HRD-94-21

136. "School-Linked Services."
    Behrman, R. E., ed. (1992).
    David and Lucile Packard Foundation, Center for the Future of Children, 300 Second St., Suite 102, Los Altos, CA 94022.
    The Future of Children, 2(1), 1–145.

Issue devoted to discussion of school-linked services, containing articles from ten authors. Outlines six critical issues as essential to successfully planning and implementing school-linked services: systemic change in the schools and child-serving agencies, targeting, financing, evaluation, state and federal leadership, and alternatives to the school-linked service approach.

137.   "School-Linked Services: So That Schools Can Educate and Children Can Learn, Part One."
   Pollard, J. S. (May 1990).
   Insights on Educational Policy and Practice, no. 20, pp. 1–6.
   Southwest Educational Development Laboratory, 211 E. Seventh St., Austin, TX 78701.

Addresses the argument of providing expanded services at local schools. Explores the types (external referral, mobile rapid response, and school-based services) and attributes (comprehensive services, shared governance, collaborative funding, and organizational models) of school-linked service delivery programs. ED 330 060

138.   "School-Linked Services: So That Schools Can Educate and Children Can Learn, Part 2."
   Pollard, J. S. (Aug. 1990).
   Insights on Educational Policy and Practice, no. 22, pp. 1–4.
   Southwest Educational Development Laboratory, 211 E. Seventh St., Austin, TX 78701.

Discusses school-linked services and these concerns: "(1) the qualities of successful collaborative service delivery programs and (2) the nature of the policy context in which they operate." Presents six policy concerns that need to be addressed by state and local policy makers, followed by strategy statements that aid in successful implementation. ERIC ED 330 062

139.   "School-Linked Services: So That Schools Can Educate and Children Can Learn, Part 3."
   Pollard, J. S. (Sept. 1990).
   Insights on Educational Policy and Practice, no. 23, pp. 3–9.
   Southwest Educational Development Laboratory, 211 E. Seventh St., Austin, TX 78701.

Offers policies for school-linked services: "ensuring comprehensive service delivery to children and families; developing alternative funding strategies; ensuring family support; ensuring personnel quality; providing leadership in the development of a broad support base; and providing leadership in the development of a broad support." Chart of programs from Arkansas, Louisiana, New Mexico, Oklahoma, and Texas is provided, each containing a contact person and phone number. ERIC ED 330 063

140.   *School-University Partnerships in Action.*
   Sirotnik, K. A., and Goodlad, J. I., eds. (1988), pp. 1–235.
   Teachers College Press, 1234 Amsterdam Ave., New York, NY 10027.

Focuses on what school-university partnerships are and what supports are required to facilitate such collaborations. Analyzes five case study partnerships and their experiences and concerns regarding implementation. Biographical sketches of contributing authors. ISBN 0-8077-2892-6

141. *Schools as Intergovernment Partners: Administrator Perceptions of Expanded Programming for Children.*

    Herrington, C. (1994), pp. 1–27.

    "Provides an analysis of the pressures being placed on schools to become more active in intergovernment programming and explores the challenges these new programs pose to educational administrators as determined by in-depth interviews with a small sample of school principals and district superintendents." Tables include estimated public expenditures on children, local providers of governmental services, and statutorily mandated responsibilities for child and youth services by policy area and by state.

142. "Schools Can Do More for Parents."

    Shields, M. (1986).

    The Exceptional Parent, Sept., pp. 21–22.

    Discusses the importance of schools' providing parents with "resource lists, sponsoring orientation sessions, and helping parents network with one another." Indicates these activities help to empower parents and dispel feelings of isolation. UMI EJ 341345

143. *The Schools Partnership Project.*

    Jewish Family and Children's Services (1992), pp. 1–78.

    Jewish Family and Children's Services, 1600 Scott St., San Francisco, CA 94115.

    Summarizes the Schools Partnership Project, implemented at six elementary schools during 1988 and 1989 with the goal "to investigate whether the emotional and academic well-being of children could be improved by providing mental health consultation services to public school personnel." Discusses basic information about the project, goals and objectives, project development, implementation, evaluations, implications, finances, practical lessons learned, and policy considerations. Appendixes include teacher demographics, description of school sites, rosters of project advisory council and JFCS board of directors, and consultation job description.

144. "Schools Reaching Out: A Portrait of Family-Community Involvement in Schools Today."

    Hollifield, J. (1992).

    Contemporary Education, 64(1), 31–34.

    Results of a research survey of forty-two member schools of the Institute for Responsive Education's League of Schools Reaching Out. These schools involve families and the community as a whole in educating children. Summarizing "the efforts of the schools and the activities they are conducting, the researchers describe (a) the level and types of activities being carried out, (b) noteworthy emerging strategies, (c) noteworthy program gaps, (d) the comprehensiveness of programs, (e) the need for evaluation, (f) the influence of formal policies, (g) the influence of informal policies, and (h) the costs of parent-community-school collaborative activities." UMI EJ 463309

145. *Shining Stars: Prevention Programs That Work. 1994 Edition.*
      Straub, B. W., and Buford, B. (1994), pp. 1–64.
      Southeast Regional Center for Drug-Free Schools and Communities, Spencerian Office Plaza, University of Louisville, Louisville, KY 40292.

Collection of prevention program summaries from across the country, all of which are part of one of three projects: Noteworthy Programs and Practices, U.S. Department of Education's Drug-Free School Recognition Program, or An Eagle's View. Each entry contains program description, program highlights, evaluation information, clientele information, and designated contact person, address, and telephone number.

146. *Size of Space and Design Criteria for Facility Spaces Associated with School Health Rooms and the Concept of Full-Service Schools.*
      Florida Department of Education (1992).
      Product of the Interagency Work Groups on Full-Service Schools (Departments of Education, Health and Rehabilitative Services, and Labor and Employment Security). Contains specifications on school health room (square footage, components of clinic space, number of beds, program description, location), reading resource room (purpose, size, requirements), and waiting room (purpose, size, requirements).

147. *Standards for Data Exchange and Case Management Information Systems in Support of Comprehensive Integrated School-Linked Services.*
      Far West Laboratory for Educational Research and Development, the Youth Law Center, and the California Interagency Data Collaboration (1995).
      Far West Laboratory for Educational Research and Development, 730 Harrison St., San Francisco, CA 94107-1242.

A guide to local integrated school-linked services sites in California and vendors who are developing and implementing case management information systems for the exchange and management of client data. Standards suggested include core data elements, computer management information systems (CMIS) functional specifications, and confidentiality.

148. "Standing up to Violence. Kappan Special Report."
      Sautter, R. C. (1995).
      Phi Delta Kappan, Jan., pp. K1–K12.

Discusses violence among youth today, specifically juvenile victimization, psychological impact of violence, significant declines in rates of arrests, differentiation between juvenile crime today and in the past, increase of school violence, sources of youth violence, psychological roots, violence predictors, violence prevention programs, school plan for safety, and creating safe schools. Provides a comprehensive overview of youth violence as well as practical applications to combat it. Also contains a list of resource reports, studies, and organizations pertaining to school violence.

149. *Starting Points: Meeting the Needs of Our Youngest Children. (Abridged Version).*
      Carnegie Task Force on Meeting the Needs of Young Children (1994), pp. 1–41.
      Carnegie Corporation of New York, P.O. Box 753, Waldorf, MD 20604.
      Task force was charged to study "the quiet crisis" in America, in the belief that an increasing number of children under the age of three are exposed to situations that have the potential to affect their normal development. focuses on promoting responsible parents, choosing good child care, ensuring proper child health, and fostering community-based resources and services.

150. *Starting Young: School-Based Health Centers at the Elementary Level.*
      Shearer, C. A., and Holschneider, S.O.M. (1995), pp. 1–33.
      National Health and Education Consortium, Institute for Educational Leadership, 1001 Connecticut Ave. NW, Suite 310, Washington, DC 20036.
      Focuses on elementary school-based health centers. Discusses such issues as what school-based health centers are, why elementary schools need them, funding, federal and state support, and how school-based health centers affect the school environment. Appendixes contain a directory of federal, state, and local programs that support school-based health centers and proposed federal legislation. Also contains a reading list of materials relating to school-based health centers.

151. *Streamlining Interagency Collaboration for Youth at Risk: Issues for Educators.*
      Guthrie, G. P., and Guthrie, L. F. (1990), pp. 1–14.
      U.S. Department of Education, Office of Educational Research and Improvement, Washington, DC 20208.
      Discusses importance of interagency collaboration and why it is essential for schools and agencies to implement such a philosophy today. Outlines four elements of integrated services: comprehensive, preventative, child-centered, and flexible. Also provides a four-step process for streamlining interagency collaboration, as well as four common "pitfalls and danger signs to avoid." ERIC ED 342 137

152. *Student Assistance Program Core Team Training Manual.*
      Florida Department of Education (1995).
      325 West Gaines St., Tallahassee, FL 32399.
      Based on Orange County's SAFE core team training manual. What to look for and what to do about alcohol, tobacco, and other drug use among students and their parents. Produced under Interdistrict Student Assistance Program Training Project, federal contract no. S207 A40002.

153. *Survey of Full-Service School Sites in Florida.*
    University of South Florida, Institute for At-Risk Children and Their Families (1993).
    Florida Department of Education, 325 West Gaines St., Tallahassee, FL 32399.
    Conducted by the Department of Dropout Prevention, Bureau of Student Support and Academic Assistance. Includes full-service school site information and the services provided at each. Source of community service inventory.

154. *Synthesis of Existing Knowledge and Practice in the Field of Educational Partnerships.*
    Grobe, T., Curman, S. P., and Melchior, A. (1993), pp. 1–42.
    Department of Education, Office of Educational Research and Improvement.
    ERIC Clearinghouse on Elementary and Early Childhood Education, University of Illinois, 805 West Pennsylvania Ave., Urbana, IL 61801.
    From the Educational Partnerships Program, looks at partnerships with regard to history and context, definition and typology, generic elements, and evaluation. Focuses on characteristics that make partnerships effective: top-level leadership; grounding in community needs; effective public relations; clear roles and responsibilities; racial-ethnic involvement; strategic planning; effective management and staffing structure; shared decision making and interagency ownership; shared credit and recognition; appropriate, well-timed resources; technical assistance; formal agreements; action and frequent success; patience, vigilance, and increased involvement; and local ownership.

155. *Tackling the Confidentiality Barrier: A Practical Guide for Integrated Family Services.*
    New Beginnings Project (1991), pp. 1–90.
    Department of Social Services, County of San Diego, Community Relations Bureau, Room 843, 1255 Imperial Ave., San Diego, CA 92101-7439.
    Focuses on barriers and how to successfully maintain confidentiality. Divided into these topics: rules and issues, policy and procedure, interagency agreements and forms, implications and recommendations, and statutes and citations. Appendixes contain federal, state, and local statutes and regulations regarding confidentiality and integrated family services.

156. "Tapping Your Community's Best Resources."
    Fertman, C. I. (1988). Executive director, Maximizing Adolescent Potentials Program, School of Education, University of Pittsburgh, Pittsburgh, Pa.
    PTA Today, Nov., pp. 18–19.
    Provides practical guidelines for assessing the "ability of various agencies to serve the needs of children, families, and the community" regarding

staff, licensing and accreditation, references, ethical and professional standards, insurance, resources, networking, and program evaluation. Offers a concrete structure from which to begin an assessment of competence of children and family service programs.

157.   *A Theory of Human Motivation.*
   Maslow, A. H. (1943).
   Psychological Review, 50, 370–396.

Briefly describes Maslow's motivation theory and hierarchy of needs. Needs higher in the hierarchy only actualize if lower ones have been met. Hierarchy of needs, from lower to higher, is physiological, safety and security, love and belongingness, self-esteem, and self-actualization.

158.   *Thinking Collaboratively: Ten Questions and Answers to Help Policy Makers Improve Children's Services.*
   Bruner, C. (1991), pp. 1–31.
   Education and Human Services Consortium, IEL, 1001 Connecticut Ave. NW, Suite 310, Washington, DC 20036-5541.

Uses a "question and answer format to help state and local policy makers consider how best to foster local collaboration that truly benefits children and families." Questions discussed are:

- What we mean by collaboration
- Which programs collaborations are designed to solve
- At what organizational level collaboration should occur
- How we know if collaboration is happening and if it is working
- How effective state-level interagency groups can be in reducing system fragmentation and improving services to children and families
- What strategies state policy makers can initiate to further collaboration at the local level
- What strategies states can employ to promote collaboration across all jurisdictions, including those where obstacles are greatest
- What the role of the private sector is in collaboration initiatives
- What the risks are in collaboration
- What problems collaboration will not solve

159.   *Together We Can: A Guide for Crafting a Profamily System of Education and Human Services.*
   Melaville, A. I., and Blank, M. J., with Asayesh, G. (1993), pp. 1–157.
   U.S. Department of Education Office of Educational Research and Improvement. U.S. Department of Health and Human Services, Office of the Assistant Secretary for Planning and Evaluation.
   U.S. Government Printing Office, Superintendent of Documents, Mail Stop: SSOP, Washington, DC 20402-9328.

Study group looked into service integration at the local, state, and federal levels, developing a practical guide for communities to improve education and human service delivery systems. Includes description of the profamily system vision, strategies to implement the system, characteristics of successful service integration, framework for progress, and four case study programs: Wallbridge Caring Communities, St. Louis; Lafayette Courts Family Development Center, Baltimore; New Beginnings, San Diego; and Youth Futures Authority, Savannah-Chatham County, Georgia. Appendixes contain checklists for progress, directory of key contacts, and organizational resources.

160. *Towards Improved Services for Children and Families: Forging New Relationships Through Collaboration. (Policy brief based on the eighth annual Symposium of the A. L. Mailman Family Foundation.).*

Blank, M., and Lombardi, J. (1991), pp. 1–14.
Institute for Educational Leadership, 1001 Connecticut Ave. NW, Suite 310, Washington, DC 20036.

Defines the concept of collaboration and the reasons it is needed. Outlines six essentials for successful integration and collaboration: a climate for change, leadership, flexibility and resources, problem-solving structures, supportive relationships, and documented results. Highlights three initiatives: "the Florida example focused on expanding and improving early childhood services before school, the Missouri example focused on expanding school-based services, and the Maryland example focused on improving the overall service system to families."

161. *Turning Points: Preparing American Youth for the 21st Century.*

Task Force on Education of Young Adolescents (1989), pp. 1–106.
Carnegie Council on Adolescent Development, 11 Dupont Circle NW, Washington, DC 20036.

Guide to restructuring middle-grades education to actualize an "effective human being." Describes these characteristics as evidence of an effective human being: intellectually reflective, caring and ethical, good citizen, healthy, and on the way to a lifetime of meaningful work. Eight principles for accomplishing middle-grade restructuring and the task force's recommendations for each are described in detail. Appendixes contain a listing of papers on the topic of adolescents, workshop meetings, consultants to the task force, and biographical sketches of its members.

162. *Turning Troubled Kids Around: The Complete Student Assistance Program for Secondary Schools. An Easy-to-Use Manual for Busy Educators.*

Johnson Institute-QVS, Inc. (1993), pp. 1–155.
Johnson Institute, 7205 Ohms Lane, Minneapolis, MN 55439-2159.

Nine-step manual details how to establish a student assistance program, "the sum total of all the things a school does to help students solve problems related to alcohol or other drugs." Steps include identifying problems, designing solutions, laying groundwork, identifying, and screening and intervening with students; also gives tips on prevention and evaluation. Appendixes include sample forms and resource list. ISBN 1-5624-6062-5

163. *Values and Opinions of Comprehensive School Health Education in U.S. Public Schools: Adolescents, Parents, and School District Administrators.*

Gallup Organization (1994), pp. 1–58.

American Cancer Society, 1599 Clifton Rd. NE, Atlanta, GA 30329-4251.

Survey questioned adolescents, parents of adolescents, and public school district administrators regarding opinions and values of comprehensive school health education. Separates results according to population; however, in the summary, important similarities and differences between the three populations are analyzed. All three sample populations viewed comprehensive school health education as more important than other things taught in school. Appendixes outline demographics and methodology.

164.   *Vision in Action: A Resource Directory.*

National Foundation for the Improvement of Education (1993), pp. 1–100.

NFIE, 1201 Sixteenth St. NW, Washington, DC 20036.

Resource directory contains brief descriptions and essential information about programs across the country that work to serve children, families, and communities: Christa McAuliffe Institute for Educational Pioneering; Dropout Prevention Program; Learning Tomorrow Program; William G. Carr Grants Program; and Hilda Maehling Grants Program.

165.   *Voices of the City: Closing the Achievement Gap. A Vision to Guide Change in Beliefs and Practice.*

Williams, B., ed., with Benard, B., Greenfield, P. M., Louis, K. S., Stevens, F. I., Wang, M. C., and Zeichner, K. M. (1995), pp. 1–117.

North Central Regional Educational Laboratory, 1900 Spring Rd., Ste. 300, Oak Brook, IL 60521.

Summarizes research and practice regarding four needs: (1) paradigm shifts in understanding social interaction, values, and standards in human development and learning in urban contexts; (2) caution against reductionist views of urban intervention limited to curriculum, instruction, and assessment; (3) challenges to current deficit and at-risk characterization of poor urban students; (4) reconceptualization of teacher preparation programs and support for organizational change in schools and classrooms.

166.   *What It Takes: Structuring Interagency Partnerships to Connect Children and Families with Comprehensive Services.*

Melaville, A. I., with Blank, M. J., pp. 1–55.

Education and Human Services Consortium, State of Florida Department of Education, Bureau of Student Services, 325 West Gaines St., Tallahassee, FL 32399-0400; http://www.firn.doe

Joint effort of twenty-two organizations to discuss comprehensive services for children and families. This monograph is divided into three components that address current status and future prospects. Discusses five elements of climate, processes, people, policies, and resources that have an impact on all collaborative efforts. Contains brief outline of elements that are important for successful, positive partnerships and collaboration. Appendixes contain program descriptions, contacts, and resource information.

167.   *What Works: Promising Interventions in Juvenile Justice.*
          U.S. Department of Justice (1994), pp. 1–248.
          National Center for Juvenile Justice, 701 Forbes Ave., Pittsburgh, PA 15219.

Report from the Office of Juvenile Justice and Delinquency Prevention provides a directory of 425 effective prevention and treatment programs for juvenile offenders. Entries are divided into these categories: academic education, behavior management, community service, crisis intervention, education and employment, counseling, intensive probation, mediation, mentoring, milieu management, outdoor activity, reality therapy, recreation and fitness, referrals, sex offender treatment, shoplifting awareness, skill development, special education, substance abuse treatment, therapeutic milieu, use of speakers, and vocational training. Each entry contains program name, address, phone number, contact person, target population, age, gender type, referrals out-of-state, capacity, average stay, target area, program type, structure, administration, staff size, staff-to-client ratio, per diem rate, annual budget, date began, evaluation date, and primary intervention.

168.   *What's In? What's Out? American Education in the Nineties.*
          Murphy, J. (1993).
          Phi Delta Kappan, Apr., pp. 641–646.

Discusses need for remodeling the education system: "if our schools are to provide us with a modern work force prepared to excel in a post-industrial, knowledge-based society, we must transform the design and structure of education; we must make a fundamental change that strikes at the core of present operations." Addresses increased standards and expectations, emphasis on outcome variables, ability versus effort, individualization of education, the age-grade link, seniority versus competence regarding the teaching staff, year-long schooling, the full-service school concept, and education as a community responsibility.

169.   *Who Should Know What? Confidentiality and Information Sharing in Service Integration.*
          Soler, M. I., and Peters, C. M. (1993), pp. 1–19.
          National Center for Services Integration Information Clearinghouse, National Center for Children in Poverty, Columbia University, 154 Haven Ave., New York, NY 10332.

Discusses the balance of confidentiality between the rights and interests of the client (child or family) and the need for interagency information sharing. Proposes to share information with agencies while respecting client rights, using certain principles and mechanisms. Also provides practical checklist of points to consider when developing procedures for interagency information sharing.

170.   "Why Blame Schools?" (Research bulletin).
        McClellan, M. (1994).
        Phi Delta Kappa; Center for Evaluation, Development, and Research, Mar. 12, pp. 1–6.
        Phi Delta Kappa, P.O. Box 789, Bloomington, IN 47402; (812) 339-1156.
Discusses rising social problems plaguing children and young people and the implication that schools are "to blame" because of poor academic conditions. The 1990 Sandia Report is discussed to point out rising test scores and provide evidence that the American educational system matches workplace needs. Concludes that, based on recent evidence of schools' academic success, students at risk face problems outside the school rather than inside, and that schools should take a leadership role in addressing children's needs.

171.   *Working Smarter in a Shared Service Network.*
        Leon County Shared Service Network (1991), pp. 1–66. 1950 West Tennessee St., Tallahassee, FL 32304.
        Bureau of Education for Exceptional Students, Florida Department of Education, Tallahassee.
Describes development and implementation of Shared Service Network Project, begun in 1990, which "incorporates a variety of community agency locations as sites for collocated education, social, health, employment, legal and cultural services for children, youth and their families." Provides information on client assessment, shared service centers, case management, funding, and future plans. Appendixes contain list of technical reports, sample newsletters, and population density maps of students, exceptional students, CMS primary medical care, and state health department's primary care program.

172.   *Working Smarter in a Shared Service Network: A Resource and Planning Guide.*
        Florida Department of Education (1991), pp. 1–65.
        Clearinghouse and Information Center, Bureau of Education for Exceptional Students, Division of Public Schools, Florida Department of Education, Florida Education Center, Tallahassee, FL 32399-0400.
Describes project activities from January to August 1991, "documenting one community's experiences in its attempt to innovatively address the needs of its children; assisting other communities in Florida which may want to review and revise their methods of service provision for children and youth; assisting other communities which are looking for ways to implement the Full-Service Schools legislation." Contains information regarding development, council membership and roles, guiding principles, client assessment, program eligibility, workgroup activities, case planning, case management, funding, resource development, and future plans. Appendixes contain a list of technical reports and county maps.

173.   *Youth and Caring: Developing a Field of Inquiry and Practice. A Report of a Lilly Endowment Research Grants Program.*
        Chaskin, R. J., and Hawley, T. (1994), pp. iii–60.

Chapin Hall Center for Children at the University of Chicago, 1155 East 60th St., Chicago, IL 60637.

Explains the Lily Endowment's Research Grants Program on Youth and Caring. Part one introduces the concept of youth and caring. Part two lists studies funded by the endowment. Part three lists commissioned papers and brief summaries. Part four is an extensive youth-and-caring bibliography divided into these topics:

- Caring: definitions, determinants of caring behavior
- Development of altruism, moral development, and moral reasoning
- Family as context
- Cultural and ethnic diversity
- Gender differences in caring and adolescent development
- Adolescents and the educational system
- Schools as a context for caring
- Service learning programs
- Primary services for adolescents
- Community as a context for caring
- Caring in the professions
- Risk factors and resiliency in youth and children

174.   *Youth Involvement: Developing Leaders and Strengthening Communities.*
Swinehart, B. (1990), pp. 1–46.
Partners for Youth Leadership, 250 Arapahoe, Suite 301, Boulder, CO 80302.

From the U.S. Department of Housing and Urban Development, addresses the issue of partnerships between young people and adults. Emphasizes treating young individuals with respect and as valuable active participants: "The purpose of this book is to provide an overview of how to build and maintain effective youth participation programs." Describes youth participation programs and how they can have positive impact on adolescents and the community. Also discusses implementation and success strategies. Appendixes contain a list of programs referred to in the document as well as national organizations that support youth participation programs, including addresses and telephone numbers.

Index

BUILDING A
Full-Service
School